IAN D. CLA[RK]

GREG MORAN

MICHAEL L. SKOLNIK

DAVID TRICK

ACADEMIC

TRANSFORMATION

THE FORCES RESHAPING
HIGHER EDUCATION
IN ONTARIO

Queen's Policy Studies Series
McGill-Queen's University Press
Montreal & Kingston • London • Ithaca

Copyright © 2009 School of Policy Studies, Queen's University at Kingston, Canada

SCHOOL OF
Policy Studies
Publications Unit
Robert Sutherland Hall
138 Union Street
Kingston, ON, Canada
K7L 3N6
www.queensu.ca/sps/

The preferred citation for this book is:
Clark, I.D., G. Moran, M.L. Skolnik, and D. Trick. (2009). *Academic Transformation: The Forces Reshaping Higher Education in Ontario*. Montreal and Kingston: Queen's Policy Studies Series, McGill-Queen's University Press.

Library and Archives Canada Cataloguing in Publication

Academic transformation : the forces reshaping higher education in Ontario / Ian D. Clark ... [et al.].

Includes bibliographical references.
ISBN 978-1-55339-265-1 (bound).—ISBN 978-1-55339-238-5 (pbk.)

1. Education, Higher—Ontario. 2. Postsecondary education—Ontario. I. Clark, Ian D., 1946- II. Queen's University. School of Policy Studies

LA418.O6A222 2009   378.713   C2009-904911-2

TABLE OF CONTENTS

ACKNOWLEDGEMENTS

This book began as a research project sponsored by the Higher Education Quality Council of Ontario (HEQCO) in which each of us were to produce an "expert discussion paper ... [that] examines and analyzes emerging and future challenges to Ontario's university and college sectors." Each discussion paper was to take "a different perspective on the most pressing issues facing the sector, as well as provide advice on how the system might respond to these challenges."

Diverse perspectives were anticipated because we each bring different histories to the task. One of us worked for 22 years in the federal government in economic and budget offices before leading the advocacy organization for Ontario's universities for nine years. Another spent his professional life as a teacher, researcher, and senior administrator in one of those universities. A third devoted much of his academic career in another Ontario university to the study of the organization and governance of higher education systems in Canada and abroad, and has a particular interest in the relationship between universities and colleges. The fourth spent two decades in the finance and post-secondary education ministries of the Ontario government before becoming a founding CEO of a joint college-university institution and a consultant in higher education.

Unsurprisingly, we soon discovered as we developed our "different perspectives" that our observations were highly interdependent and there would be merit in trying to produce an integrated analysis of the forces reshaping higher education. Perhaps surprisingly, we discovered after a number of exchanges of drafts and animated discussions that we all found it to be more constructive and stimulating to write the manuscript as joint authors rather than producing separately authored chapters.

Our first debt is to the Higher Education Quality Council of Ontario, which provided financial support for the research and wide latitude for us to define and carry out the project. We are especially grateful to the Honourable Frank Iacobucci, the Council's chair; James Downey, its president; and Ken Norrie, its vice president (research). Each has provided consistent support for our work as well as valuable comments on the manuscript. That said, the views expressed in this book and the suggestions for improvement in Ontario's higher education system are those of the authors and not necessarily those of any institution, including the Higher Education Quality Council of Ontario.

We have been assisted and encouraged by our many friends and colleagues in Ontario's colleges, universities, and government ministries. We would like to thank the following people who reviewed an early draft of the text: Bob Christie, Marjorie Clark, Paul Davenport, Marie-Lison Fougère, Robert (Squee) Gordon, David Lindsay, Henry Mandelbaum, Janet Mason, Leah Myers, Bonnie Patterson, Robert Prichard, Janice Gross Stein, Carolyn Tuohy, and Richard Van Loon. Their feedback proved crucial in shaping the direction of our book. We are grateful, too, to the many colleagues in universities, colleges, and government who provided assistance in locating and understanding data.

We would also like to thank Kelsey Norman, Vass Bednar, and Mary Catherine Lennon for their research and editorial assistance, and McGill-Queen's University Press and its three anonymous reviewers for very useful comments.

Any errors or omissions are solely the responsibility of the authors.

IDC, GM, MLS, DT
September 2009

INTRODUCTION

The thesis of this book is that the present approach to the provision of baccalaureate education in Ontario is not sustainable and is in need of significant modification. The stage for the present approach was set by two higher education policy decisions that were made in the 1960s: (1) that the colleges would have no role in the provision of baccalaureate credit activity; and (2) that the publicly supported universities would have complete autonomy in deciding on their purpose, mission, and objectives. While the universities had been primarily teaching institutions until the 1960s, since then a single idea of the mission of the university—the research university—has been adopted by all. A key element of the research university model to which the university community in Ontario has subscribed is that of the teacher-researcher ideal: that undergraduate students should be taught only by professors who are active researchers.

Not only have all the universities embraced the research university model, but in the past two decades there has been a growing expectation from the public and the government for universities to produce knowledge that will enhance Canada's economic well-being and international economic competitiveness. This new model has fostered substantial growth in university research, brought changes to the traditional research paradigm, and introduced new costs—both human and financial.

At the same time as the universities have experienced growing internal and external pressure to expand research, particularly research that is anticipated to have commercially valuable applications, the pressure to expand accessibility to baccalaureate programs has continued unabated. Any further increases in the university participation rate—already high by international standards but seen as necessary by many to the province's future competitiveness and productivity—will now require making substantial advances with respect to groups that historically

Academic Transformation: The Forces Reshaping Higher Education in Ontario, I.D. Clark, G. Moran, M.L. Skolnik, and D. Trick. Montreal and Kingston: McGill-Queen's University Press, Queen's Policy Studies Series.

have been underrepresented in higher education. The academic success of the additional members of these groups may require more attention and resources than universities have provided their students in the past. Another ingredient in this scenario is that a substantial portion of the growth in the demand for baccalaureate education has been in career-focused programs rather than in the liberal arts and sciences.

As it struggles with the challenges of massive increases in enrolment, Ontario is relying exclusively on a publicly supported system of research-focused universities—the most expensive type of post-secondary institution—to provide baccalaureate education to a population of students with increasingly diverse educational requirements. Ontario appears to be unique among jurisdictions of comparable size and rates of participation in baccalaureate programs in relying exclusively on a system of publicly supported research-focused universities for the provision of baccalaureate education. Besides being expensive, this model provides insufficient variety in the types of baccalaureate experiences available to students relative to the diversity of backgrounds, situations, aspirations, and learning styles. At the same time, serving the needs of a much larger student body while also meeting societal expectations of knowledge production creates substantial resource allocation tensions for individual professors and institutions that might be better met within a more diverse post-secondary system.

In the year 2000, some policy changes were made to ameliorate the problem described here, but these have not changed the situation appreciably. The *Postsecondary Education Choice and Excellence Act* made it possible for both the colleges and private post-secondary institutions to offer baccalaureate programs. However, these programs in the colleges account for only about 2 percent of undergraduate enrolment, and only two secular post-secondary institutions have obtained approval to offer baccalaureate programs, involving a small number of students in three specialized programs.

Besides the frequent statements from the universities themselves that they do not have sufficient funds to fulfill their mission (at least the way they believe that should be done), another indicator that the present approach is not sustainable is the increasing reliance on part-time faculty to deliver undergraduate programs. Ironically, while the universities have resisted the idea of having any university-level institutions in Ontario whose mission is primarily that of teaching, many of them employ large numbers of faculty whose job consists solely of teaching. In some universities, part-time and temporary faculty now do half or more of the teaching in the largest undergraduate faculties.

The seven chapters in this book are grouped into four sections. The first section, composed of Chapter 1, elaborates on the basic thesis of the book, placing it in an historical perspective. We argue that the original rationale for the exclusion of the colleges from baccalaureate credit activity was dependent upon the fact that teaching was the predominant function of the universities at the time, and that the ascendancy of the research university model has now undercut that rationale. The chapter also describes major changes in the environment of higher education since the 1960s, notably those associated with the emergence of a global knowledge society, and the implications of these changes for higher education in Ontario. This opening chapter identifies two societal demands that have had the most formative impacts on higher education in recent years, impacts that will continue to be felt into the foreseeable future: first, accommodating a substantial increase in overall participation in higher education, particularly to baccalaureate programs, and enhancing accessibility for members of groups that historically have been under-represented; and, second, accelerating the pace of knowledge production, particularly of knowledge that has commercial value and enhances Ontario's international economic competitiveness. Besides an ever-growing increase in the private demand for higher education, the push for greater accessibility is fuelled also by governments' belief that a more educated populace is necessary for collective economic well-being. The chapter notes that responses to these two demands—for ever greater accessibility and for knowledge production—are the principal ways in which post-secondary education fulfills its obligation to serve society. Two other societal expectations regarding the conditions under which the teaching and research functions are carried out have had important related constraints on the response of Ontario's post-secondary system's adaptation in recent years: that Ontario should perform both its teaching and research functions at a high level of excellence, and that it should do so in a financially efficient and equitable manner.

Chapters 2 and 3 explore in more detail the two major forces that have driven change in the system, forces that are far from played out: substantial increases in the participation rate and in enrolment, and a new research paradigm arising from governmental expectations that research in post-secondary institutions, particularly universities, will be a key driver of the province's success in a globally competitive, knowledge-based economy. Chapter 2 relates Ontario's experience since the 1960s in attempting to make post-secondary education more accessible. It documents achievements and identifies issues, problems, and lessons. Chapter 3 describes both the internal and external forces that have pushed Ontario universities toward the research university model. It describes the federal and provincial programs that have been introduced since the mid 1990s to encourage and support an expansion of university research, and it discusses some of the important issues that have arisen with the intensification of the university's research function within a new and unfamiliar research paradigm.

Chapters 4, 5, and 6 examine the factors that have constrained and shaped the college and university response to these two large forces: the funding systems, quality assurance and accountability, and the structure of the Ontario system itself. Chapter 4 describes the funding arrangements for Ontario's universities and colleges, and traces the resultant financial circumstances within which post-secondary institutions have functioned since the 1960s. We suggest that the one-size-fits-all funding mechanism that has been in operation over this period has militated against the kind of institutional differentiation that has evolved in many other jurisdictions and that we believe, would better meet Ontario's current and future needs. The chapter shows that recent trends in funding for these institutions have not been as negative as is commonly thought, at least prior to the global economic recession that began in late 2008. This pattern of funding, however, must be seen within the context of the rising expectations of the system in both teaching and research that have brought with them substantial new costs for individual institutions that are not captured in traditional per-student analyses. In this chapter we discuss themes emerging from the relationships among operating revenue, average salary of full-time faculty, teaching loads, student-faculty ratio, and the proportion of faculty who are part-time. Important among these themes is the observation that if the average salary of full-time faculty increases faster than operating revenue, and teaching loads remain constant or decline, then universities have little choice but to increase the student-faculty ratio and/or increase the proportion of part-time faculty. Chapter 5 describes the accountability and quality assurance arrangements and measures that are presently in place for Ontario post-secondary education, and identifies some problems associated with them. For example, it is suggested that the principal performance indicators are not well aligned with provincial goals for post-secondary education, and that the predominant quality paradigm in the university sector militates against some changes that might enable the post-secondary system to meet societal expectations more effectively.

Building on the historical sketch provided in Chapter 1, Chapter 6 elaborates in some detail on the present design of Ontario's post-secondary system and the logic underlying that design. In this chapter we argue that while the present design may have been suitable for the conditions of the 1960s when it was introduced, changes in both the internal and external environments of post-secondary education since then have made it obsolete. We note also that most other jurisdictions of Ontario's size have made considerable changes in the design of their post-secondary systems since the 1960s, while Ontario has not. We suggest that while the inaction in this regard in Ontario compared to other jurisdictions may be explained in large part by lack of the political appetite for change in Ontario, it is due also to inadequate structures and processes for system-level governance of post-secondary education.

In the final section, Chapter 7, we suggest a number of broad conclusions and their implications for the future development of the Ontario post-secondary education system. A dilemma in dealing with the issues identified in this book is how much emphasis to place on advocating for change within existing institutions, particularly the universities, as opposed to proposing new forms of post-secondary education and new types of institutions. As we describe later, previous recommendations for changes in the existing universities of the type discussed in Chapter 7 have been strongly criticized by senior figures in the university community, although it is not clear just how widely shared these criticisms are. Although we think that some new forms of provision of baccalaureate education are necessary, it is simply not financially feasible—especially in current economic circumstances—to rely solely on new providers of baccalaureate programs for change in the way that baccalaureate education is provided.

We believe that the global economic recession that began in 2008 adds urgency to the need for change. Although the length and depth of the recession remains uncertain at the time of writing, it is clear that the combined financial crisis and economic contraction will have profound effects on government and institutional finances, and some of these effects are described in Chapter 4. At the same time the likely permanent shrinkage in many of Ontario's traditional industrial sectors makes it all the more important for the province to build on its strength of a relatively well educated population in order to respond to the economic opportunities of tomorrow. The global recession makes more obvious that change is needed, and will increase the expectation and acceptance of bolder action by government and institutional leaders.

In summary, the goal of this book is to elaborate our thesis that Ontario's present approach to the provision of baccalaureate education is not sustainable. We will marshal evidence and argument in support of this thesis, and suggest modifications to the curent approach. It is not our intention to provide a comprehensive text-book like description of Ontario's post-secondary education system, although in order to achieve our purpose we have to provide a considerable amount of historical and descriptive material pertaining to post-secondary education in Ontario. Nor is it our goal to provide and discuss a litany of problems currently facing post-secondary education in Ontario. However, the central problem that is the focus of our attention does have many different aspects and ramifications, and we follow several of these threads in our analysis. The unifying theme of this book is provided by two broad forces that have washed over post-secondary education in recent decades and continue to do so: demands for increased participation in baccalaureate education and for increased contributions through research to economic competitiveness and wealth generation in a global economy. Because both these forces are most relevant to the central role of the university, our primary emphasis is on the province's universities. We also examine the important contribution that colleges can make to baccalaureate education. Although we do not aim to describe the overall state of education in the colleges, it is important to appreciate how demands on the colleges for the various types and levels of education that they provide may influence the extent and nature of their possible contributions to meeting the province's needs for baccalaureate education.

Finally, this book is about trends and issues in higher education for a single sub-national political jurisdiction, Ontario. While book-length treatments of the subject investigated here are far more common for national than for sub-national jurisdictions, there are two factors besides local interest that make a study at this level particularly relevant, and possibly of interest to people outside Ontario. One is the size. Ontario is the largest province of Canada, with 39 percent of the population, and 41 percent of the full-time post-secondary students in Canada. With about three dozen public post-secondary institutions and over six hundred thousand full-time post-secondary students, Ontario has a post-secondary education system that is as large as that of many nations. Second, and more importantly, in a federal system like Canada's, the key policy and funding decisions pertaining to post-secondary education are made at the provincial level. In fact, as Jones has argued, "there is no such thing as a national system of higher education in Canada" (Jones, 1997, ix). Rather, higher education is best viewed "as a collection of different provincial/territorial systems operating in parallel" (1997, x). Thus, an examination of the systemic dynamics of higher education policy-making and its impacts must necessarily be conducted at the sub-national level. Of course, national governments in federated political systems do have varying types and degrees of influence on higher education, and this is certainly the case in Canada. While our focus in this book is Ontario, we are necessarily mindful of the federal policy context and national (and international) environment in which Ontario higher education operates.

Annexes at the end of this book provide a Glossary of Acronyms and Terms, a Chronology of Key Events, and a listing of Universities and Colleges in Ontario.

1

TRANSFORMATION ... AND THE NEED FOR FURTHER TRANSFORMATION

In 1963 the Ontario post-secondary system consisted of 14 universities which had a combined full-time undergraduate enrolment of 35,000, seven institutes of technology which had a combined enrolment of just over four thousand (of which one institution, Ryerson Institute of Technology, accounted for nearly two-thirds of the total), 11 teachers colleges, close to 60 hospital schools of nursing, and the Ontario College of Art. For the most part the post-secondary system had evolved sporadically to this point, with little deliberative planning. New institutions had come into existence as a result of independent decisions of churches, community and other interest groups, employers, and professional associations. In the years following World War II, the provincial government had taken some initiative in regard to the creation of new institutions, but no mechanism for ongoing system planning had been established. Nor was this collection of post-secondary institutions and facilities yet thought of as "a system."

Faced with projections of enormous growth in the youth population (Jackson, 1963), government departments and some groups of educators began to think seriously about the need for expansion of facilities for post-secondary education. In addition to the anticipated population increase, growing awareness of an explosion in knowledge and rapid changes in technology also contributed to the interest in the province's future needs for post-secondary education. A similar realization that it would be necessary to plan in order to meet imminent needs for post-secondary education was also apparent in other provinces (Dennison and Gallagher, 1986; Skolnik, 1997). The responses to this realization varied. New Brunswick

Academic Transformation: The Forces Reshaping Higher Education in Ontario, I.D. Clark, G. Moran, M.L. Skolnik, and D. Trick. Montreal and Kingston: McGill-Queen's University Press, Queen's Policy Studies Series.
© 2009 The School of Policy Studies, Queen's University at Kingston. All rights reserved.

and Quebec each established a royal commission to document needs and develop plans (Royal Commission, 1962; Royal Commission, 1963). In British Columbia, the president of the provincial university took the initiative himself to produce a plan for the development of the province's post-secondary education system, and that plan was largely implemented by the provincial government (Macdonald, 1962).

In Ontario, detailed deliberations about future needs for higher education were conducted by two distinct agencies: the Department of Education, which included senior officials of the Department and the active involvement of the Minister of Education; and the Committee of Presidents of the Provincially Assisted Universities of Ontario, the predecessor of the Council of Ontario Universities. The important decisions that exerted an enormous shaping influence on post-secondary education which continues to this day were made by the Minister and provincial government. It is unclear just how much direct influence the Committee of Presidents had on those decisions, though the decisions were in the main consistent with the wishes of the Committee.

In sheer enrolment numbers the expansion of post-secondary education over the past four and a half decades has been extraordinary. Enrolment measured in full-time equivalent students (FTEs) now totals about 400,000 in the universities and 200,000 in the colleges. The more than twelve-fold increase in enrolment that has occurred in post-secondary institutions constitutes a quantitative transformation of post-secondary education. On the other hand, this increase in enrolment was accomplished without adding many new institutions. Although there are 19 universities now, all but one of the additional ones existed in a different form in the 1960s, and there are only two more colleges now than when that sector was designed in the mid-60s. The enormous expansion in the size of post-secondary institutions, and changes in their external and internal environments have created strains and problems that are the subject of this book.

SOME FACTORS THAT HAVE SHAPED THE SYSTEM

Two factors that had a particularly significant impact in shaping post-secondary education in Ontario in the last half of the twentieth century were the absence of a private degree granting sector and the decision that the colleges would not have a university transfer function. Several of the universities were originally private institutions, but over the years came into the public system, the last doing so in 1973. As the government authorized the establishment of new publicly funded universities, it responded negatively to attempts by groups that wished to start new private degree granting institutions. Eventually it became formal policy not to allow private degree granting institutions in Ontario, a policy that continued until the year 2000. Relying exclusively on publicly funded institutions to meet the rapidly increasing demand for degree level education had two consequences of note. It made the financial well-being of the post-secondary education system almost totally dependent on what the government felt that it was able and willing to provide for that purpose. Post-secondary education thus became hostage to trends in government revenue, competition from other sectors and interests, and the whims and fashions of politics. As tuition also was strictly controlled by government, residents of Ontario were—in contrast to residents of the United States, and many countries in Asia and South America—unable to exercise their preferences for spending on post-secondary education within their province, except insofar as they could influence the political process. The other consequence was that the post-secondary education system was deprived of the potential for institutional differentiation that private institutions can—but not necessarily will—provide (Levy, 1999). Differentiation is not constrained for private institutions in the way that it often is for public ones which are subject to a common financial and regulatory framework. This factor is potentially significant since, as we argue throughout this book, a lack of institutional differentiation has been a major problem of post-secondary education in Ontario.

The other shaping factor that had perhaps even further-reaching implications was the decision that the new colleges established under a 1965 Act of the Legislature would not have any role in the provision of degree credit courses. This meant that the entire responsibility for all degree credit education in Ontario would rest on publicly supported universities. Ontario university presidents lobbied vigorously to exclude colleges from degree credit activity. This was in contrast with the position taken by universities in several American states, where university presidents strongly advocated that colleges provide the first two years of undergraduate arts and sciences courses. The presidents in these states wanted the colleges to shield their institutions from the burden of serving large numbers of first and second year students, many of them underprepared for academic studies, so that the universities could concentrate on upper division courses, graduate studies, and research. In this connection, Clark Kerr, President of the University of California from 1958 to 1967 said:

> I considered the vast expansion of the community colleges to be the first line of defense for the University of California as an institution of international academic renown. Otherwise the University was going to be overwhelmed by large numbers of students with lower academic attainments or attacked as trying to hold on to a monopoly over entry into higher status. (Kerr, 1978, 26)[1]

---

[1] University leaders in many other states, such as Illinois, Washington, Texas, and Florida, displayed similar attitudes to Kerr's about the value of having comprehensive community colleges. However, there were some states in which

The government's decision that colleges would not have a transfer function was one of Ontario's most widely discussed and second-guessed educational policy decisions of the twentieth century (for analysis of the arguments pro and con and reports of the debates, see Bartram, 1980; Fleming, 1971; Smyth, 1970). However, a few aspects of that decision have not received much attention. One is the question of why the presidents of Ontario universities took such a different position on this issue than their counterparts in many American states. It is insufficient to say that Ontario universities were acting out of self-interest, as that begs the question of just what decision would best serve their interests. Likely, Ontario universities took a different tack than their US counterparts because at the time teaching was the overwhelmingly predominant function of Ontario universities, which were not yet as involved in graduates studies and research as the leading state universities in the United States, such as the University of California. Many of Ontario's universities were small and new, and some were located in communities with a small population of prospective students. Teaching undergraduates was seen by Ontario universities as their major source of revenue, and they didn't want to compete with the colleges for that revenue stream. Be that as it may, the government had undertaken its own analysis of the situation, and did not have to accept the recommendations that it received from the university presidents. However, it was intensely concerned about providing the technical education that it felt was essential for Ontario industry, and feared that such education would be neglected if delivered in institutions that also provided academic education.[2]

For nearly three decades after the colleges were created, the two post-secondary sectors developed in isolation from one another. The main focus of the colleges was preparation for employment, which included

---

university leaders worried, as did their Ontario counterparts, about the potential competition from colleges. Perhaps the most interesting comparison is with Indiana. Leaders of the public universities there were successful in keeping the government from establishing community colleges. However, the Indiana universities established their own two-year branch campuses which would provide the opportunities that community colleges did in other states, and the state also established technical colleges (Dougherty, 1994, 156-157). It is noteworthy that the state universities identified by Dougherty as supporters of a transfer role for colleges were all flagship campuses of state university systems. Even for those institutions, Dougherty notes that the strength of their support tended to fluctuate with their own enrolment and revenue prospects. There was less support for transfer from the less prestigious, and hence less secure, public universities.

[2] Stoll found support for this view in an analysis of original letters, memoranda, handwritten notes, and other documents sent to and from the Minister of Education and the Executive Assistant to the Minister pertaining to the establishment of the colleges (Stoll, 1993).

short term training and retraining, as well as pre-employment programs of longer duration, up to three years. They also offered academic up-grading, adult education, and community education activities. By the 1990s, with the baccalaureate becoming important for several of the fields for which the colleges had been providing programs, and with the increased interest in baccalaureate attainment generally, the colleges became concerned about creating degree completion opportunities for their students. Accordingly, they started giving considerable attention to finding ways of providing such opportunities. This included seeking transfer agreements with universities, developing joint programs, and when both of these approaches turned out to be insufficient, seeking to award baccalaureates on their own.

INCREASING EMPHASIS ON RESEARCH

Among the changes that have occurred in the universities since the early 1960s, the most significant is their transformation from being predominantly teaching institutions to the present situation in which teaching and research are of approximately equal importance.[3] This can be seen, for example, in university mission statements, most of which give about equal emphasis to each of these two functions. It can also be inferred from statements about norms or expectations for allocation of faculty time. For example, at one university there is an explicit statement that the "distribution of effort" for a faculty member shall be 40 percent teaching, 40 percent scholarship, and 20 percent service, unless there is an agreement otherwise in writing between the faculty member and the dean. Similar statements about the normal allocation of effort between teaching and research appear in faculty evaluation policies and collective agreements. The 40-40-20 distribution is not unique to institutions that receive the largest amounts of sponsored research funding. For example, the same distribution of effort among functions is found at an institution that *Maclean's* magazine classifies as primarily undergraduate. The only explicit statement on division of faculty effort among functions that we were able to find in which there is a difference between the proportions of effort on teaching and research was one in which the division of time among teaching, research/scholarly/creative activities, and service is

---

[3] In a 1994 discussion paper, the Ontario Council on University Affairs observed that until the 1950s Ontario universities were primarily teaching institutions, but that in the 1960s a new paradigm of excellence emerged with research productivity at its pinnacle (Ontario Council on University Affairs, 1994). This change was under way in the early to mid 1960s when the decisions about post-secondary education discussed here were made, but the full extent of the transformation and its implications was not yet appreciated.

stated to be 50, 35, and 15, respectively. That modest exception aside, the norm in the Ontario university system is for faculty to spend about the same proportion of their time on research as on teaching.[4]

Underlying the norm that each faculty member should divide his or her time equally between teaching and research is the idea that the teacher-researcher model provides the best possible education—that students learn best when their teachers are also active scholars. Although this idea has the status of an article of faith within the Ontario university community, it is not supported by the enormous body of empirical research that has been conducted on the relationship between teaching and research. Nevertheless, based upon commitment to this idea, Ontario universities have opposed any suggestion that the province should have a university whose mission is predominantly that of teaching, and in which faculty are expected to devote a substantially smaller portion of their time to research than to teaching. It is largely for this reason also that Ontario universities have been reluctant to award credit for courses in the colleges and have opposed degree granting for colleges. The irony is that a substantial proportion of undergraduate courses in Ontario universities are not taught by teacher-researchers, but by part-time faculty who have little or no opportunity to participate in research.

Frequently in discussions about higher education one hears the term "research university." Different observers use the term in different ways, and there is no commonly accepted definition of a research university. The term is generally used to refer to an institution that gives substantial attention to the research function. Thus, it is reasonable to refer to a university in which faculty are expected to spend as much of their time on research as on teaching as a research university, or as a research-oriented university, in order to distinguish it from an institution in which faculty are expected to spend a substantially smaller proportion of their time on research than on teaching.[5] Unlike many other jurisdictions, Ontario does

---

[4] The institutions referred to in the paragraph above are, in order of the references to them, Guelph, Toronto, Brock, and Carleton.

[5] In the 1980s, the term "research-intensive university" was used by a government appointed commission to differentiate among universities on the basis of the proportion of their revenues that was derived from sponsored research (Commission on the Future Role, 1984). While the proportion of revenue derived from sponsored research may be a useful indicator for some purposes, it is but one indicator of effort devoted to research. It is also an indicator that is biased toward institutions that have relatively larger faculties of medical and natural sciences. For providing information on the availability of faculty time for teaching, the allocation of faculty effort between teaching and research is a better indicator than the proportion of revenue derived from sponsored research. The actual distribution of effort between these functions might be a better indicator, but in the absence of available data, the institutional norm is probably a good proxy.

not have a university in which faculty are expected to spend a substantially smaller percentage of their time on research than on teaching. In that regard, we may describe all Ontario universities as research universities, or research-oriented universities, and observe that there is not much differentiation among the universities in the norm for how faculty should divide their time between teaching and research.

In the previous section, we referred to two factors that have had an influence on the shape of higher education in Ontario, the absence of private universities, and the decision that the colleges would not offer degree credit courses. The decision that all Ontario universities would be research universities was not made by the government. Rather, it was the result of the government allowing each publicly funded university to determine its own mission. The government has given each university a broad charter and the freedom that enables it to shape its mission and priorities as it wishes. An important element of the freedom referred to here has been the provision of a single operating grant to each institution that the institution is free to allocate as it chooses. Within this framework, each university has made the decision itself to be a research university.

CONSEQUENCES

As a consequence of the factors just described, Ontario has been attempting to serve a large and rapidly increasing demand for baccalaureate education *exclusively* through publicly funded universities in which faculty typically spend only 40 percent of their time on teaching. The ambitiousness of this undertaking is heightened by the province's apparent intent to have one of the most highly educated populations in the world.[6] While Ontario has been remarkably successful given the ambitiousness of

---

[6] The Higher Education Quality Council of Ontario reported that with 26 percent of its population aged 25-64 with a university degree, Ontario ranked behind only the United States and Norway at 30 percent, and Netherlands at 28 percent among OECD countries. Ontario was tied with Denmark and Iceland (HEQCO, 2009, 22). Looking at the proportion of the population aged 25-34 with a university degree provides a better indicator of recent trends, and on that index, Ontario at 33 percent has overtaken the United States at 30 percent. For this age group Ontario trails only Norway at 40 percent and Netherlands at 34 percent, and is tied with Korea (derived from OECD, 2008 and Statistics Canada, 2006). The competition for international leadership in educational attainment is likely to become more intense. Australia's Education Minister announced her government's intention to increase the proportion of the population aged 25-34 with a baccalaureate or higher degree from 32 percent to 40 percent by 2025 (Maslen, 2009). The Minister noted that Germany, Sweden, the United Kingdom, and Ireland had also announced similar or higher targets for educational attainment.

the goal, it is also not surprising that the universities have been voicing anguished concern for over three decades about inadequate funding. The crux of the problem is that Ontario is attempting to rely on a single approach to the provision of baccalaureate education—the most expensive approach—for all baccalaureate education, while aiming to have among the highest participation rates in the world.

Providing the amount of baccalaureate education in the way that the university sector wishes to supply it requires more money than any Ontario government has been willing, or felt itself able, to provide. This problem has been described by a series of advisory bodies over the past three decades, with little government response. The Committee on the Future Role of Universities in Ontario in 1981 (Committee on the Future Role, 1981)—known as the Fisher Committee, after its Chair, Harry Fisher, Deputy Minister of Education and Colleges and Universities—observed that there were only two ways out of this impasse: either the government had to provide a massive increase in the level of public funding or the structure of the university system had to be radically altered to make it more economical. The Committee suggested that one such alteration might be to have only one full spectrum university, no more than four full service universities that offered a restricted range of high quality programs at all degree levels, and four or five special purpose universities. The remainder would be closed or restructured.

Shortly after the government received the report, it appointed a Commission, headed by Edmund C. Bovey, a board chair of one of the universities, that was asked to develop "an operational plan" for the university system that would provide for "more clearly defined, different and distinctive roles for the universities" (Commission on the Future Role, 1984). However, the Bovey Commission ignored this request, and instead focused on funding arrangements within the existing structure, recommending that institutional differentiation be achieved through evolution in a competitive context. The Commission disliked the idea of any central agency designating the missions and roles of the individual institutions. The antipathy of Ontario universities to any form of central direction has been a recurring theme in dialogues about higher education policy. In the mid-1960s, the Committee of Presidents of Ontario's universities commissioned a former president of the University of Saskatchewan, J.W.T. Spinks, to conduct a review of graduate studies and research, and make recommendations on the development of these activities. Spinks shocked the Committee with his conclusion that there was a need for some type of centralized planning for the development of the university system. He observed:

> The most striking characteristic of higher—not only graduate—education in
> Ontario is the complete absence of a master plan, of an educational policy,

and of a co-ordinating authority for the provincially-supported institutions. (Spinks, 1966, 77-78)

The Committee of Presidents was so dismayed with this observation that it released the Spinks Report during the Christmas holidays when Spinks had gone home and the report was likely to get the least attention (Monahan, 2004).

The most detailed and substantial examination of the relationship between research and teaching in Ontario universities, and of its implications for funding and policy was a 1994 discussion paper produced by the Ontario Council on University Affairs. This paper was produced at the request of the Minister of Education and Training, who asked the Council for advice on how the universities could increase enrolment by up to 19 percent, become more accessible to underrepresented groups, give more emphasis to teaching, and do better at facilitating movement of students from college to university without a significant increase in funding. The conclusion in the discussion paper was that the only way the university sector could accommodate a substantial increase in enrolment and give more attention to teaching without an increase in funding was to reduce the effort devoted to research. Based upon its review of the literature on the relationship between teaching and research, the discussion paper concluded that the present emphasis on research in Ontario universities could not be justified in terms of its contribution to undergraduate education.

As for persuading the universities to shift resources from research to teaching, the discussion paper observed that within the existing funding arrangements, the decision about the allocation of resources between teaching and research is the prerogative of the institution, and that institutions would not willingly make such a shift. Therefore, the paper suggested changing the funding system in such a way as to separate funding for research from funding for teaching. This would allow the government to decide how much to allocate to research and how much to teaching, i.e., shift that decision from the institution to the government. The university community was deeply opposed to the discussion paper's suggestion of an incremental shift in the balance between research and teaching (for an analysis of university responses to the discussion paper, see Skolnik, 1995). One response accused the Task Force of wanting to forbid faculty from doing research.

Raising the question of the appropriate relationship between teaching and research, even in the sober, scholarly way of the discussion paper, did not have salutary consequences. Neither action nor further discussion was initiated by the government on the report, and when a subsequent government moved to abolish the Ontario Council on University Affairs, the university community did not come to the Council's defence.

Although questions about the economic viability of the present model of providing baccalaureate education have been at the heart of the inquiries just summarized, the interest in modification of this model is not motivated solely by affordability concerns. There are also concerns about the quality of undergraduate teaching in institutions that are strongly committed to research, particularly for students whose academic backgrounds differ from those who made it to university in earlier generations. There is also concern about whether the universities can make sufficient improvements in accessibility while at the same time devoting more of their resources and effort to the production of knowledge that has commercial value and will enhance the province's productivity and economic competitiveness. Also it seems likely that as the pool of baccalaureate students expands, larger numbers of incoming students will be seeking applied, job oriented education. Fully addressing this demand could threaten to disrupt the balance that the university has always strived for between its economic role and its broader intellectual and cultural role, as Wolf has described so poignantly (Wolf, 2002).

Government decisions about Ontario's post-secondary system that were made in the 1960s, particularly to exclude colleges from any involvement in degree credit activity while at the same time to leave it entirely to each degree granting institution to determine its own mission, may have been appropriate at the time—although there is room to question whether it is ever prudent to give publicly funded institutions the complete authority to determine their own mission. On the other hand, hindsight shows the consequences of having decisions that should be inter-related made independently. If the government had known that all the universities were soon going to become so research-oriented, it might have decided differently.

At the time that these government decisions were made, the goal was to increase the participation rate in baccalaureate programs from just over 5 percent to something in excess of 15 percent. Given the pace of change in social and economic affairs over the past decades, it would be rather surprising if the forms and models of post-secondary education put in place then would still be the most suitable when the province nears the point of universal post-secondary education, with the participation rate approaching 50 percent. The problem is not so much with the original decisions about the design of the post-secondary system, but with the fact that the question about how best to organize baccalaureate education has not been revisited in a systematic manner since then. While there have been some piecemeal adjustments, for example, in 2000 allowing the colleges to offer a limited number of baccalaureates in applied fields of study, there has been no serious rethinking of the design of the entire post-secondary system by those in a position to do something about it since the 1960s.

THE BROADER CONTEXT FOR RETHINKING ONTARIO'S APPROACH
TO THE PROVISION OF BACCALAUREATE-LEVEL EDUCATION

In the previous section, we highlighted a few studies in the past three decades that have indicated a need to rethink Ontario's approach to the provision of baccalaureate level education, and we noted that little action or even deliberation has occurred in response to such calls. The problem which the Fisher Committee and the OCUA Task Force described has grown more serious since those reports first appeared. This is so for several reasons. One is the worsening of the financial situation of post-secondary education in terms of the gap between what is needed to finance baccalaureate education at the scale now desired and the manner in which the universities wish to provide it. Increases in the scale of post-secondary education contributed to a widening of this gap even before the global economic recession, which has exacerbated this problem substantially.

Another reason is an intensification of some of the trends and concerns that were identified in the OCUA discussion paper: pressure to increase access to the baccalaureate, particularly for groups that have been underrepresented in baccalaureate studies, and to improve the quality of undergraduate education and degree completion rates. In large part these concerns reflect a strengthened commitment in our society to social equity, but increasingly they reflect also the recognition of the importance of achieving the full development of our human resource potential for national and provincial economic well-being and social development. The latter recognition is part of Canada's and Ontario's response to the challenges of globalization. At both the national and provincial levels, governments have identified higher education and research as among the most important elements in ensuring that the nation and province have the talent and innovation to successfully compete in the increasingly competitive international economy. Rather than merely being something to pursue in order to satisfy curiosity and advance the career interests of faculty, research is now seen as vital to the prosperity and economic security of the nation and province. Accordingly, governments have introduced substantial new programs of support and increased funding for higher education research.

Many of the factors now shaping the environment in which Ontario post-secondary education will pursue the objectives of increasing accessibility and contributing to the province's economic competitiveness are closely related to two major phenomena: democratization and globalization.

Democratization

Democratization has many facets that are relevant to the future development of post-secondary education. One of the most important of these is the idea that all members of society should have equal access, in a meaningful way, to the resources that society makes available for post-secondary education and to the opportunities resulting from that experience. Access, equity, and opportunity in regard to post-secondary education are not totally under the control of the post-secondary educational system, but neither is the post-secondary system a helpless bystander in regard to these matters. It can be expected that the post-secondary system will increasingly be held to rigorous accountability standards for its own performance with respect not just to providing equitable access, but also to fostering student success, particularly for students from historically disadvantaged groups.

Another aspect of democratization that is related to access and student success, but goes beyond those concerns, is the expectation that organizations given public funding and granted special privileges will behave in ways that further the objectives for which such funding and privileges are given. This means that there may be increasing public interest in the decisions and performance of universities and colleges, and these institutions may be under growing pressure to justify their decisions and behaviour. Expectations for greater accountability and transparency could have implications for institutional autonomy, and, at the least, autonomy will need to be justified on the basis of institutions' service to society rather than being taken for granted.

A third important aspect of democratization is the movement toward greater diversity among the staff of colleges and universities with respect to such characteristics as gender, ethnicity, and background. As a consequence of this increasing diversity, one can no longer assume widespread agreement with the institutional norms, values, and assumptions pertaining to academic work that have been so prevalent in Canadian academic life over the past several decades, including ideas about what constitutes quality in academic work. Also it may be increasingly difficult to gain consensus on institutional priorities and important academic decisions, and traditional governance processes may come under considerable strain.

Globalization

"Globalization" is a term for a set of phenomena that, taken together, has several important implications for higher education. First and perhaps foremost, globalization has heightened the public perception of the importance to the province's economic well-being of the knowledge and skills produced by post-secondary institutions through their teaching and research. The heightened public interest in the contribution of higher education to economic growth and security puts considerable stress on colleges and especially universities in dealing with the age old tension between economic and broader intellectual and cultural objectives.

Though not necessarily mandated by globalization, one element in the response of many governments, including to some extent Ontario's, has been increasing reliance on market and quasi-market forces. A manifestation of this in Ontario has been at least a slight opening of what had been a closed system to greater competition in the provision of degree level education. With the present international economic distress, many governments are rethinking the balance between government direction and reliance on market forces, and it is unclear where this process will lead, and what its implications may be for Ontario post-secondary education. The broader debate about the benefits of regulation and de-regulation provide an important part of the context for addressing the issues that are central to this book.

In a related vein, a third important implication of globalization for post-secondary education has been increased uncertainty about the levels of funding available for universities and colleges and greater pressure on these institutions to be, and be seen to be, more efficient. This is yet another factor that will contribute to the pressure for greater accountability. Because the public understands the teaching function of the university better than the research function, it may be necessary in the coming period of financial stringency to do a better job of explaining and justifying expenditures on research.

Globalization has spawned apparent pressure toward blurring the boundaries between higher education and industry from two directions. There is both pressure on universities for increased collaboration with the business sector in order to help make Ontario industry more economically competitive, and to adopt decision-making and operational processes associated with the business sector in order (allegedly) to make institutions more efficient. These pressures have met with some resistance on many university campuses among faculty who are sensitive to the differences between the values and conventions of academe and those of business. However, as is common in periods of great change, there are some contradictions in the reactions of higher education stakeholders to these pressures. For example, often the same faculty who object most strongly to the university adopting practices that they associate with industry are the ones who have been most avidly seeking to bring trade unionism to the campus.

Finally, globalization has generated pressure for greater commonality of structures, processes, and standards in post-secondary education worldwide. Harmonization of various facets of post-secondary education across jurisdictions is sought in part to facilitate mobility of students, graduates, and faculty, and in part to create a level playing field for competition among providers of post-secondary education. The international focal point for efforts in this direction has been the Bologna Process, through which 45 European nations have undertaken to harmonize their structures for post-secondary education in order to create an integrated European

Higher Education Area. In some respects, the Bologna Process is aimed at helping Europe achieve something that already exists to a considerable extent in North America, a uniform structure of degrees. However, looking at the Ontario post-secondary situation through the lens of the Bologna Process may shed light on some unresolved issues, for example the ambiguous status of baccalaureates awarded by Ontario colleges. In Europe, opinion seems to be divided as to whether Bologna is leading to a convergence of degrees between the university and non-university sectors, and this issue has been the subject of considerable attention (Machado et al., 2008).

One of the goals of the Bologna Process is harmonization of quality standards among jurisdictions. Given the diversity of quality assurance models and processes within Ontario and Canada, the Bologna Process may generate pressure to achieve greater consistency among quality standards throughout Canadian higher education, and comparability with other nations in this regard.

SERVING SOCIETY

The factors described in the previous section, particularly globalization, have given a new sense of urgency and direction to the role of higher education in serving society. Although the university may have originated in the desire of scholars to understand the world around them, as historian Nathan Schachner noted, it was not long before popes, kings, and emperors discovered how to use this astonishing new resource to serve their own ends (Schachner, 1938). Thus began the long struggle between town and gown for control of the university, a struggle that has been a central element in the history of the university.

In a related vein, Brubacher described two directions in which the university has always been pulled: serving truth and serving society (Brubacher, 1977). While it may be possible to reconcile these apparently conflicting directions philosophically by observing that in the long run nothing serves society better than truth, in the short run the goals of scholars often seem in conflict with the goals of the governments that provide the funding necessary for the operation of the institution. For example, while some curiosity driven research may produce tangible benefits for society within a reasonable time frame, other research of this type may yield identifiable benefits for society only in the very long run or not at all. Further, governments may perceive that greater benefits of the kind they value will accrue more from some disciplines than others, and thus for example, governments may provide greater financial support for research in the natural sciences and medicine than in the social sciences and humanities.

In the long history of the university, there has frequently been a tension between the pursuit and transmission of knowledge for its own sake on the one hand, and on the other the more instrumental pursuit and trans- mission of knowledge to serve specifically defined ends. The pendulum between these orientations has swung back and forth over time; often the reaction to excessive preoccupation with one orientation has resulted in a move to create more balance between the two. However, it may well be that the trend toward universal higher education, supported by public funding, will change the university forever. No society can afford to sup- port all of its young people for four years of post-secondary education that has no instrumental purpose.

The origin of the community colleges was quite different from that of the universities. Community colleges in Canada were established by provin- cial governments to pursue specific objectives set by those governments. However, the kinds of conflict over priorities that have been endemic to the university sector are not totally foreign to the college one. While col- leges have since their founding had a major responsibility for workforce preparation, their mission has also included helping individuals to change and enrich their lives, and helping communities to improve their quality of life. In order for colleges to accomplish these goals, it has been important for them to provide "an environment in which learning is revered and in which opportunities for personal advancement abound" (Dennison, 1995, 282). With globalization have come pressures that have made it difficult for colleges to maintain this kind of environment. Commenting on the changes that have occurred in community colleges in both Canada and the United States as the pressures of globalization have been felt during the last two decades of the twentieth century, Levin observed that "the mission of the community college had less emphasis on education and more on training; less emphasis on community social needs and more on the economic needs of business and industry; less emphasis upon indi- vidual development and more on workforce preparation and retraining" (Levin, 2001, 171).

Higher education in Ontario has undergone two types of transforma- tion since the early 1960s. One, associated with the enormous increase in enrolment, is the transformation from elite to universal higher edu- cation; the other is from serving society primarily through its teaching function to becoming also a major producer of knowledge that is vital to the innovativeness and competitiveness of Ontario industry. These transformations have created serious strains that limit the effectiveness of the post-secondary system. As a consequence, it is necessary to further transform the system in order to enable it to carry out its present respon- sibilities more effectively. In this attempt, attention should be given also to the importance of maintaining, if not strengthening, the capacity of the system to perform its traditional intellectual and scholarly functions, as well as to seeking a healthy balance between these traditional functions and the newer functions which it has been called upon to perform for society.

Within the context just outlined, this book examines the achievements and problems experienced in Ontario post-secondary education in its simultaneous pursuit of the accessibility and knowledge production objectives described in Chapters 2 and 3, while still employing a model for baccalaureate education that was developed through provincial and institutional decisions made some decades ago that we describe in further detail in Chapter 6.

2

THE CHALLENGE OF ACCESS

MOVING FROM AN ELITE SYSTEM TO A NEAR-UNIVERSAL SYSTEM

The dominant story in Ontario higher education over the past half-century, as in many other jurisdictions, has been the transition from an elite system to a mass system and then from a mass system to a near-universal system. Enrolment growth has been due primarily to higher participation rates, and only secondarily to growth in the normal source-age population. Using Trow's demarcations (Trow, 1973), Ontario passed from an elite system of higher education to a mass system in the late 1960s, when the share of young people attending higher education passed 15 percent. Ontario is on the brink of passing the 50 percent threshold that separates mass from universal systems of higher education. These figures measure full-time equivalent post-secondary enrolments as a share of the population aged 18-24, as shown in Figure 2.1.

By other measures Ontario already meets Trow's standard for universal higher education. Slightly over half of Ontarians aged 25-34 have attained a post-secondary education (Higher Education Quality Council of Ontario, 2007). Eighty-three percent of Ontarians aged 24-26 say that they have attended university, college, or other post-secondary institution for at least some period of time, without necessarily graduating (Shaienks, Gluszynski, and Bayard, 2008).

Total enrolments in Ontario's post-secondary education system, measured in full-time equivalents (FTEs), have grown nearly six-fold since the late 1960s. The number of university students has grown from fewer than 100,000 to almost 400,000. The college system, which was in its infancy in the late 1960s, has grown to nearly 200,000 FTEs, as shown in Figure 2.2.

Academic Transformation: The Forces Reshaping Higher Education in Ontario, I.D. Clark, G. Moran, M.L. Skolnik, and D. Trick. Montreal and Kingston: McGill-Queen's University Press, Queen's Policy Studies Series.
© 2009 The School of Policy Studies, Queen's University at Kingston. All rights reserved.

FIGURE 2.1
Post-secondary enrolments as a share of the population aged 18-24, Ontario,
1950-51 to 2007-08 (percent)

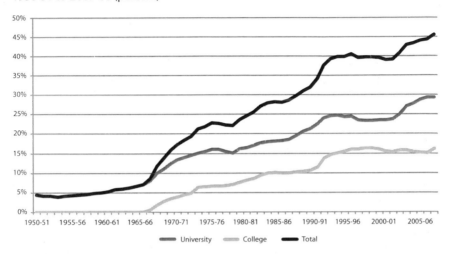

Source: Ontario Ministry of Training, Colleges and Universities and Ontario Ministry
of Finance.

FIGURE 2.2
Post-secondary enrolments, Ontario, 1967-68 to 2007-08 (FTEs)

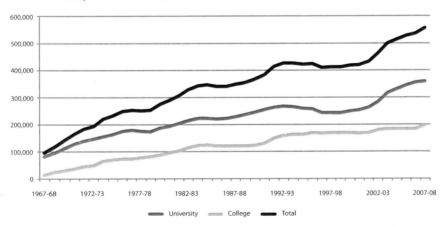

Source: Ontario Ministry of Training, Colleges and Universities.

This growth has had almost no impact on the overall structure of the
higher education system put in place in the mid-1960s, but it has had
an enormous impact on individual universities and colleges. Most institutions have grown substantially. The average college numbers about
8,000 students today, compared with 3,000 in 1973. In the same period,

the average university has grown from 10,000 to almost 20,000 students. Put another way, the majority of Ontario's university students are now enrolled at a university with more than 30,000 students, and the majority of college students are at a college with more than 11,000 students.

THE COMING BOOM IN ENROLMENTS

The sharp rise in the number of students applying to attend higher education in this decade, especially in the university sector, suggests that the half-century-long increase in higher education participation rates is by no means over. Students and their parents correctly sense that a post-secondary education will significantly increase the likelihood of accessing secure employment with the prospect of career advancement.

On a province-wide basis, population growth by itself will place little pressure on post-secondary enrolments over the next decade. The Ontario Ministry of Finance projects that the Ontario population aged 18-24 will grow slowly to 2014 and then decline, so that in 2021 it will be about equal to its 2005 level.

The pressure for growth will come from rising participation rates. University participation rates have been on a continuous upward trend since the early 1950s, with only a few brief pauses. Assuming that these rates continue to rise in accordance with the long-term trend, and that Ontario wishes to continue to accommodate the demand as it has in the past, it is reasonable to expect that university undergraduate enrolments in 2021 will be 60,000-100,000 higher than in 2007.[7]

---

[7] This is a consensus estimate based on our own analysis and on projections from other sources. We have projected that the number of undergraduate students who will want to attend university in Ontario will be 60,000-100,000 higher in 2021 than in 2007, an increase of 17-28 percent. We have also projected that, if historical patterns of student demand continue, the demand to attend GTA universities will grow by 29-39 percent by 2021 over 2007 levels, while the demand to attend non-GTA universities will grow by 11-22 percent. The higher end of this projection is based on an extrapolation of the average increase in participation rates from 1997 to 2007; the lower end assumes that participation rates in future will grow at only half the rate of increase of the 1997-2007 period. A separate projection based on an extrapolation of the average increase in participation rates since 1950 suggests an increase of 53,000-86,000 FTEs from 2007 to 2021. Ryerson University has estimated that the number of students wanting to attend university in the GTA "may be 34-49 percent higher in 2021 than it is today" (Ryerson University, 2008)—equivalent to an increase of 36,000-65,000 students. A University of Toronto report says that, "The Government of Ontario expects growth in demand for undergraduate university places to be especially intense in the Toronto region. Conservative projections call for 40,000 new places in Toronto" (University of

College enrolments are more difficult to project. The demand to attend college is sensitive to economic circumstances: enrolments grew sharply during the recessions of the early 1980s and early 1990s, and then in each case levelled off at their new higher levels. Based on assumptions similar to those for universities—that long-term participation rates continue to rise in accordance with the long-term historical trend, and that Ontario wishes to continue to accommodate the demand as it has in the past—it is reasonable to expect that college enrolments in 2021 will be 35,000-50,000 higher than in 2007.[8] Much of the rise in applications to college is likely to take place over the next several years, as the current economic downturn drives more young people to seek a college education and more laid-off workers to prepare for a new career.

TABLE 2.1
Projected growth in post-secondary enrolments in Ontario (FTEs)

	Enrolments (FTEs, 2007)	*Projected growth 2007-2021*
University undergraduate	354,000	60,000-100,000
College post-secondary	183,000	35,000-50,000

The demographic outlook in the Greater Toronto Area (GTA)[9] is sharply different from that in the rest of the province. Fuelled by continued high levels of immigration, the number of young people in the GTA is expected to grow almost continuously over the period to 2021. In the rest of Ontario, the number of young people will grow modestly to 2014 and then decline. By 2021, the total number of young people in Ontario will be about the same as in 2009, but they will be heavily redistributed: there will be more people age 18-24 in the GTA than in the rest of the province combined, as shown in Figure 2.3. This means that the expected growth in demand to attend university will be heavily concentrated in the GTA. This will also be true for colleges, but to a lesser extent, because colleges in all regions will see increased demand from laid-off workers.

To accommodate so many additional students in the GTA will be an enormous challenge. All of the existing universities and most of the colleges have grown substantially since the late 1990s. All face shortages of space and, in some cases, shortages of developable land.

Toronto, 2008, 7). Media reports suggest that "between 40,000 and 75,000 places will be needed in the city" by 2014 (Church, 2007.)

   [8]This figure includes diploma and certificate students only. It excludes apprenticeships and short-term training.

   [9]The Greater Toronto Area is defined to include the City of Toronto plus the Regional Municipalities of Durham, Halton, Peel, and York.

FIGURE 2.3
Ontario population aged 18-24

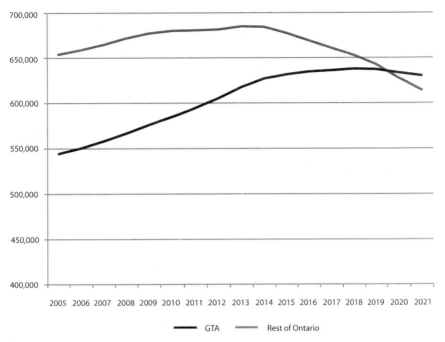

Source: Ontario Ministry of Finance (2008).

Despite the projected population decline outside of the GTA, the enrolment outlook for most universities and colleges outside Toronto is far from bleak. Higher participation rates will offset the effect of population decline in most regions of the province. There has historically been a net flow of university-bound GTA students to non-GTA universities, reflecting both the supply of spaces and student preferences. In 2007, 54 percent of university-bound secondary school students who lived in the GTA chose to enrol at a university in the GTA, and 46 percent enrolled at universities elsewhere in the province. Conversely, 91 percent of university-bound students who lived outside the GTA attended university outside the GTA, and only 9 percent attended GTA universities. For these reasons, most universities outside the GTA will maintain their enrolments over the coming decade or experience modest growth. For many colleges outside the GTA, the demographic picture is less sanguine: only 13 percent of students entering college from the GTA enrolled in non-GTA colleges in 2008. A few institutions will have difficulty maintaining enrolments, especially in Northern Ontario, where the youth-age population is expected to decline by 22 percent between 2005 and 2021.

Supply or Over-supply?

The sharp growth in projected demand raises the question of whether that demand should be met. There is nothing inevitable about such a policy response. The United States—which holds first place among OECD countries for higher education attainment levels among 55-to-64-year-olds, but ranks only fourth place among 35-to-44-year-olds and tenth place among 25-to-34-year-olds (OECD, 2007)—can be seen as an example of a country that has, comparatively speaking, placed a lower priority in recent decades on access to higher education than on other public and private goods.

The standard argument for expanding participation in higher education is that more years of education lead to higher incomes, and these incomes produce net benefits for both the individual and society. However, the relationship between actual learning in post-secondary institutions and subsequent economic success is difficult to demonstrate with certainty. Universities and colleges benefit from a number of phenomena that make the institutions attractive to students, employers, and alumni, but have very little to do with what students learn there. These include:

- Sorting. The challenge of being admitted to a post-secondary institution and surviving to graduation performs a sorting function that employers and others can use as a convenient signal of innate ability and future potential. The validity of this signal is only partly related to what students actually learn in their courses.
- Credentialing. Universities and colleges are near-monopoly providers of credentials that are either absolutely required or strongly recommended for entrance into a variety of professions and careers. People will want to come to the institutions to acquire this credential almost regardless of what they learn.
- Blossoming. Universities and colleges are places where many people spend their first years of adulthood—years when they gain independence from parents, form relationships, and learn about life. Many look back on these years with relish, and post-secondary institutions are the beneficiaries of this nostalgia, no matter what took place in the classroom.
- Bonding. Relationships made during these formative years often last a lifetime, and become the basis of valuable professional and social networks. Again, this is almost independent of the teaching that takes place in the classroom.
- Branding. Given that so much of the value of the university degree or college diploma is associated with the place rather than the learning, and given the intense competition among institutions for resources and students, it is not surprising that branding is becoming more important for all institutions. The most basic brands are the terms "college" and "university." The second level of brand is the specific

institution. The efforts of post-secondary institutions to "build their brand" are likely to get stronger without necessarily offering evidence of the learning associated with the program of study.

Yet even economists who are highly sceptical of government-led expansions of higher education agree that education is positively related to economic productivity. Their argument is that education has multiple economic effects—improving productivity, helping employers identify prospective employees with high innate abilities, and assigning standard credentials for certain baskets of knowledge and ability—and that these effects are difficult to disentangle. (See, for example, Wolf, 2004.)

Since the late 1950s, every Ontario government has committed itself to providing a place in post-secondary education for all qualified students who wish to attend. This policy was initially controversial—the president of the University of Toronto, Sidney Smith, told a national conference on university enrolments in 1955 that "[w]e are admitting many young men and women who have neither the brains nor the moral stamina to pursue advanced studies" (Globe and Mail, 1955)—and some university administrations argued that the projected rise in university applications should be an opportunity to set more demanding admissions standards. Their opposition was short-lived. Governments have justified accessibility both as a matter of individual right and as a means of economic development. Indeed, they have seen little need to distinguish between these two rationales, since the individual's interest in personal development and the government's interest in economic development have been seen to coincide.

We might propose two tests to determine whether further expansion is warranted. The first is a market test: Do workers with a post-secondary credential earn more than those without one? An indicator of the economic demand for higher education can be found by measuring the gap in earnings between workers with a university or college education and workers without. In Canada, the earnings gap between workers aged 25-34 with a high school education and those with a post-secondary education widened between 1980 and 2005, although earnings of less educated workers improved somewhat in the early 2000s as a result of the boom in oil and gas, mining, and construction (Chung, 2006, and the literature review in Emery, 2004). Other research confirms that workers with an advanced education earn more, and are more likely to be employed full-time and full-year, than workers who are high school graduates only, holding demographic factors constant. Higher education creates a more flexible workforce, encourages social and economic mobility, and reduces reliance on government income support programs (Institute for Competitiveness and Prosperity, 2007a). Government-sponsored surveys of recent graduates in Ontario over the past decade suggest that graduates from university and college programs fare well in the labour market on average, although the transition to the workforce is difficult for some graduates. Criticisms of programs that have no clear career orientation overlook the ways in which some—though not all—of these programs have incorporated experiences that prepare students to apply their education in the workforce, including co-op terms, work placements, practicums, field research projects, and other forms of applied learning. According to the Higher Education Quality Council of Ontario,

> Recent research has found that, over the past two decades in Canada, the earnings and employment gap between occupations that normally require PSE and occupations that do not has been fairly constant. In other words, the strong rise in demand in high-skilled occupations has been adequately supplied—but not oversupplied—by the growing number of well-educated workers. (HEQCO, 2009)

A second test of whether Ontario is over-supplying the market for higher education is a competition test: What do other successful jurisdictions do? The Martin Prosperity Institute has compared Ontario with 21 other jurisdictions with similar populations and economic structures. Ontario ranks 16th out of 21 in its share of the population aged 25 or older who hold a baccalaureate. (Massachusetts ranks first.) Ontario ranks slightly better in the share of the population holding graduate and professional degrees, at 12th out of 21. The Institute concludes that "The province underperforms considerably on both measures of human capital" (Martin Prosperity Institute, 2009).

With the development of New Growth Theory, the expectation that investments in education and technology will lead to higher living standards has become near-universal. Factors that provide incentives for knowledge creation (such as research and development, the education system, entrepreneurship, tolerance for diversity and openness to trade) are at the heart of government economic development strategies in much of the developed and developing world (Romer, 2007).

Looking at the evidence as a whole, there is little to suggest that Ontario is producing "too many" highly educated workers or that the province would be more likely to prosper by encouraging qualified students to forego advanced education in favour of directly entering the workforce after high school. In any case, government has the capacity to monitor the economic outcomes of graduates in the workforce and, if these should weaken relative to outcomes for secondary school graduates, to adjust course.

THE NEW STUDENTS

What will cause the demand to attend post-secondary education in Ontario—which is already high by many international standards—to climb even higher? Increasingly, students see higher education—whether it leads to a degree, a diploma, or certification in a skilled trade—as essential to economic security. While higher education offers no guarantees, a student who completes a post-secondary credential is statistically more likely to gain employment that is relatively stable, relatively well-paying, and more likely to lead to career advancement, compared with a student who enters the labour market directly from secondary school. As long as this substantial gap in employment prospects continues, it is reasonable to expect that an increasing share of academically qualified students will seek to enter university or college—as has been the case in Ontario almost continuously for more than a half-century.

Participation rates are already high among demographic groups that traditionally have been most likely to attend universities—that is, young people in families with above-average incomes and in which parents hold a post-secondary diploma or degree. Nevertheless, there is room for participation among these groups to continue to grow.

With appropriate policy supports, these students will increasingly be joined by others from traditionally underrepresented groups—including students with low or moderate family incomes, students from families with no history of attending higher education, First Nations students, students with disabilities, and others. For individuals from historically disadvantaged groups, and for individuals whose families are new to Canada, higher education may be the surest step to full participation in mainstream economic, social, and political institutions. For governments whose economic strategies depend on increasing the share of workers whose skills and abilities can attract well-paying employers and investors, expanding higher education to include non-traditional groups is essential to success.

Overcoming the barriers or deterrents to participation in these underrepresented groups will require expanding the capacity of post-secondary institutions to accommodate them. But it will also require new responses from universities and colleges combined with government initiatives necessary to address students' interest in, and preparation for, higher education.

Family income and parental education

The largest single pool of potential new entrants to higher education is young people from moderate- and low-income families and from families with parents who did not attend higher education themselves. Both factors matter. They are closely intertwined, and affect prospective students for many years prior to the student reaching post-secondary age. Young people from families falling in the lower ranges of family income, and from families where the parents did not attend post-secondary education, continue to be relatively less likely to participate in and graduate from Canadian universities.

In 2001, children from families earning more than $100,000 were about two-and-one-half times as likely to attend university as children from families with annual incomes of less than $25,000 (Berger, Motte, and Parkin, 2007). Families with moderate incomes were more similar to poor families than to well-off families: participation from families with incomes from $50,000 to $75,000 was similar to that for families with incomes below $25,000. The income-related gap in university participation was essentially unaltered between 1993 and 2001 in spite of substantial increases in overall enrolment in Canada's universities (Drolet, 2005). That is, the increased enrolment during this period was drawn from those groups that have traditionally displayed higher participation rates.

Colleges are more successful than universities in attracting students from across the income and education spectrum. In sharp contrast to the pattern in universities, participation rates at Canada's colleges are not closely tied to family income (Drolet, 2005). College participation among children from families falling within the lowest income quintile is not significantly different from that of those from families in the highest income bracket. This same pattern holds for Ontario's colleges: college applicant rates across income levels approximate closely the percentage of the total Ontario population represented by those groups.

The patterns of associations of university and college participation rates with family income are substantially mirrored by their associations with parental education. The likelihood of university participation is a direct function of the parents' education: children of parents with education at the high school level or less, college, or university, display rates of 53, 68, and 81 percent respectively. Statistics for college participation again contrast with university patterns: the educational profile of the parents of college students is very similar to that of the overall population aged 45-64 (Colleges Ontario, 2007, 13). The participation gap associated with family income and parental education in universities, and the clear absence of such a gap in Ontario's colleges, proved fairly constant during the 1991-2001 period. When both factors are taken into account, parental education is a better predictor of participation rate than family income (Drolet, 2005).

Studies taking into account a broader range of factors suggest that non-financial factors account for fully 84 percent of the gap in university attendance between children from families in the highest income quartile and those in the lowest (Frenette, 2007).[10] These factors may include

---

[10] A second independent analysis by Johnson (2008) of data from the same survey came to parallel conclusions regarding the relative importance of factors other than finance in impeding access. See also Berger, Motte, and Parkin (2007).

quality of high schools, school grades at age 15, academic performance on standard tests, whether the student has discussed or planned for higher education, and parental encouragement.

There is evidence that, for a minority of students, substantial annual increases in tuition discourage enrolment. These impacts would be stronger were it not for the effect of government financial aid programs (Johnson and Rahman 2005; Johnson, 2008). The impacts are not confined to low-income students, but may be felt by middle-income students in the absence of adequate financial aid—as has been found, for example, during the period of rapid increases in tuition associated with the deregulation of professional programs in Ontario in the late 1990s (Frenette, 2005).

There is also evidence that university and college age students who cite affordability as an impediment to attendance may, in fact, be referring to factors other than direct tuition costs. Some have concluded that the investment of time and money in post-secondary education cannot be justified on the basis of its long term returns. For others who recognized the longer-term benefits of a post-secondary education, a lack of confidence in their ability to succeed made the investment too risky.

These findings suggest some of the complexities in understanding and improving participation among young people from low-and moderate-income families. Financial and non-financial factors are not easily disaggregated, and they affect students over a period of many years. Many of the non-financial factors cited as being the greatest deterrents to university attendance by children from lower income families have financial origins. Each of these variables is, at least in part, likely to have roots in the relative financial disadvantages of the family but at a time much earlier than the age at which decisions are made to attend higher education. Underrepresented groups such as low-and moderate-income families and students whose parents did not attend higher education are highly likely to face simultaneously several, rather than only one, of these significant deterrents to participation. Financial, academic, and motivational or informational impediments tend to co-occur within these groups.

Compounding the problem of lower rates of participation among children of families with lower incomes and first generation university students is the fact that such students are more likely to encounter difficulties and fail to complete their degrees once enrolled (Engle and O'Brien, 2008; Berger, Motte, and Parkin, 2007). Improved access will need to be accompanied by new approaches to supporting completion.

Students from immigrant families

Most of Ontario's population growth over the coming decades will be attributable to international immigration. Census data show that, as of 2006, young people aged 25-34 with immigrant parents are, on average, 50 percent more likely to attend and complete university education than children of Canadian-born parents. This gap is partly due to the higher education levels of the immigrant parents.[11] With policy changes that have favoured immigration by degree-educated professionals, there is a growing population of recent immigrants who are more likely than the Canadian-born population to want their children to earn a degree and who are willing to make significant financial sacrifices for this purpose.

Immigration will have two effects on Ontario's higher education system: it will increase the number of students wanting to attend, leading to higher participation rates, and it will tend to concentrate demand on urban areas that attract the most immigrants. Cities that attract immigrants will see their populations grow, while most not attracting immigrants will see their populations stabilize or decline. Recent immigrants are more than twice as likely to settle in the Greater Toronto Area as in any other city in Ontario, as shown in Table 2.2. Among other Ontario cities, only Ottawa, Hamilton, Kitchener, Guelph, London, and Windsor attract immigrants approximately in proportion to their share of the population. Other cities—including some with major post-secondary institutions—attract few immigrants relative to their populations.

The situation in the GTA will differ from that in most of the rest of Ontario, and Ontario's situation will differ from that of most other provinces, where the normal post-secondary-age population is expected to decline starting in the mid-2010s before recovering in the 2030s (Berger, Motte, and Parkin, 2007).

Will the impact of immigration be mitigated by the dispersal of immigrants to centres outside the GTA? For decades there has been a two-way flow of post-secondary students, especially university students, from the GTA and vice versa. While this flow will continue, the future growth in participation by immigrants and by students from low- and moderate-income families suggests that the share of GTA students wishing to attend university outside the GTA may be somewhat lower in future.

Research suggests that immigrants prefer to settle in communities where they have family or friends. They tend initially to be more reliant on friends and family to link them to employment. There is little dispersal to other cities in subsequent years, due to the attraction of an established immigrant community and the generally strong economic opportunities offered by large urban centres. There is evidence that, when immigrants

---

[11] This figure includes students with at least one immigrant parent; the students themselves may or may not be immigrants. (Abada, Hou, and Ram, 2008; Sweet, Anisef, and Walters, 2008). The phenomenon of high immigrant participation in education is not unique to Canada: at the University of California, 61 percent of students are foreign-born or have at least one parent who is foreign-born (Brint et al., 2007).

TABLE 2.2
Distribution of recent immigrants to Canada by selected census metropolitan areas (percent), 2006

	Total population	Total immigrant population	Recent immigrants	Ratio of recent immigrants to total population
Canada	100.0	100.0	100.0	...
Toronto	16.2	37.5	40.4	2.5
Windsor	1.0	1.2	1.2	1.2
Kitchener	1.4	1.7	1.5	1.1
Ottawa – Gatineau	3.6	3.3	3.2	0.9
Hamilton	2.2	2.7	1.9	0.9
Guelph	0.4	0.4	0.4	0.9
London	1.4	1.4	1.2	0.8
St. Catharines – Niagara	1.2	1.1	0.7	0.6
Oshawa	1.1	0.9	0.4	0.4
Kingston	0.5	0.3	0.2	0.4
Barrie	0.6	0.4	0.2	0.3
Brantford	0.4	0.3	0.1	0.3
Peterborough	0.4	0.2	0.1	0.2
Thunder Bay	0.4	0.2	0.1	0.2
Sudbury	0.5	0.2	0.1	0.1

Note: "Immigrant population," also known as "foreign-born population," is defined in the 2006 and 2001 Census as persons who are, or have been, landed immigrants in Canada. "Recent immigrants" refer to immigrants who came to Canada between 1 January 2001 and 16 May 2006. This ratio shows whether the share of recent immigrants in a given location is higher than the share of the total population in the same location. For example, if 5 percent of recent immigrants live in a place and the same share (5 percent) of the total population lives there, then the ratio will be 1.0.

Source: Statistics Canada, Census of population (2006).

move after they arrive, the net effect is to concentrate the effects of immigration rather than to disperse immigrants across the country.[12]

GTA students who enrol at non-GTA universities today come, on average, from higher-income families. As demand grows in the coming years among students from low- and moderate-income families who at

---

[12] For a review of this literature, see Matthews (2006, 44-64).

present are less likely to attend university, there will be strong financial reasons for these students to want to live with family for at least part of their university years.

In addition, many full-time students rely on part-time employment to fund educational and personal expenses. At one GTA university, two-thirds of students reported working for pay during the academic year in 2005. Among those students who work off campus, the median student works 11-20 hours per week. Like older workers, students often find jobs through personal contacts and word-of-mouth. Students connected to the GTA labour market may be reluctant to leave their jobs for smaller cities where their job prospects are less certain.

Aboriginal students

Aboriginal students in Ontario are approximately as likely as non-aboriginal students to hold a college diploma or certificate, but they are only one-third as likely to hold a university degree. To close this gap would require an additional 900 aboriginal students to enter Ontario universities each year for 20 years. First Nations students are more likely to fall within the broader categories of children from families of lower income and those with parents who have not participated in post-secondary education, and face the same barriers as non-aboriginal children in those groups. A particular barrier is that, at the time of the 2001 Census, 43 percent of aboriginal people age 20-24 had not completed high school, compared with 16 percent of the non-aboriginal population. For aboriginals on reserves in Ontario, the non-completion rate is 55 percent (Mendelson, 2006). Newer data from the 2006 Census show that, nationally, the university education gap between aboriginal and non-aboriginal Canadians grew between 2001 and 2006: the share of aboriginal adults with a university degree grew from 6 to 8 percent, while the share for non-aboriginals grew from 20 to 23 percent (Statistics Canada, 2006b).

Improving high school completion rates among aboriginal students may be the largest single measure that will lead to improved post-secondary participation. Post-secondary participation rates among aboriginal youth completing their high school education approach those for the non-aboriginal population: in fact, 65 percent of aboriginal youth who finished twelfth grade in 2003 had pursued some post-secondary studies within two years, compared to 80 percent of non-aboriginal respondents (Berger, Motte, and Parkin, 2007, 21). Efforts by universities and colleges to enhance the experience of aboriginal students, coupled with financial aid, will be significant factors for closing the remaining gap.

Gender issues

Perhaps the most striking trend in post secondary enrolment over the past four decades has been the growth of participation by women. The number of women enrolled in Canada's universities expanded from approximately 75,000 in 1966 to 465,000 in 2006 (AUCC, 2007). Women now comprise approximately 58 percent of undergraduates, 50 percent of master's students and 45 percent of PhD enrolment. Women also now make up the majority of students in Ontario's colleges: in 2005-06, women made up approximately 58 percent of applicants and registrants and 60 percent of graduates. The steady increase in female enrolment follows directly on the removal of barriers to their participation; this has been a historic period of increases in educational, lifestyle and career choices for women in Canadian society. In both colleges and universities, the relative proportion of men and women varies substantially across programs.

What is less easy to explain is the substantial under-participation by men relative to women: men are now only two-thirds as likely to attend higher education as women. While there is no reason to expect exact parity, the difference suggests that a large number of male students who might benefit from higher education are not attending.

HISTORICAL RESPONSES TO DEMANDS FOR GREATER ACCESS

How have Ontario's higher education institutions responded to growing demand in the past? Borrowing from Trow, we can think of government advisors and institutional leaders in higher education as responding to change along two dimensions. The first is their attitude regarding the proper forms and functions of higher education, where orientations can range from "traditionalist" at one end to "reformist" at the other. The second is their attitude toward the growth of higher education, where orientations can range from "elitist" to "expansionist."

This typology produces four combinations of policy orientation as illustrated in Table 2.3.

TABLE 2.3
A typology of responses to changing conditions and expectations in higher education

		Attitude towards the purposes and forms of higher education	
Attitude towards growth		*Traditionalist*	*Reformist*
	Elitist	Traditionalist elitists	Reformist elitists
	Expansionist	Traditionalist expansionists	Reformist expansionists

- The "traditionalist elitists" would retain the forms, functions, and enrolments roughly as they were in the mid-20th century.
- The "reformist elitists" would like to maintain a highly selective university system with high academic standards but would make changes to account for recent developments in technology, pedagogical theory, professional requirements, and societal expectations for fairness (perhaps including such reforms as needs-blind admission policies); this group would also be likely to support a much-expanded college system for those who do not meet the academic requirements to be admitted to university.
- The "traditionalist expansionists" would prefer to expand enrolments to provide higher education opportunities but at the same time to retain the best of what developed in universities and colleges when higher education was an elite activity.
- The "reformist expansionists" would seek the necessary changes to the forms and functions of higher education to accommodate much higher enrolments at a lower per-student cost to meet the resources available.

Ontario has gained significant experience over the past half-century in expanding its higher education system to meet growing student demand (Trick, 2005). Throughout this history, the decision-making process has been dominated by traditionalist-expansionist thinking. Student demand to attend post-secondary education has rapidly increased on five occasions: (1) the expansion of post-secondary enrolments from the mid-1950s to 1971 as the first part of the post-war baby boom entered the system; (2) the growth in university enrolments from 1986 to 1992 associated primarily with increased female participation rates; (3) and (4) the rapid expansion in college enrolments from 1978 to 1983, and again from 1990 to 1993, associated with the recessions in those periods; and (5) the increase in enrolments beginning in 2002, especially in universities, associated with the double cohort of entering students following Ontario's secondary school reforms. This experience is instructive because it tells us about the political and institutional dynamics of policy development during periods of enrolment growth.

The early baby boom expansion, mid-1950s to early 1970s

Projections of increased demand became widely known across Canada in 1955 and were generally accepted (including by the Ontario government) by 1957. These initial projections substantially underestimated the demand that materialized, but they were enough to spur the provincial government to action. The provincial government took the lead in ensuring that there would be a space in Ontario's universities for every qualified student who wished to apply. It introduced bills to create each of the new universities, creating a system in which each university was formally equal, was autonomous from government in most internal matters, and had the mission of granting degrees at all levels of study and in a wide range of disciplines. The government granted start-up funding for the new institutions until they reached viable size, and it provided financial incentives for established universities to expand. In 1963, having approved the establishment of universities in all regions, Premier Robarts placed a moratorium on the creation of new universities for at least fifteen years. In 1964—after the new universities were established—the government created a separate department to manage its relationships with the universities. The government also recognized the labour market need for nondegree graduates in applied arts and technology and so created a province-wide system of colleges.

The primary response of the established universities was to expand their own enrolments and—recognizing that the number of students was likely to exceed the number of spaces they could supply—to support the creation of new universities and the college system. The established universities worked to create an institutional framework to maximize their individual and collective autonomy in managing the university system. This framework included: a voluntary collective organization that united the older and newer universities and that had a significant capacity to gather information and develop policy options; a government department whose statutory powers allowed it to fund universities but not directly to interfere in their autonomy; a college system that would run in parallel with the universities, without offering degrees or university transfer courses; and a university funding formula, negotiated with the government, that would treat older and newer universities equally while at the same time providing substantial financial benefits to universities that had large enrolments in graduate programs.

Meanwhile, the new universities and colleges created during this period were fully occupied with establishing themselves as permanent entities whose enrolment base would make them viable for the future. A particular concern among new universities was to expand in ways that would cause them to be perceived as fully equal to the older universities—notably through the creation of master's and doctoral programs. In the college sector, much attention was devoted to developing a full range of programs and to creating academic processes that would formalize programs formerly taught in technical institutes or in non-post-secondary settings.

The growth in university enrolments from 1986 to 1992

After the first part of the baby-boom passed through the higher education system, and with the slowdown in government revenue growth in the 1970s, the practice of projecting enrolments and planning for growth fell by the wayside. The 22 percent growth (46,000 FTE students) in university enrolments between 1986-87 and 1992-93 was largely unpredicted. The biggest single contributor to this growth was the rise in the female participation rate to match and then exceed that of males. Additional contributors were the growth in participation among students in rural areas, increased immigration, and a shift in student preferences in the late 1980s from colleges to universities.

The provincial government's immediate response to the unexpected growth in admissions was to offer universities full funding if they would accept the incremental students. As the pattern of increased participation became more evident, the government in 1988 launched an exercise to project university enrolments through the early 1990s. Based on this projection, the government approved a five-year increase in university funding. Through its advisory body, the Ontario Council on University Affairs (OCUA), the government established a process to allocate future enrolment growth among the universities. At full rates of funding, the universities offered almost twice as many spaces as would be needed to meet the projected demand growth. The OCUA recommended an allocation of the available spaces, based on its own formulas and a qualitative evaluation of university growth proposals. Capital funding was increased somewhat but nevertheless supported the construction of only five to seven new buildings in a typical year. In addition, the government made available $40 million over four years, distributed by formula, for capital needs.

The growth in student demand was a disappointment to many universities that wished to stabilize their undergraduate enrolments and concentrate on developing their research enterprises. (In 1986, the universities persuaded the government to move to a so-called corridor system of funding that provided each university with stable funding even if its enrolment did not grow.) Nevertheless, the availability of full funding for incremental enrolments caused all universities to want to grow. This was true even though, by 1986, Ontario ranked near the lowest among the provinces in per-student operating funding, and even though the capital funding provided by the government was less than would be needed to accommodate the enrolment growth.

Growth in college enrolments from 1980 to 1984 and from 1989 to 1993

Ontario's colleges have experienced two major surges in enrolment, neither of which was projected. College enrolments grew by 49.5 percent (31,500 FTE students) between 1978 and 1983, and by a further 33.3 percent (40,300 FTE students) from 1989-90 to 1993-94. The first surge was linked to the back-to-back recessions of 1979-80 and 1981-82—Ontario's largest economic setback since the Great Depression. The second was linked to the even deeper recession of 1990-92.

Both periods of enrolment growth took the government by surprise. In the early 1980s, the government expected that college enrolments would decline in the 1980s following the decline in the population of K-12 students. The government restrained the growth of both capital and operating funding, fearing that the system would over expand (Drea 2003, 185). In the late 1980s college enrolments did in fact decline slightly as student demand shifted towards universities. The growth after 1989 was therefore a second surprise. With no time to develop a system-wide plan for growth, the government provided some incremental operating funding in the early 1990s, but then actually cut college operating grants in 1993-94 as part of a government-wide restraint program. The primary policy tool for encouraging growth was the college funding formula, which automatically reallocated funds away from colleges that grew more slowly than the system average rate, towards colleges that grew more quickly.

All colleges chose to grow during the periods 1978 to 1983, and again from 1989 to 1993. Enrolment growth exceeded the growth in government funding, so that by the mid-1990s college funding per student was less than in the late 1980s. Even though these two periods of growth were recession-driven, college enrolments did not decline after each recession ended. Instead, most colleges maintained their enrolments at their new (higher) level as the economy recovered and expanded.

Another outcome of rapid enrolment growth was the imposition through the collective bargaining process of limits on the workloads of full-time faculty. The rapid escalation of enrolments from 1978 to 1983 was a key factor leading to a strike by full-time faculty in 1984—the first such strike in the college system's history. The strike's end saw the appointment of an arbitrator who reviewed the growing workloads of college faculty and imposed a comprehensive formula to limit faculty hours (including time spent on preparation, marking, and other duties). With modest changes this workload formula remains in place today.

The double cohort, 2002 to 2007

Reforms to the education system introduced in the late 1990s shortened the normal secondary school program for university-bound students from five years to four—meaning that two cohorts of secondary school graduates would seek to enter university in 2003. In 1999, the provincial government and the universities agreed on enrolment projections that would grow university enrolments by 58,000 spaces (25 percent) by 2004-05. Separately, the provincial government and the colleges agreed on enrolment projections that would see college enrolments grow by 30,000 (18 percent) during this same period. It was further agreed that, with normal population growth and constant participation rates, enrolments were likely to remain at or above these levels through most of the period to 2021—in other words, the system expansion to respond to the double cohort would be permanent rather than temporary.

The provincial government's initial response was to provide capital funding to institutions in return for commitments that, in total, ensured there would be adequate physical space for the incremental students. The government then agreed to provide full operating funding to the institutions for their incremental enrolments. Actual enrolments in the university sector proved to be much higher than initially projected, and additional funding was eventually provided.

All universities and colleges agreed to grow during this period, and many universities grew their first year undergraduate enrolments by 40 percent or more. This growth took place even though the financial terms offered by the government were, on the surface, unattractive; the capital funding provided was less than needed to maintain space-per-student ratios, and the operating funding was offered at rates that universities and colleges had deemed to be inadequate. Many universities incurred substantial debts to fund their share of the cost of expansion, to be repaid from future operating revenues.

Responding to demands from employers

In addition to these large system-wide expansions, from time to time provincial governments have offered universities targeted funding to expand spaces in specific programs in response to labour market shortages. Normally the provincial government has given each university wide latitude to decide which undergraduate programs it wishes to offer, and to shift enrolments from one program to another as capacity and demand warrant. Since its inception in 1967, the university funding formula has authorized all universities to offer programs from a long list of "core" programs without special funding approval. The government's funding approval is required to initiate certain specialized programs, typically those with a professional focus.

Most commonly provincial intervention has involved spaces in the regulated professions—notably education, nursing and medicine—where employment is restricted to those holding a specific qualification, and where government is directly or indirectly the major employer. Universities have normally been willing to fully supply (or over-supply) the number of spaces the government requested, in exchange for this funding. In some cases, for short periods applications from students have been insufficient to fill the spaces.

The move to knowledge-based strategies for economic development has also led the provincial government to attempt to address supply constraint in engineering and related programs. In 1989, the government designated science and engineering programs as one of five priorities for enrolment expansion. Universities' willingness to respond meant that the available funding was over-subscribed, and spaces were rationed with priority given to expanding established programs.

A much larger program was offered in response to the shortage of spaces in computer science and software engineering during the technology boom of the late 1990s. In response to industry concerns, the provincial government approved the Access to Opportunities Program (ATOP), which offered incremental (but less-than-full) operating funding to universities that would double their enrolments in these programs, while placing significant responsibility on industry to fund some of the cost of expansion. In addition, the government offered to deregulate tuition fees in these programs at participating universities.

While the industry proposal that led to ATOP suggested that the program be limited to universities with a strong record in these program areas, the government rejected this approach. The offer to participate in ATOP was made to all universities, and all universities accepted it despite the fundraising onus placed on them. One university succeeded in negotiating a lower threshold for participation. The government also offered funding to all colleges to expand technology-related programs.

WHAT PATTERNS CAN WE OBSERVE?

The episodes discussed above reveal several patterns in how higher education has historically been managed in Ontario.

Government commitment to access and equality

Provincial governments of all parties have had a strong commitment to increasing access as the number of qualified applicants to university and college has grown. This commitment has been shared (or has not been challenged) by the universities and colleges. In cases where enrolment growth was foreseen in advance, there has been effective use of bilateral processes involving the provincial government and the university sector and/or college sector to plan for growth.

Provincial governments of all parties have also tended to treat all universities equally and all colleges equally. Within each sector, there has been reluctance to expand universities or colleges based on differences in mission or program strength.

Aversion to system planning

Many important outcomes in higher education in Ontario throughout the period prior to the early 2000s did not reflect any province-wide plan. There was no consistent attention to enrolment planning, whether through projections or targets. Where projections were developed, they almost always underestimated the actual growth in student demand that materialized.[13] With occasional exceptions (primarily in selected professional programs), the provincial government expressed no view about the mix of programs that universities and colleges should offer. The government generally has avoided setting goals or targets for the balance between graduate and undergraduate programming in universities, or for the balance between non-degree and degree programs in colleges.

Further, the government avoided recognizing differences in student demand growth by region. The major capital expansions during the early 1960s and the early 2000s supported universities and colleges in all regions of the province, without explicitly attempting to match the growth in post-secondary places to the growth in local populations. Regional policy has been expressed through special grants for northern (and, in the case of colleges, rural) institutions. These grants are intended to recognize differences in costs rather than differences in regional demand.

Issues relating to the quality of students' education were generally absent from government policy until the mid-1990s. Until that time provincial governments showed little or no interest in measuring quality, and they denied the relevance of the input indicators that suggested quality might be declining (e.g., ratio of full-time faculty to students; use of part-time faculty; average class sizes; growing use of large lecture classes; average physical space per student; quality of physical space—deferred maintenance). In recent years, the provincial government has placed quality issues more firmly on the agenda, but difficulties in defining and measuring quality have inhibited progress.

There has been reluctance to undertake analysis or to engage in public discussion about what higher education should cost, or how per-student costs should grow over time. The funding available to universities and colleges was largely a function of provincial fiscal policy and tuition policy rather than of a detailed analysis of the actual cost of achieving specified outcomes. Universities were better able to weather the government funding reduction of the 1990s than were colleges, primarily because government and university administrations shared the view that university students could and should pay more of the cost of their educations. This view was much less prevalent in the college sector, reflecting in part the more diverse financial backgrounds of college students.

---

[13] The principal exception was in the university sector in the early and mid-1970s, when projections of continued growth made in the late 1960s did not materialize.

Institutional behaviour

Within this policy environment, institutions have had considerable freedom to plan and realize their own aspirations, subject to resource constraints. Based on the episodes we examined, we can make several generalizations about institutional behaviour.

There is much evidence that institutions tend to increase enrolment for the purpose of maximizing total revenues (rather than, for example, attempting to maximize average revenue per student). This behaviour may seem puzzling for institutions which make continued reference to the need to protect quality. There are two plausible explanations. The first is short-term financial exigency: many institutions, especially since 1993, have needed to expand year-over-year revenues at less than "full funding" simply for the purpose of funding inflation and capital-related debt costs in the near term. The second explanation is more subtle. Some institutions may have been implementing a strategy of long term expansion at full funding by carefully selecting the periods and the programs to expand, and by betting that the government would within a few years agree to pay for "unfunded students."

There is also evidence of prestige-maximizing behaviour, especially in the university sector where prestige is closely linked to research and graduate studies. Universities with well-established research programs succeeded during this period in persuading the federal government to create new programs that tended to reinforce their research strengths. Fearing relegation to a second tier, universities with less-established research programs sought federal and provincial funding to initiate new graduate programs and new research programs. Some colleges sought to expand their missions by establishing a larger role in degree-granting and in applied research.

Institutions have continued to value and protect their autonomy. Increasingly, institutions have argued that public interest would best be served by allowing each institution to differentiate itself. Autonomy is seen as being the key to this differentiation.

The government of Canada has played the largest role in strengthening differentiation over the past decade, especially in the university sector, by creating programs that reward established research strengths while providing relatively modest offsets to strengthen the research capacity of universities with small research programs. Yet the existence of large funds for research and related purposes has had the ironic effect of encouraging all universities to adopt research as a primary mission. This tendency of all universities to adopt similar missions in order to pursue new revenues can also be seen in the competition for new graduate funding in the 2000s and in the competition to expand computer science and engineering programs in the late 1990s.

In sum, in the period from the 1960s to the early part of this decade, these basic behaviours—revenue maximization, prestige enhancement, and protection of autonomy—have dominated the university sector and, to a lesser extent, the college sector. They have tended to reward post-secondary leaders who saw enrolment expansion as a route to the higher revenues that would allow their institutions to move as far as possible towards the more prestigious roles that characterized elite universities in the pre-baby boom period. There has been less reward for reformers who would seek to improve educational quality without expanding enrolment, or who would attempt to offer a high-quality education in new ways in order to serve more students within constrained budgets.

WHAT IS DIFFERENT THIS TIME?

Meeting the growing demand for higher education in the next ten to fifteen years will raise challenges that Ontario has not seen in recent decades. The growing demand to attend higher education is increasingly focused on degrees rather than diplomas or other shorter credentials. While a sharp spike in college applications can be expected during the current economic downturn, the long-term trend in demand from both students and prospective employers is for education that leads to a degree.

Yet some of the largest universities are near the limit of their willingness to accept more undergraduate students. All of Ontario's universities have grown substantially since the late 1990s. Growth has been stronger in the GTA on average. This growth has placed substantial pressure on the campuses of the three large GTA universities. All face shortages of space and, in some cases, shortages of developable land. The largest, the University of Toronto, already ranks among the biggest universities in North America, with more than 60,000 full-time students on three campuses. For the first time since Premier Robarts placed a moratorium on new universities in 1963, it appears that the growing demand for undergraduate education will only be met by creating new post-secondary institutions or new campuses of existing institutions.

Traditional patterns of government-university behaviour may be adequate to meet this demand. In other words, the government might simply offer the universities money to create spaces and see which universities wish to grow—recognizing that the large GTA universities may participate at modest levels, so that other universities will need to take up the slack through new campuses or other approaches that accommodate the high demand growth in the GTA. This traditionalist-expansionist behaviour would be in keeping with how similar pressures have been resolved since the 1960s. The government could address students' demand for higher education while maintaining a system in which all universities are formally equal. Universities would maintain their autonomy, and those that chose to grow would receive the benefit of increased revenues. Meanwhile, all universities would continue to press the government for increased resources for research and for graduate programs.

This traditional pattern of behaviour, if it were to materialize, would ignore other forces that are re-shaping the higher education system. In the following chapters we consider three of these forces. The high costs of top-quality research and graduate programs make it increasingly unlikely that each university can expand in these areas at the same rate as—or faster than—it grows its undergraduate enrolments. Growth in the per-student cost of instruction is outstripping governments' and students' ability to pay. The increased demand that the higher education system account for its results in preparing students for the future means that academic quality is increasingly under the microscope. Each of these forces will challenge traditional patterns of responding to increased student demand.

3

KNOWLEDGE PRODUCTION: THE CHALLENGE OF CONTRIBUTING TO PRODUCTIVITY, COMPETITIVENESS, AND SUSTAINABILITY

No longer quiet enclaves removed from the busy world, [universities] had emerged as the nation's chief source for the three ingredients most essential to continued growth and prosperity: highly trained specialists, expert knowledge, and scientific advances others could transform into valuable new products or life-saving treatments and cures.

Derek Bok
Universities in the Marketplace (2003, 1)

Former Harvard President, Derek Bok, takes this assertion as the stepping off point for his reflections on the rise of commercialization in the American university and the threats and opportunities this process poses for those who would seek to maintain the core values of those institutions. The statement captures the essence of a fundamental change in the role of institutions of post-secondary education within the societies they serve. This altered role has been shaped by two important changes in society's expectation of colleges and universities that have prompted a fundamental transformation in Ontario's post-secondary education sector—a transformation that seems set to continue for the foreseeable future.

Academic Transformation: The Forces Reshaping Higher Education in Ontario, I.D. Clark, G. Moran, M.L. Skolnik, and D. Trick. Montreal and Kingston: McGill-Queen's University Press, Queen's Policy Studies Series.
© 2009 The School of Policy Studies, Queen's University at Kingston. All rights reserved.

In the preceding chapter, we described and discussed one of these two related expectations: demand for increased access that has seen higher education in the province move from the well-established elite model—with it roots stretching back to Oxbridge and beyond—to a near universal system that now approaches a participation level of 50 percent. The second aspect of this emerging new role is captured by the final phrase in Bok's assertion, that is, the belief that research performed in post-secondary institutions must serve the need for wealth-generation of our province and country, and the well-being of its people, in a much more direct and engaged manner than has previously been the case.

HIGHER EDUCATION AND INCREASED PRODUCTIVITY AND COMPETITIVENESS

Berger, Motte, and, Parkin (2007) use the term "substantial consensus" (13) to describe the idea that a post-secondary education is essential to current and future employment in a post-industrial economy where knowledge has replaced labour and raw materials as the key determinant of productivity and competitiveness. This case is often bolstered with reference to Canadian employment statistics that show an increase of two million in the number of jobs filled by those with a university education between 1990 and 2006 while, in the same period, jobs filled by those without a post-secondary education fell by 1.3 million (AUCC, 2008c). Higher education, moreover, is widely viewed as essential not only to an individual's employability and economic welfare (as discussed in detail in Chapter 2) but also to the competitiveness of the province and the nation (see, for example, publications of Ontario's Institute for Competitiveness and Prosperity, including *Realizing Canada's Prosperity Potential* 2005; Homer-Dixon, 2001; AUCC, 2005, 2008b, 2008c; Berger, Motte, and Parkin, 2007; Jones, McCarney, and Skolnik, 2005a; Fallis, 2007).

The global recession that began in 2008 prompted Alex Usher (2008) of the Educational Policy Institute to pointedly observe that "the party's over" for Canada's post-secondary sector. The main thrust of Usher's message, however, is that the period in which Canada's prosperity flowed from a booming commodities market, disguising the demise of its manufacturing sector, ended resoundingly with the international financial crisis. Usher further asserts that, even in the absence of this crisis, such an exclusive dependency on commodities could never support the innovation necessary to promote productivity and competitiveness in the modern economy. This argument has special weight for Ontario where manufacturing rather than commodities has been the foundation of its traditional prosperity. Usher makes the case, then, as have many others in Canada—and particularly in Ontario—that the essential fuel for the engine of such innovation is the education and research housed in universities and colleges, and that, fortunately, this fuel is a truly renewable resource.

At the heart of this linkage of higher education to the future prosperity and quality of life of the province is a belief that competitiveness in a global economy is dependent on the knowledge and innovation that derives from a post-secondary education. Although the increased demand for Canadian commodities has sustained significant growth in employment in recent years, particularly in oil-rich provinces, these positions are vulnerable to declines in demand or exhaustion of those resources. Many commentators have asserted that the country's longstanding dependency on natural resources has contributed to Canada's persistent failure to realize its full potential prosperity, and that this is due in large part to the fact that Canada lags behind its competitors in productivity. In turn, productivity can only be enhanced through innovation and increases in efficiency that in a knowledge-based economy are dependent upon a highly qualified work force (see Institute for Competitiveness and Productivity, 2007b).

Although such arguments regarding the route to increased global competitiveness most often are cast in terms of productivity and wealth-generation, it is clear that these objectives are also closely linked to a broader conceptualization of improved quality of life. That is, for example, as many have argued, increased societal productivity is a prerequisite for addressing the challenge of the increasing number of Ontarians living in poverty. The case is made that poverty is a function of an inequality of access to higher education and training that substantially impedes full participation in the new economy. Thus, increased enrolment of those currently underrepresented in post-secondary education can be seen as both a key element of increasing the province's competitiveness and a route out of poverty for individuals (The Institute for Competitiveness and Prosperity, 2007b).

A parallel analysis of education's relation to wage differentials in the United States between the late 19th and early 21st centuries leads to this same conclusion. Goldin and Katz (2007) tracked the fluctuations in the college wage premium—the earnings differential associated with a college (university) education—between 1890 and 2005. They describe a steady decline in the premium through the 1960s, reflecting a narrowing of the wage differentials across the income scale as participation in higher education increased, keeping pace with or exceeding demand for an increasingly well-educated workforce. The rate of increase in the supply of college-educated workers then declined from 1980-2000 while the demand for such workers in the emerging knowledge-based economy increased at an unprecedented rate. As a result, the college wage premium rebounded by fully 23 percent between 1980 and 2005, returning to the same level as that of the early part of the 20th century. The authors conclude that the failure of higher education participation to keep up with demand for more highly qualified workers had resulted both in a serious threat to the American economy and a widening of economic and social inequality in the society.

RESPONDING TO DEMANDS FOR KNOWLEDGE CREATION:
THE EMERGENCE OF A NEW PARADIGM FOR UNIVERSITY
RESEARCH

Universities and knowledge creation

Arguments that locate the higher education of individuals at the heart of Ontario's future productivity, competitiveness, and citizens' well-being have been inseparably linked within a broader model that also saw university based research become a pillar of government economic development strategies. This model did not emerge until long after the foundations of Ontario's higher education system had been established. Until the late 1970s, Ontario had no explicit higher education research policy. The university funding formula established in 1967 simply provided an operating grant to cover the costs of both instruction and research, with no guidance to universities on how much they should deploy to fulfill each of these roles. Nor were there separate provincial programs to develop the universities' research strength. The federal government was able to support university research through the National Research Council and the forerunners to the present granting councils. This active federal research role—coupled with the urgent pressure of providing space for growing enrolments—meant that defining a university research policy was simply not a priority for the provincial government in the 1960s and most of the 1970s.

The economic slowdown of the 1970s, coupled with competition from Alberta, Quebec, and other jurisdictions, led the Ontario government to re-think its role in economic development. Leaders of universities with resource-intensive research programs urged the government to develop a strategy based on knowledge creation, with government programs that would offer funding not linked to growing enrolment to universities. Consistent with principles embedded in the 1967 funding formula, the (Bovey) Commission on the Future Role of Universities in Ontario argued in 1984 that every university must have a "core research function"—composed of "scholarly inquiry, critical appraisal and weighing of evidence"—co-existing with educational activity in all disciplines. At the same time, however, Bovey argued that certain universities had become involved in "resource-intensive research" and incurred costs for infrastructure, overhead, and capital that went beyond what the 1967 formula had been intended to pay for. Moreover, the observations of the Commission for the first time underscored the fact that research activities and associated costs were not distributed across institutions according to the same pattern as student enrolment. There no longer existed a uniform, coherent relationship between the demands of research in these disciplines and the numbers of students involved in undergraduate and graduate programs (Commission on the Future Role of Universities in Ontario, 7-8).

The most influential and enduring contribution of the provincial government in the 1980s to recognizing universities' role in research-based economic development was the creation of the Ontario Centres of Excellence. In creating these seven centres in 1987—with $204 million in government funding over five years—the government adopted a new strategy for relating to universities that set a precedent for the future development of other research-related programs. The strategy had three parts: (1) developing the program by engaging participants other than the universities' administrations, including both leading researchers from Ontario and elsewhere, and representatives from knowledge-intensive industries; (2) focusing on promoting research excellence, especially in the natural sciences, but without a link to university enrolment levels; and (3) assigning the continuing management of new research programs to the ministry responsible for economic development rather than that responsible for universities. The federal government followed suit in establishing the National Centres of Excellence in 1989, a program that closely paralleled the structure and objectives of its provincial predecessor.

In 1995, feeling the impact of federal and provincial expenditure-cutting budgets of the early 1990s and recognizing the futility of pursuing a common position among the diverse array of institutions in the Association of Universities and Colleges of Canada (AUCC), an alliance of the ten Canadian universities with the most resource-intensive research programs—known as the G-10, which later became the G-13[14]—helped persuade the Chrétien government to commit to a significant investment in university research. This initiative, with modifications, eventually won the support of AUCC. The result—the 1997 creation of the Canada Foundation for Innovation (CFI), with initial funding of $800 million—marked the first large-scale attempt to reshape university research in Canada so as to build on established research strengths that could contribute to economic development. The foundation was mandated to award funding for university research infrastructure, such as upgrading laboratories and purchasing equipment, on the understanding that, on average, 60 percent of funds would come from provincial or private sources. Funding was

---

[14] The universities that are members of the Group of 13 (G-13) are: University of Alberta, University of British Columbia, University of Calgary, Dalhousie University, Université Laval, McGill University, McMaster University, Université de Montréal, University of Ottawa, Queen's University, University of Toronto, University of Waterloo, and University of Western Ontario.

restricted to the fields of health, environment, science, and engineering—
an unsubtle judgment on the potential contributions of other disciplines
to Canada's future economic needs.

In spite of their previous lack of enthusiasm for the initiative spear-
headed by institutions involved in the most resource-intensive research,
the potential benefits of a large new program whose awards would be
based on independent peer reviews was quickly apparent to universities with a modest history of winning peer-reviewed grants. Following
extensive debate between the universities and federal officials involved
in creating the CFI and within AUCC itself, it was determined that $40
million—about 5 percent of the fund—should be earmarked for a "Research Development Fund"—identical in purpose to the CFI's main funds,
but reserved for universities that were receiving less than 1 percent of
sponsored research funding in Canada.

Such "capacity building" elements subsequently became a standard
feature in most national and provincial funding aimed at the promotion
of research and graduate education. The motivation for the inclusion of
such a mechanism appears to be linked to the need to respond to political
demands and to a discomfort with any approach that deviates too starkly
from an "across the board" distribution of funds that would ensure an
acceptable level of resource allocation across geographical locales and
institutions. Even though one can argue that the modest size of the new
fund preserved the differential intent of the CFI and subsequent related
programs, the impact was to support homogeneity rather than diversity
and to dilute—at least to some degree—the focused differential investment in established capacity and research excellence among universities.

The case presented by the G-10 universities was strongly aligned with
the federal government's emerging interest in creating policies for the
knowledge-based economy, and both of these were supported by media
reports about the importance of knowledge-based investments in stemming the emigration of distinguished researchers. The government and
the universities agreed—the inclusion of the modest capacity-building
Research Development Fund in the CFI not withstanding—that excellence should be the primary criterion for funding and that distributional
equity should receive minimal consideration. The federal government
demanded—and the universities accepted—that each university should
prepare a strategic research plan, and that the CFI should have authority
to reduce unnecessary duplication and encourage joint projects such as
digital libraries and high-speed computing. This emphasis on explicit
planning and the association of these plans with decisions regarding
funding marked another important change in direction, notably at odds
with the long tradition of investigator-driven research without formal
links to institutional or government plans and priorities.

The design of the CFI—taking applications from individual universities,
and awarding funding based on established research strengths—made

it clear that the federal government accepted the G-10's argument that investments in research infrastructure need to be concentrated at specific universities, and it largely rejected the argument of some universities that the program should attempt to create research capacity at all universities. This approach differed from that of the federal and Ontario Centres of Excellence, which consciously sidestepped the geographic issue by funding networks of outstanding researchers who usually represented more than one university. The CFI managed the geographic issue through the simpler device of a modest set-aside for equalization, and this was supplemented by the federal government's (far more expensive) creation of a special fund for Atlantic Canada. The need to resolve such persistent resistance to the consequences of frank differentiation remains a perplexing challenge in research funding programs in Ontario and Canada.

The CFI quickly set the pattern for expanded federal and Ontario investments in university research. Less than three months after the federal announcement of the CFI, the Ontario government created the Ontario Research and Development Challenge Fund (ORDCF)—with $500 million in provincial funds over ten years, through which the government hoped to leverage $3 billion in additional research investments. Two years later the provincial government created the Ontario Innovation Trust with a mission to match CFI funding for research infrastructure—freeing the ORDCF to fund the costs of researchers' salaries and other personnel-related expenses. A new Ministry of Energy, Science and Technology (MEST) was created in 1997 to house the ORDCF and other research-related programs, so that—while there was much cooperation among ministries—the new programs were shielded from the equality-related debates that characterized the universities' relationship with MTCU.

At the provincial level, new research-related expenditures after the creation of the ORDCF were frequent, and the decision to direct most funding to universities with well-established research programs found increasing acceptance—sometimes grudgingly—within the university community. New programs were established to support newly-hired faculty with the costs of equipping their labs and to provide more scholarships for graduate students. The government established ongoing funding to help universities with the overhead costs of research grants received from the provincial government. After the 2003 election, MEST was reconstituted as the Ministry of Research and Innovation, which absorbed the responsibilities of the ORDCF and introduced new programs to support research and commercialization.

More significant, both politically and financially, was the province's implicit invitation to the federal government to expand its research-related programming for universities. This invitation—coupled with a growing federal budget surplus and the skilful advocacy of the universities with resource-intensive research programs—meant that almost every federal budget from 1997 to the mid-2000s featured a major new investment in university research. These investments were consistent with the federal government's new paradigm for supporting the knowledge-based economy and were increasingly easy to afford in a period of growing budget surpluses. The federal government agreed to expand the CFI three times in its first four years, and the original $800 million became $3.65 billion by the end of 2008. CFI commitments to Ontario universities totalled $983 million by the end of 2008—with three-quarters of this amount concentrated on six of the 18 universities. In most cases matching funding was provided by the Ontario government.

In the 2000 federal budget, the government provided $900 million to support the hiring of 2,000 new faculty at Canadian universities. These Canada Research Chairs were distributed to universities based on each university's share of grants from the federal granting councils over the preceding three years—a formula that surprised even some of the universities that benefited from it, since the chair holders would have responsibilities for teaching as well as research. In defence of this allocation, federal officials asserted that a formula based on anything other than research could be challenged as an intrusion in the provincial field of education. Learning from the dispute over the CFI, the federal government agreed that every university should receive at least one CRC, irrespective of its level of federal research funding—effectively reallocating 6 percent of the chairs to small institutions. Even with this set-aside, Ontario's six largest research universities accounted for 80 percent of the CRCs allocated in Ontario by the end of 2008.

These new research programs were complemented by the restoration and expansion of funding to the three federal granting councils—the Canadian Institutes for Health Research (CIHR), the Natural Sciences and Engineering Research Council of Canada (NSERC), and the Social Sciences and Humanities Research Council of Canada (SSHRC). The councils themselves were transformed to fit more closely with economic development ambitions. The most explicit expression of this policy was the emergence of the CIHR from the Medical Research Council of Canada (MRC), bringing with it a core objective of aligning research with priority societal health objectives. At the same time, there was a growth in the share of all Tri-Council funds devoted to special strategic research initiatives as opposed to the historic investigator-driven programs, although each of the three councils have continued to assign priority to the support of this more traditional role. As with new programs such as the CFI, the Tri-Council strategic programs typically called for multi-centred research groups and partnerships with the private or public sector focused on strategic areas of research.

The transforming impact of these changes can perhaps best be seen in SSHRC. Funding at this agency in the past had very much been dominated by single investigator-driven research grants in which practical application was a minor consideration. The mid-1990s saw the emergence at SSHRC of a series of major programs that contrasted sharply with this traditional pattern of research support. They featured, by design, an emphasis on knowledge mobilization for the solution of societal problems, multi-disciplinary research teams from multiple universities, and collaboration with both the broader public and private sector. Examples of such programs include the Community University Research Alliance, the Major Collaborative Research Initiatives, the Knowledge Impact in Society program, and the SSHRC Knowledge Clusters.

A more recent, and a critical piece, of the emergence of a substantially new paradigm for the support of university research by the federal government was the decision to begin paying the indirect costs incurred by universities receiving funds from the three granting councils. Again drawing from its CFI experience, the federal government introduced a sliding scale so that every university received funding under the Indirect Costs Program equal to 80 percent of its first $1 million in research grants, with the percentage falling in steps to about 20 percent of any grants above $7 million.

The impact of the new federal government strategy can be seen in the four-fold increase in federal research funding to universities over the past decade—from $733 million in 1997-98 to $2,924 million in 2007-08. Of the 2007-08 total, 43 percent was associated with programs that simply did not exist at the beginning of this period. Funding for the three granting councils and the Networks of Centres of Excellence program increased by 130 percent over the decade (AUCC, 2008c).

The conceptual rationale of the new strategy

The task of discovery and knowledge production has long been fundamental to the vision of universities and colleges. So, too, has been the assumption that the knowledge emerging from the research and scholarship activities within the institutions will lead to new products, practices, and applications of all kinds that will produce wealth and contribute to the betterment of our societies and of humankind as a whole. Prior to the emergence of the knowledge economy and the globalization of the marketplace, however, it was generally held that the vast majority of research and scholarship within the academy would focus on increasing our basic understanding of the workings of the natural and human world. Furthermore, the specific directions of that research should be set by the interests and curiosities of the faculty members of the college or university rather than by the demands of particular problems or opportunities outside the campus walls. Complementing the work within the campus walls, "others could transform (the knowledge produced therein) into valuable new products or life-saving treatments and cures" (Bok, 2003, 1).

As illustrated by the nature of the funding programs that emerged in Ontario and Canada in the 1980s and 1990s, there has been a considerable shift over the past two decades in this traditional relationship where—using some exaggeration—uncovering knowledge of basic processes was the purview of those within the campus boundaries and the transformation of this knowledge was left to those outside the ivory tower. The conceptual origins of the transformation of this model of university research can be traced to widespread discussions taking place during this period that were effectively summarized by Robert Prichard in his 2000 Killam Lecture shortly after he ended his term as President of the University of Toronto. Not only did Prichard describe the seminal events of this era but he embedded these in a logical framework that represented a fundamental shift, what he labeled a "new paradigm," in the relationship between Canada's universities and the federal government.

Prichard sketched the history of the association of the federal government and the country's universities. This relationship was historically balanced on three pillars: support of higher education by way of transfers to the provinces; direct funding of research through the national granting councils; and direct financial aid to students across Canada. The budget of 1997 marked a turning point in that relationship. By this point in time, there was a growing realization at all levels that the country's performance in an increasingly globalized economy was insufficient to ensure Canada's place among the world's nations and the future well-being of its citizens. At the same time, it was increasingly clear that success in this global economy would demand a shift from an economy based on commodities and natural resources to a foundation built on intellectual capital. It was this intellectual capital that would support the innovation and effectiveness needed to raise productivity and Canada's faltering record of global competiveness.

The conceptual foundation of the new economic strategy described by Prichard can be found in a series of pivotal federal government reports that first emerged following the creation of the CFI and continued after the election of the federal Conservative government in 2005. The first of these, from the federal Council of Science and Technology Advisors (1999), called for future funding programs on a scale never before seen in Canada, based on a research paradigm that was equally unfamiliar. It argued for the creation of an integrated "system of innovation"—a network of innovative research activities linking exploration of basic science through the development of related technology and its application to the enhancement of the Canadian economy and society at large. The authors' recommendations were based on three principles that have echoed throughout federal and provincial research and development initiatives since that time: (1) the *alignment* of publicly-supported research activities with the mandate and priorities of the government; (2) the requirement of explicit *linkages* between players from the government, private and university sectors as a condition of receiving public research funding; and (3) *excellence* in research. The report placed special emphasis on the need to more effectively recruit the university and private sectors into this process through focused partnerships.

The evolving impact of the ideas expressed in the Council of Science and Technology Advisors report can be seen in two federal government policy documents that followed. *Achieving Excellence* (Government of Canada, 2001) and *Knowledge Matters* (Government of Canada, 2002) were explicitly presented as the two pillars of "Canada's Innovation Strategy." Echoing the theme of the earlier report, this strategy developed the notion of innovation to embrace domains ranging from skills training to higher education to the venture capital necessary to promote the translation of new ideas into products and services in the marketplace.

A parallel study to these federal reports was commissioned by the Ontario Ministries of Training, Colleges and Universities, and of Energy, Science, and Technology, and by the Ontario Jobs and Investment Board. This 1999 report entitled *Growing Ontario's Innovation System: The Strategic Role of University Research* was authored by Heather Munroe-Blum (1999), the Vice-President for research at the University of Toronto with the support of James Duderstadt, Past-President at the University of Michigan and Sir Graeme Davies, then Principal and Vice-Chancellor at the University of Glasgow. These authors arrived at largely the same conclusions as those in the federal policy documents, emphasizing alignment with government priorities, linkages across sectors, and excellence. The provincial study underscored even more sharply than the federal reports the key place of university-based research for success in the emerging global economy, an emphasis captured by the title of a summary of the report: *Road Map to Innovation Through University Research*.

These arguments and the recognition of the centrality of basic and strategic research to the country's prosperity and quality of life continue to be reflected in the most recent statement of the federal government's strategy in this domain: *Mobilizing Science and Technology to Canada's Advantage* (Government of Canada, 2007). Despite differences associated with the passage of time and changes in government, the three principles of the Council of Science and Technology Advisors report can still be found—reworded, but their import intact. The 2007 document reemphasizes the importance of promoting world-class excellence, focusing on priorities, and encouraging partnerships, and it adds a fourth principle—enhancing accountability.

In adopting this strategy, the federal government has attempted to address a structural weakness in Canada's economy. Canada ranks next-to-last among the G-7 countries in private-sector research and development (measured as a share of GDP)—reflecting the role of resource industries in the economy and the legacy of branch-plant manufacturing. In contrast, federal and provincial expenditures on research, including university research, have had the consequence of positioning Canada first among the G-7 in publicly-funded research. Summing the private and public expenditures, Canada ranks fifth among the seven countries. (Government of Canada, 2007, 26). While it remains to be seen whether university research can address Canada's longstanding shortfalls in research and development, the experience of the past decade has demonstrated the close alignment and growing interdependency between the governments' economic development strategy and universities' ambitions to expand their research programs.

Martha Piper, the former President of the University of British Columbia, was an advocate closely associated with these policy arguments and the resultant unprecedented increases in federal investment in university research in the 1990s and early part of the following decade. She compellingly, and successfully, argued for the critical role played by research in the medical, natural, and engineering sciences in productivity and economic competiveness. Throughout this same period, however, she also has been among Canada's most forceful and effective advocates of bringing the human sciences to bear on some of the more intractable threats to Canada and, indeed, the broader world (Piper, 2002; 2008; see also Neuman, 2005). Piper points to issues and problems whose resolution, although undeniably linked in part to technological expertise and innovation, is fundamentally rooted in the maladaptive dynamics of human interpersonal and intergroup relationships. Such issues include the following: the growing income and well-being gap between the rich and poor, a critical issue within both developing and developed countries (UN-Habitat, 2008); challenges to maintaining adequate health care; global warming and the degradation of the world's environment; ethnic conflict and resettlement of refugees; globalization and immigration; and, most recently, the collapse of communism and fundamental challenges to free-market capitalism.

If Ontario's post-secondary sector is to play a central part in addressing these pressing issues, a transformation of the traditional research paradigm in the human sciences is required that parallels that which has taken place in the medical and natural sciences over the past two decades. Such changes would need to occur both within the walls of the academy and, more significantly, in the engagement and partnership with other sectors of society, both private and public. All sectors—post-secondary, government, public, and private—have a considerable distance still to travel before the potential expressed in Piper's vision could be fully realized.

Expanding graduate programs

The core underpinning of the rationale for this new research paradigm is the expectation that the province's post-secondary sector will play a dominant role in the production of the discoveries and knowledge that will form the foundation for the province's and the country's future productivity and competitiveness. The training and education of highly qualified individuals by the universities and colleges is an equally important and complementary component of this model. The dramatic increase in access to Ontario's post-secondary institutions was addressed in Chapter 2. This increase has not only occurred in programs targeted at studies that one might normally associate with the global knowledge economy, but also involved substantial increased enrolment in traditional liberal arts and science programs. Such widespread growth across undergraduate programs indicates a recognition by individuals—and, in turn, by their employers—of the value, not only of the particular knowledge associated with higher education in specific fields, but also of the more general critical thinking, communications, and interpersonal skills that stem from the university and college experience.

The desire of every university to participate in meeting the need for knowledge creation, however, has been most vividly mirrored in the universities' response to opportunities to increase enrolments in master's and doctoral programs. Indeed, the creation of highly-qualified personnel, in the form of graduates with an advanced understanding of research methods and the capacity to undertake research and apply it, is an integral part of a university research program.

Ontario's higher education system imposes no statutory limitations on each university's power to confer master's and doctoral degrees.[15] In other words, there is no statutory limit on the ambitions of any university to offer, over time, a comprehensive range of programs at the graduate and undergraduate levels that mirror those of the largest universities in the province. As a result, the number of master's and doctoral spaces that each university can offer is determined by the willingness of the government to fund them, rather than by the design of the system. New programs are subject to approval by the Ontario Council on Graduate Studies, an arms-length affiliate of the universities' voluntary association, the Council of Ontario Universities; and established programs are subject to regular quality reviews by the same body.[16] In years when new government funding has been available, the amount of annual government

---

[15] The three newest universities—the University of Ontario Institute of Technology, Algoma University and the Ontario College of Art and Design—do not yet have full legislative authority to grant master's and doctoral degrees. The statutes creating UOIT and Algoma each permit Cabinet to confer such authority; once Cabinet does so, the authority cannot be reduced except by an act of the Legislature. OCAD's statute authorizes it to confer graduate degrees at the master's level only.

[16] The understanding between the government and the universities since the creation of the Ontario Council on Graduate Studies in 1966 has been that the government would only fund new graduate programs which had been approved by the OCGS, and only if the government determined that there was a societal need for the new program.

funding per PhD student has been approximately ten times as high as that for a first-year Arts student.

In spite of the relatively high cost of mounting and sustaining graduate programs, the universities' response to government offers of fully-funded graduate spaces over the decades has been enthusiastic, reflecting not only the universities' mandate to meet individual and societal demand but also the prestige associated with graduate instruction and research, the desire of newer universities to model themselves on the older institutions, and the attractiveness of the government grant. One participant in the 1960s recalled that the "scramble to get into graduate studies ... resembled a gold rush" (Corry, 1981, 189). A recommendation in 1966 to establish an overarching "University of Ontario" with executive authority to coordinate the expansion of the university system and prevent unnecessary duplication (Commission to Study the Development of Graduate Programs in Ontario Universities, 1966) was immediately rejected by the provincial government and by the existing universities. The universities' behaviour led to sharp criticism from a 1972 advisory commission, which found that "graduate programs had proliferated across the Ontario university system without adequate attention to the need for quality, specialization, responsiveness to regional wants, and economy" (Commission on Post-Secondary Education in Ontario, 1972, 140). The government deliberately limited funding for new graduate programs in the 1970s and adopted an explicit policy of not approving new doctoral programs at five so-called "emergent" universities—a ban that was lifted in the following decade. During this period the Ontario Council on University Affairs oversaw the creation of a series of five-year plans to guide the growth of graduate programming. As undergraduate enrolments increased in the late 1980s, the provincial government offered targeted funding to increase graduate enrolments with the stated purpose of replacing the retiring professoriate; spaces were rationed because the universities' desire to expand exceeded the available funding.

The case for the most recent expansion of graduate education was laid out in the Council of Ontario Universities' 2003 document, *Advancing Ontario's Future through Advanced Degrees*. In essence, the Council's task force argued that the dramatic expansion in undergraduate enrolment of recent years (fuelled by government funding during the period of the double cohort) would drive a parallel increase in demand for graduate spaces, spaces that simply would not exist without new investment. The COU task force augmented their case with data demonstrating that the demand for graduate degrees in the emerging economy was in fact growing at an even greater rate than that for undergraduate education. A significant percentage of posts demanding graduate-level education in Canada and Ontario in recent years have been filled through immigration in the absence of qualified Canadian degree holders. A recent report of the Association of Universities and Colleges of Canada (2008b) reveals that half of the growth between 2001 and 2006 in jobs held by people with doctorates were filled by immigrants who earned their degrees outside of Canada. Finally, it was noted that a substantially higher percentage of the US population hold both master's and doctoral degrees than in Canada and that per-capita production of graduate students in Ontario is lower than in US states with similar economies.

On the basis of such considerations, the Ontario government expanded funding for graduate enrolments through its Reaching Higher plan. The government provided funding to increase graduate enrolment by 12,000 from 24,616 in 2002-03 to 36,616 in 2007-08. Further funding was available to increase enrolment by an additional 2,000 students by 2009-10. By that year, Ontario universities are expecting to exceed their growth targets, with a total of 42,000 graduate students—a near-doubling of graduate enrolment over the decade. The distribution of this funding has raised many of the same issues that were seen with the initial CFI funding, with universities having modest graduate enrolments successfully seeking special consideration in order to narrow the gap with others.

Colleges and applied research

Although its greatest impact has been within the province's universities, the federal and provincial governments' adoption of knowledge-based economic development strategies has created new opportunities for colleges as well. At the urging of leaders from a number of colleges who wished to expand their applied research—that is, research directed primarily towards specific practical or commercial objectives—the legislation creating the CFI listed colleges as eligible recipients. This marked the first formal recognition of colleges as part of the national knowledge creation strategy. The precedent set by the CFI was followed with the creation of the Ontario Research and Development Challenge Fund and the Ontario Innovation Trust, both of which recognized colleges as eligible for funding.

Colleges' role in applied research was legally recognized in the *Ontario Colleges of Applied Arts and Technology Act* in 2002. The statute's careful wording does not list applied research as an object of the colleges (the objects are education, meeting the needs of employers, and supporting community economic development), but the act says that a college may undertake applied research as a means of achieving those objects.

Applied research nevertheless accounts for only a modest share of colleges' overall activity. A 2004 study estimated that 2 percent of Ontario's full-time college faculty engage in applied research, development, and commercialization activities, and about 20 percent of college faculty hold research-based master's or doctoral degrees (Association of Colleges of Applied Arts and Technology of Ontario, 2004). CFI funding to colleges to date has been small: by the end of 2008, seven Ontario colleges had received a total of $6.8 million as lead institutions on CFI projects, while others have benefited as partners in larger projects. Funding from CFI and other programs has permitted many Ontario colleges to establish applied research centres in specific fields. A significant barrier has been the absence of ways for college faculty to be relieved of other responsibilities in order to conduct applied research. Following the success of a pilot program started in 2004, NSERC in 2008 created the College and Community Innovation (CCI) Program to fund release time from teaching for college faculty members engaging in research. The CCI will provide $48 million in grants nationwide over five years.

CHALLENGES EMERGING FROM THE NEW KNOWLEDGE PRODUCTION MODEL

Ontario's post-secondary institutions have responded impressively to the increased, and previously unaccustomed, role that they are currently expected to play in sustaining the province's wealth and well-being. This adaptation, however, has entailed major challenges, even threats, to an expanded and transformed role in education and research. The AUCC *Momentum* (Association of Universities and Colleges, 2008c) report on university research and development in Canada explored these challenges within the framework of five "drivers of change": (1) a worldwide recognition that research and development is critical to a society's prosperity and well-being; (2) the global competition for highly qualified graduates of post secondary institutions who fuel these endeavors; (3) the increasing complexity and associated costs of research; (4) the enhanced demands for accountability and, thus, measurement of the impact of investments in research and development; and, finally, (5) the fact that partnerships and collaborations well beyond individual institutions are an expected part of the modern research enterprise.

Aspects of these five issues have been addressed previously in this chapter and in other parts of the book. We end this chapter by highlighting four related areas that seem to us to pose particular challenges to Ontario's higher education institutions as they continue to respond to the growing and shifting societal expectations of them in the domain of knowledge creation.

The threat of institutional and individual over-commitment

The aggregate of the internal and external forces impinging on Ontario's post-secondary institutions, and especially its universities, has had a formidable impact on the scale of responsibilities in the sector. On the one hand, as described in Chapter 2, colleges and universities grapple with the enrolment associated with a shift from an elite to a mass—and, arguably, a universal—system of higher education. At the same time, expectations have grown for them to play a more direct role in training the highly qualified personnel and generating the knowledge that is required in a knowledge-based economy. These expectations emphasize vocationally oriented programs and professional and graduate education, as well as the expansion of research activities, especially in the area of knowledge transfer or mobilization essential to the province's productivity and competiveness that are often in collaboration with the private sector. Many of these forces have been building at a remarkable rate for 10-15 years and they show no signs of abating.

As we have described here and in Chapter 2, Ontario's post-secondary system has responded effectively to these pressures and the opportunities that they have represented to expand and diversify its activities. There is a real question, however, regarding the limits of the flexibility of the system, of its individual institutions and, indeed, of its individual members of faculty. The performance to date has been impressive: the accommodation of a substantially increased participation rate through massive expansions of undergraduate admissions and enrolment; the diversification of undergraduate programs, particularly into more vocationally oriented domains; the substantial expansion of graduate enrolment, here again, accompanied by the creation of new programs in priority areas; and, dramatic increases in research, especially within the new, more complex, knowledge mobilization paradigm. In the face of all this change, educational standards and program quality have been maintained at levels that, by most available yardsticks, rival those of any other jurisdiction. Finally, all of this has been accomplished in a period when per-student funding from government grants and tuition barely kept pace with the Consumer Price Index.

The mechanisms by which this apparently remarkable increase in productivity—viewed in classic terms as both increased value of the product and enhanced efficiency of operations—has been achieved are not well researched. Little study has been devoted to understanding the changes within the institutions that lie behind this adaptation of the post-secondary system in Ontario. Signs of those changes, however, can be seen across the system. There can be little doubt, for example, that increased graduate enrolment and research productivity in Ontario's universities have only been possible because full-time, tenured members of faculty now devote a greater percentage of their energies to these domains. At the same time (and as discussed in Chapter 4), larger classes and the use of teaching-only full-time and, especially, part-time instructors has both taken up the slack of this change and accommodated the larger enrolments at the undergraduate level.

This is not to suggest that full-time research-oriented members of faculty have abandoned the undergraduate classroom, which remains a significant part of their responsibilities; rather, it is being squeezed by other rapidly expanding components. The pressures remaining on full-time members of faculty, then, are high and continue to grow, especially since part-time faculty carry few responsibilities beyond those associated with the direct teaching and administration of their classes.

Both the provincial government and the post-secondary institutions must ask whether an extension of this pattern of adaptation is sustainable or desirable. Without substantial expansion of the institutions through government grants that recognize the true dimensions of their expanded role, key elements of performance will be strained and impaired. We are already seeing unfavourable comparisons in explicit measures of the quality of the Ontario student experience relative to US public institutions reflected, for example, in some aspects of the National Survey of Student Engagement (NSSE), particularly among the larger, more research-intensive universities (Higher Education Quality Council of Ontario, 2009; Kuh, 2003; Maclean's, 2009; National Survey of Student Engagement, n.d.). In the 2008 results of this survey, those Ontario universities who are among the country's top research-intensive institutions (Toronto, Queen's, Western, Ottawa, McMaster, and Waterloo) consistently ranked below smaller less research intensive counterparts on a variety of measures of their students' engagement in their academic programs.

Parallel issues regarding the competitiveness and performance of research programs led by over-burdened members of faculty must also be considered. That is, in addition to the danger that the demands of the new research paradigm could diminish the capability of members of faculty to contribute to undergraduate teaching, these same pressures of individual over-commitment also threaten to shift the traditional balance of university research away from basic processes toward strategic problems or opportunities. This danger was the theme of an address by Michael Lazaridis (2004), the co-founder and CEO of Research In Motion, who underscored the point that basic research continues to be the fundamental source of the innovation that is so essential to successful competition in the global knowledge economy. As the most capable and successful researchers and scholars are drawn into the rich funding associated with more strategically oriented projects, he fears that their essential contributions to basic research could diminish.

These concerns are compounded by the fact that the major recent research funding programs not only require, as a result of their scale, the devotion of considerable individual time and energy for the direct execution of the work but, because of the new funding paradigm, also involve new levels of complexity that were not typically associated with more traditional research. The requirements of programs such as the Canada Foundation for Innovation, the strategic research initiatives of the national granting councils, and direct research collaborations with the private sector involve levels of collaboration across disciplines, sectors, and geography, and of accountability to the funding agency that are unprecedented. These additional demands further tax the time, attention, and energies of the individual researcher.

The pressures of over-commitment stemming from both the substantial increases in level of research activity and the costs of increased complexity associated with the new strategic knowledge production research paradigm are also observable at the level of the institution. Most obviously, of course, individual members of faculty comprise the academy and are the basis of its teaching and research activity. Over-commitment at the level of these individuals translates into a threat to the basic integrity of the institution as a whole.

The strains on the institution, however, go beyond this. The costs of increased complexity to the university itself are nowhere better illustrated than by the ubiquity of institutional offices of research services and vice-presidents for research. Our survey of Ontario's universities in 2009 revealed that all but one feature both the position of vice-president research and associated offices of sizes that vary with that of the institutions. This costly infrastructure is essential in the knowledge production paradigm of today's research-intensive university, but was the exception rather than the rule as recently as the early 1990s. The vice-president for research and her staff offer services essential to the direct research activities of the institution: setting strategic research direction, identifying and encouraging individuals and groups to pursue available funding opportunities, supporting the preparation of complex granting applications, coordinating increasingly demanding ethical reviews for research involving human and animal participants, research accounting, and assisting with the demanding reporting requirements associated with the newer major funding programs. Increasingly these offices also take the institutional lead in the establishment and maintenance of international research collaborations.

Another example of increased costs associated with the new research paradigm can be found in the universal presence of vice-presidents for external relations and their sizeable offices. These organizational structures are necessary to meet increased expectations of private fund raising and relations with alumni and the broader university community, including the provincial and federal governments. Although clearly involved in raising funds and advocating for university initiatives beyond research, the period of greatest proliferation and expansion of these external offices corresponds to the rise of the new research paradigm and the flow of additional research funds from government. This is no mere coincidence. As previously mentioned, a key component of the new paradigm is involvement of the private sector through obligatory matching contributions to the costs of the funded research. Obtaining these very substantial funds has been a Herculean task requiring a substantial infrastructure and associated ongoing investment by the universities. The administrative costs of the increased complexity associated with the new research paradigm in this domain have been very substantial indeed.

The instructional strains of commitment arising from the new paradigm stretch to other costly areas well beyond the administrative structures and processes exemplified by the external and research portfolios. These include the considerable costs of renovations and of the new physical facilities associated with expansion of the research enterprise and associated graduate programs. Equally, the research-intensive model has dramatically increased the competition for leading researchers, bringing with it substantially increased salary costs both for leading researchers and for the staff necessary to attract them. Although some of these costs are balanced by capital funding though programs such as the CFI and by personnel funding of the CRC program, the real costs outstrip the revenues available through these funding opportunities.

As we argue in Chapter 4, this pressure to offer differentially higher salaries driven by market competition for the very best researchers may have contributed indirectly to another increased cost for the institution. That is, the provision of salaries necessary to attract and retain the most productive researchers raises issues in the academy of salary anomalies— differences in salaries across disciplines and individuals that arise from the institutions' response to market forces. Not only have the salaries of some individuals more than others been subject to market forces associated with recruitment and retention, but some entire disciplines more than others have been subject to the same forces over the past 10-15 years, e.g., computer science, software engineering, and business. The resulting differences in remuneration have become major factors in faculty negotiations that have tended to drive all salaries upward irrespective of specific market forces.

The various challenges raised by the new, knowledge production research paradigm are compounded by the striking homogeneity of the Ontario university system (a topic more fully discussed in Chapter 6). In a nutshell, without denying differences in style, size, and disciplinary emphasis, all of Ontario's universities consider themselves research-intensive. Even the smallest most recently established institutions have striven to and succeeded in establishing research-based graduate programs at the master's and doctoral level in an increasing array of disciplines. This pattern of homogeneity reaches down to the level of the individual member of academic staff with expectations of responsibilities equally divided between teaching and research—between the diffusion and creation of knowledge. A winter 2009 survey of Ontario's universities found that all but two nominally assigned equal weighting to both teaching and research in the appointment conditions of tenured or tenure track faculty. As pressures for research increase, the pressures of over-commitment and conflict with teaching responsibilities at both an individual and institutional level increasingly are facing essentially all Ontario's universities—not only those with the largest involvement in research and graduate studies.

The forces toward homogeneity and away from diversification arise from many sources: the absence of formal government policy of differentiation; uniform base funding policies; the "capacity-building" elements of most recent large research funding programs; an academic culture that associates excellence in research, more than education, with higher status in a competitive environment; and other pressures that are discussed elsewhere in this book. In the context of this chapter, however, the trend underscores the question of whether this uniform application of the traditional research-intensive model of the university is sustainable within the institutions and across the system given the expectations of the province and country, and the associated changes that are transforming post-secondary education in Ontario.

The consequences of the new research paradigm for disciplines outside of its focus

The culture of the 21st century research-intensive university has had a substantial impact in all disciplines despite the emphasis of recent government policy and funding for research and development on science and technology. The majority of the new strategically focused research funding, although not entirely excluding scholarship in the arts, humanities, and social sciences—the human sciences, has been directed at research in the sciences, medicine, and engineering. In spite of this lack of access to the lion's share of the recent increases in funding, expectations of substantially greater productivity from faculty in the human sciences have increased in lock-step with that of their colleagues in the disciplines more strongly associated with science and technology.

In fact, throughout faculties of arts and social science in the province there are significantly increased pressures to obtain external grant funding, to work in collaborative as opposed to single-scholar research programs, to publish more frequently, to involve, and provide research stipends to, graduate students, and to embrace more fully the value of publication through journal articles as well as the traditional pattern of monographs requiring years of preparation before publication. All these changes represent quite substantial modifications to the research traditions in many of these disciplines. These shifts toward a more science-based model of scholarship have inevitably been accompanied by arguments that traditional levels of teaching responsibilities of full-time members of faculty should be reduced to accommodate greater involvement in the research endeavor—a pattern that has been common in science-based disciplines for some time. The issues of individual over-commitment, and the associated shift in the balance between teaching and research, thus have not been restricted to those faculty members in disciplines that were the intended focus of the knowledge production research paradigm.

Thus, despite the new research paradigm's differential emphasis on research in the natural and medical sciences, and engineering, the impact that this paradigm has had on the style and level of research has been widely felt across the academy. In addition to the danger of over-commitment represented by these rapidly growing responsibilities, the expansion and change of roles have posed a number of other threats that will continue to play out in the province's institutions. Prominent among these is a more direct impact of differential distribution of increases in research funding across the disciplines.

Since the recent federal and provincial funding programs have emphasized linkage between research and the global knowledge economy, they have been structured to target activities that the sponsoring governments believe best serve competitiveness and productivity. The over-riding priorities of wealth generation and health have thus focused research support in the natural and biological sciences, medicine, and engineering—seldom directly involving the arts and social sciences, except in a supporting role. Although these latter disciplines have had access in principle to some of these programs, actual allocations of funds have been disproportionately small (for example, 20 percent of Canada Research Chairs are allocated to SSHRC-related disciplines, and SSHRC usually receives smaller percentage increases to its budget than CIHR and NSERC).

The disproportionate direction of funds to work in other disciplines by these substantial new research programs has created some disquiet among advocates of the human sciences. These concerns have been compounded by the justifiable perception that, without careful planning and monitoring, these investments in other areas of the university tend to siphon off existing institutional support for the disciplines in the social sciences, arts, and humanities. To some degree, in fact, such a shift is an implicit element of programs such as the CFI and CRC in that they call upon universities to identify areas of priority and to build on these strengths, not only through funding programs but by differential allocation processes based on existing operating funds. Given the emphasis of such programs on the natural, medical, and engineering sciences, it is inevitable that these priority areas and associated investments in large part lie outside of the human sciences.

In addition to this deliberate emphasis on areas other than the arts, humanities, and social sciences, such provincial and federal funding initiatives have almost without exception required much closer engagement and collaboration with the private sector than in the past. In fact, in many cases access to government funding was only possible if matching funding could be obtained from the private sector.[17] Although

---

[17] Many provinces, including Ontario, provided generous matching funding for some programs, most notably, those of the Canada Foundation for Innovation (CFI).

exceptions to the rule are provided by several notable successes, this requirement has proven to be a particular challenge for researchers outside of the sciences, engineering, and medicine where research projects more easily correspond to profit-related objectives of the private sector. The matching-fund requirement thus has been another source of tension within academic communities where research in all domains has traditionally been of equal importance and value, and quality the sole valid arbiter of support.

These two consequences of a greater engagement by universities in supporting the economic productivity of the province—a tendency for less support to research programs in the arts, humanities and social sciences, and a requirement for more direct engagement with the private sector—are seen by many as challenging two of the foundational features of the academy, both relating to institutional autonomy: disciplinary breadth in teaching, and research and investigator-driven scholarship. This threat is taken up in a collection of thoughtful essays on the place of higher education in the 21st century knowledge-driven economy that emerged from a conference held at the University of Toronto in 2002. The collection's title, *Creating Knowledge, Strengthening Nations,* nicely captures the conference's theme and the tone of most of the papers (Jones, McCarney, and Skolnik, 2005). One of those essays, however, reminds us of the tension that inevitably exists between the more traditional, non-economic functions of the university and the pressures associated with responding to the expectation that the institution's educational and research activities fuel wealth generation (Skolnik, 2005a).

An emerging paradox may well soon compound the tensions associated with this challenge of balancing pressures to contribute to economic objectives with the non-economic values and goals of the traditional academy. That is, it may soon be seen as ironic that many of the world's most pressing challenges—ultimately with substantial economic implications—will require the engagement of just those disciplines that have been systematically excluded from most recent investments in the post-secondary sector. It will be discoveries and effective applications in the human sciences that will hold the key to addressing critical issues that include climate change, non-fossil alternative fuels, conservation, terrorism, crime, and many of the other threats that plague the same societies that now see their economic success as tied to the knowledge held and produced by its institutions of higher education. The role of the human sciences in addressing such challenges is likely to involve both direct applications of knowledge from these disciplines and other applications that successfully link knowledge and developments in science and technology to the solution of human problems. It is perhaps at this interface of technology and human factors where the greatest contributions of the human science will be made. Although wealth generation will be no small part of creating a successful future, the current implications of the term "knowledge economy" may prove to be far too limited.

With application comes commercialization

The quotation with which this chapter begins is taken from *Universities in the Marketplace,* Derek Bok's exploration of the same themes that we have identified as being at the core of the forces that have so transformed Ontario universities over the past 15 to 20 years. His treatise starts from the same emphasis on the link between university research, on the one hand, and productivity and competitiveness in today's economy, on the other. His arguments, however, quickly evolve into a focus on the relation of knowledge production to commercialization, and the impact of this process on the nature of the university.

Bok used this dynamic of commercialization to explore some of the same substantive matters that we deal with here—the associated over-commitment of the individual or institution and its impact on undergraduate teaching, on the traditional commitment to basic research, and on research beyond the boundaries of science and technology. Many in the academy in the U.S., as in Canada (see Emberley, 1996; Readings, 1996), have looked on with anxiety as universities have become more reliant on non-public funding and have pursued revenue through patents, licensing, and the other commercial products of applied research, fearing that the forces of profit and the market place will undermine the traditional values of the academy rooted in the search for truth and knowledge.

Giving careful consideration to the basis for such concerns, Bok acknowledged the negative side of the pursuit of profit in the university—perhaps best illustrated by the excesses of college-level football and its place on many US campuses. In the end, however, he concluded that the values of the academy and its place in the broader culture make the university a more robust counterweight to such commercial forces than other authors have suggested. In fact, he cited a number of impacts of strategic research in partnership with the private sector that have enhanced the public service of the university. Importantly, these examples included the stimulation of basic research through collaboration with colleagues in the private sector and the active return on public investment represented by licensing and patent revenues that then supported the university's primary functions of teaching and basic scholarship. At the same time, Bok enumerated a list of less positive effects that must continue to be of concern, including the danger of profit-driven exclusive licensing of discoveries that then limit the development of broader benefits to the public, and an increasingly narrow focus of individuals and institutions on the commercial benefits of research that undermines commitment to the educational endeavor.

It would be more difficult, at least at this time, to argue that commercialization itself has been the force driving these same changes in Canadian universities. Of course, it would be naïve to suggest that there have not been cases where the prospect of profit to the individual member of faculty and/or the institution has had the deleterious impact suggested by Bok. There is little compelling anecdotal or empirical evidence, however, that the substantial changes associated with the new knowledge generation model of research in Canada can be attributed to commercialization or profit making per se. Rather, the motivation of the individual researcher and institution seems to remain largely a function of the opportunity to access funding that then enables a scale and type of research that was previously impossible. This said, many of both the positive and negative consequences of the changes are, as we have argued, parallel to those that may well be driven more directly by the commercial marketplace in the US. It may also be that Canada's institutions are simply lagging in time behind our traditionally more entrepreneurial American neighbours.

Change is hard—the academy adjusts to the evolution of universities and colleges

The arguments in an essay by Cameron predate many of those reviewed here—that universities must increasingly contribute in more direct ways to the wealth and well-being of our societies and communities, particularly by activities that increase productivity and competitiveness (Cameron, 2002). Fulfilling such an expectation requires an openness to change and innovation as well as a nimbleness that has not always characterized our institutions in the past, and that meets with considerable suspicion and resistance on our campuses.

It can be argued that this essential conservatism is—by design—built into the governance of our universities. (This is less true of Ontario's colleges where the faculty is less directly involved in the management roles.) University governance is marked by a level of decentralization that is matched in few other institutions. At every level, consensus is the holy grail of decision-making and its pursuit can easily lead to the delay or derailing of substantial proposals for change. Exhaustion often, in the end, is the most potent and deciding factor in these processes.

Individual members of the academy who play critical roles in these decision-making processes have sometimes shown a resistance, if not an outright hostility, toward change. The position is reflected vividly in the titles of many books emerging during the period of transformation explored here: e.g., *The University in Ruins* (Readings, 1996); *Zero Tolerance* (Emberley, 1996); *No Place to Learn* (Pocklington and Tupper, 2000); *Counting Out the Scholars* (Bruneau and Savage, 2002); and *Ivory Tower*

Blues (Côté and Allahar, 2007). These examples are only a few of the collections of passionate arguments made in reaction to many aspects of transformation described in this book, associated in one way or another with both the increased participation rates in colleges and universities, and the new research paradigm. Without evaluating the validity of these arguments in favour of some vision of the *status quo*, or perhaps the *status quo ante*, often these arguments, raised within the traditional university governance structure, can generate a powerful resistance to change. At the same time, these books and, more broadly, the proponents of the arguments contained therein, also sometimes identify many of the same shortcomings of the current university system raised in this book. In contrast to the themes presented here, however, their solutions more often point to a return to an older model of post-secondary education than to substantially new directions.

In exploring the post-secondary institution's ability to respond to the changes now demanded of it, Cameron (2002) asserted that the cumbersome nature of the collegial decision-making process and the longstanding inherent resistance to change of our post-secondary institutions has been markedly compounded by the near-universal unionization of faculty associations across the country. As Cameron reflected, the bicameral structure of the university deliberately assigned the role of directing the academic activity to the Senate and the task of protecting the public interest to the Board of Governors. The model produces a sometimes uncomfortable but more or less workable balance. With unionization and the powers associated with formal labour legislation, especially the threat of strike, a third force is introduced that was unplanned for in the bicameral model. Cameron argued that the faculty union's explicit and proper interest in the welfare and interests of the individual faculty member has substantially disrupted the balance intended by the original model. The net impact, he argued, is conservative, further resisting change and impairing the nimble response required of universities shouldering the societal expectations of the early 21st century in a global, quickly evolving economy.

Many institutional responses to such external and internal forces meet with stubborn internal resistance because some members of faculty and their unions see these changes as threatening their interests and, more broadly, the collegial tradition. The increased involvement of university researchers with the private sector and reliance on non-governmental funding both in research and through fund-raising, for example, have already provided targets for some within the institutions. Other areas where change might also meet with resistance from the more conservative elements of the academy include the following: the adoption of a greater student-service orientation; competition and differentiation among institutions; accommodations necessary to address the needs of underrepresented student populations; further increases in enrolment based on an ever higher participation rate; and, acknowledgement and formal acceptance of the universities' reliance on part-time and/or full-time teaching-only faculty for instruction as opposed to pursuing support for the traditional teacher/researcher model.

Some cautions regarding an uncritical advocacy of service to the knowledge economy and wealth-generation

During the 1960s there was widespread enthusiasm similar to that of our current era for the role of post-secondary education as a major contributor to societal economic success (Skolnik, 2005a). Such arguments, in combination with the coming of age of the post-war baby-boom generation, led to a major increase in participation rates and in the number of colleges and universities across Canada and in Ontario. The tensions associated with this growth and the system responses need to be taken into account as we contemplate the consequences of similar expectations being applied to our post-secondary institutions in the early years of the 21st century.

At the same time as universities and colleges legitimately build arguments for increased support and funding based on evidence of the role they can play in wealth generation, competitiveness and, perhaps, the direct solution of some of societies' most pressing societal threats, they must also consider the appropriate limits of such arguments. Such reflections will need to embrace a variety of questions that have been raised by a range of critics of the direction of the modern university, including:

- the extent to which Ontario's largely undifferentiated college and university sectors can be sustained in the face of participation rates associated with mass or near universal post-secondary education;
- the possibility that such changes demand a re-evaluation of the relative roles of colleges and universities within the province;
- the implication of the fact that a wide range of professional and, indeed, non-professional positions see a post-secondary degree or, to a lesser extent, diploma as a necessary credential. Some would argue that the credential has grown in importance less on the basis of the substantive particular skill needs, but more as a convenient filtering or sorting mechanism or, at most, as providing the opportunity for a general maturing prior to shouldering the responsibilities of the workplace.

Although these caveats demand an ongoing evaluation and refinement of the new knowledge production model of university research, as is the case with increased participation in post-secondary education, reality has made a substantial component of this debate academic—in a figurative sense. That is, there is incontrovertible evidence that higher education and university-based research are now viewed as key components of increased productivity and global competitiveness in today's knowledge economy. Ontario's future post-secondary system must be well-adapted for this reality.

CONCLUDING THOUGHTS ON KNOWLEDGE PRODUCTION

This chapter has explored a second major transformative force that has compounded the impact of unprecedented increases in participation rates and enrolment in Ontario's post-secondary institutions over the past two decades: the emergence of a new research paradigm emphasizing a close alignment with societal and governmental objectives, collaboration with the government and private sectors, and a rigorous accountability for the excellence of the research. The impact of this new paradigm has been focused on the province's universities. The rationale for this substantial change in expectations of research can be found in a series of federal and provincial policy documents exploring competitiveness within a rapidly shifting global economy. These documents concluded that the future well-being of Ontario and Canada would require a deliberate emphasis on increased innovation and productivity necessitating both an increase in the number of well-educated workers for the knowledge economy and a focus on research that would fuel this new economy and replace Canada's long-standing reliance on raw materials, commodities, and traditional manufacturing. These arguments almost universally identified research in Ontario's universities as critical to the endeavour's success. Rapid investment in post-secondary education sectors in many parts of the world, in developing as well as developed nations, speaks to a universal acceptance of this model.

On the basis of these arguments, the 1990s and early 2000s saw new federal and provincial research support programs that provided hundreds of millions of dollars of investment in support of this new knowledge production paradigm. The universities have adjusted remarkably quickly to the challenge represented by these programs even though they have demanded a considerable change in the operations both of the institutions and individual members of faculty. Although it will be some time until the long-term impact of these investments on the province and the country's productivity and competitiveness can be evaluated, it is clear that the universities have responded enthusiastically and effectively to the incentives provided by the programs. The increase in targeted, collaborative research that was the objective of these programs is underway.

The response of the universities to the objectives of the new research paradigm has not been without costs—to both the institutions and individual researchers. The necessary adaptations have resulted in strains and conflicts with other critical elements of their mandates, including the commitment to undergraduate education. As a result of the relative homogeneity of Ontario universities, these pressures are felt more or less across the system. If Ontario's universities are to continue to meet the province's expectations and needs as actors at the centre of future productivity and competitiveness, and at the same time continue to offer outstanding educational programs, more fundamental shifts in the nature and workings of the post-secondary system will be required.

In the following three chapters, we explore elements of the post secondary system in Ontario that have constrained and shaped the past, and will determine the future response of colleges and universities to massive increases in enrolment and adaptation to the demands of research within a direct knowledge production paradigm: funding mechanisms, expectations for accountability, and the structure of the system itself.

4

Financial Pressures and the Transformation of the Professoriate

Government funding for universities, adjusted for enrolments and inflation, has declined over the past two decades. At the same time, revenue from student tuition and mandatory fees has increased more quickly than inflation. In this chapter we will show that when these are added together, total operating funding for universities, adjusted for enrolment growth and CPI inflation, has been remarkably stable: university funding per student from operating grants and student fees, adjusted for CPI inflation, has remained approximately constant over the past two decades.

For colleges, the data we present show that the history is different, but the endpoint is the same. Colleges' total funding per student from operating grants and student fees fell sharply in the 1990s, but has recovered in the current decade. Colleges' funding today from grants and fees, adjusted for enrolments and CPI inflation, is about the same today as 20 years ago.

The problem we examine in this chapter is that per-student costs tend to grow more quickly than CPI inflation. Compensation costs—which account for about three-quarters of university and college budgets—face pressures from wage settlements, progress-through-the-ranks increases for faculty, and higher employee benefit costs. Other costs such as utilities may climb faster than CPI inflation as well. In the meantime, there has been a long-term shift among full-time university faculty towards greater research responsibilities and reduced undergraduate teaching loads. As we noted in Chapter 3, the heightened competition among institutions for research grants, capital grants, high-quality students, private-sector partnerships, and gifts from donors has also imposed new costs. As

Academic Transformation: The Forces Reshaping Higher Education in Ontario, I.D. Clark, G. Moran, M.L. Skolnik, and D. Trick. Montreal and Kingston: McGill-Queen's University Press, Queen's Policy Studies Series.
© 2009 The School of Policy Studies, Queen's University at Kingston. All rights reserved.

average per-student costs have climbed more quickly than CPI inflation, most institutions have responded by increasing the student-faculty ratio and increasing the proportion of teaching done by lower-cost part-time and temporary faculty.

These facts suggest some of the financial challenges in planning for future enrolment growth. Any institution whose per-student costs grow more quickly than per-student revenues is going to face an annual budget crunch. One-time fixes—such as an infusion of government funds or a large hike in tuition fees—may provide a temporary respite but not a long-term solution. As noted, the most common response to date has been to increase class sizes and make greater use of part-time and temporary faculty. If continued indefinitely, these responses will be unlikely to provide a high-quality education to the increasing number of students, many from disadvantaged backgrounds, who are seeking a baccalaureate education.

How has Post-secondary Funding Changed over Time?

The debate over higher education funding in Ontario is heavily coloured by perceptions of history. It is widely believed in the university and college sectors that the fundamental problems of higher education can be attributed to government funding cuts. From this premise, the conclusion is often drawn that solutions are to be found in a restoration of government grants or, alternatively, in higher tuition fees. Our review of historical revenue data leads us to a more nuanced conclusion that takes into account both revenues and costs.

Our initial focus here is on revenue from provincial operating grants, tuition fees, and mandatory student fees. The largest share of the ongoing operating costs of a university or college is funded from these sources. There are of course many other sources of funding: research funds from the federal government, such as those from the national granting councils and the Canada Foundation for Innovation; research grants from the provincial government; other research grants and contracts; education and training contracts with industry; donations and endowment income; and revenue from ancillary services such as parking and food services. But these other sources of revenue are usually tied to the conduct of a specified task or project, and many are not reliable from year to year. Operating grants, tuition fees, and mandatory student fees—where institutions have substantial discretion over how to allocate revenue—are therefore our focus here.

It is indisputable that per-student revenue from these sources, adjusted for CPI inflation, fell in the 1970s and early 1980s in both the university and college sectors. The creation of the new universities and the colleges in the 1960s was followed almost immediately by the recession of 1970-71 and a slowdown in the long-term growth rate of provincial revenues.

In the university sector, government funding per FTE student, adjusted for CPI inflation, fell sharply in the 1970s, and tuition fees were frozen for most of these years. The net effect was that total university operating revenue from government grants, tuition, and fees, per student, fell by about one-quarter by the early 1980s (measured in constant dollars), as shown in Figure 4.1. In the college sector, the pattern in the 1970s was similar but more severe, with college funding from government grants and tuition, per student, falling by about one-third in constant dollars, as shown in Figure 4.2.

Since the mid-1980s, government strategies for funding enrolment expansion in a constrained fiscal environment have differed between the two sectors.

In the 1990s, faced with historically high deficits, the provincial government reduced its funding to universities in absolute terms on two occasions; however, during these years, the government permitted substantial increases in tuition, including tuition deregulation in some programs and partial deregulation of mandatory student fees. As a result, total university operating revenue remained in the range of $13,000 (constant 2007 dollars) per FTE from the mid-1980s to the mid-2000s. Recent increases in government funding have increased the total to about $14,000, as shown

FIGURE 4.1
Universities: Total operating revenue from government grants, tuition, and fees, per FTE, 1970-71 to 1982-83
(constant dollars, 1970-71 = 100)

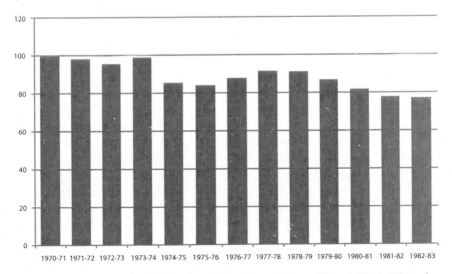

Source: Ontario Council on University Affairs, *Seventh Annual Report* (1981, 34), and *Eleventh Annual Report* (1985, 61). Data for 1980-81 and later have been re-based by the authors.

FIGURE 4.2
Colleges: Total operating revenue from government grants,
tuition, and fees, per FTE, 1971-72 to 1982-83
(constant dollars, 1971-72 = 100)

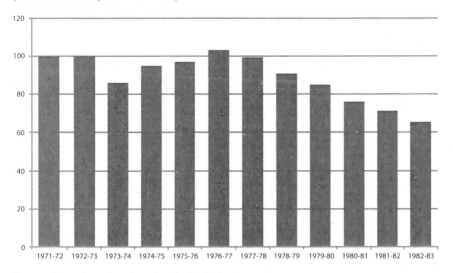

Source: Drea (2003) and authors' calculations.

in Figure 4.3. These figures do not include the effect of direct operating grants from the federal government to universities under the Canada Research Chairs program and the Indirect Costs Program; the combined revenue from these two programs averaged $450 per FTE student in 2008, although the amounts varied widely by university.

The pattern for the colleges since the mid-1980s is different from that for the universities. College enrolments grew substantially during the recession of the early 1990s with no increase in public funding. College tuition fees increased after 1993, but governments (and most college administrators) did not believe that college students could, or should, pay fee increases comparable in dollar terms to the increases that university students were paying. These factors meant that there was a sharp decline in total operating revenues per FTE from 1990 to 1996. Recent increases in government grants, coupled with increases in tuition and mandatory fees, mean that total funding per student from these sources has almost returned to its mid-1980s level, as shown in Figure 4.4.

Another way of looking at post-secondary finances is to consider the share of total economic output that is devoted to government operating grants to colleges and universities. In effect this is a public perspective: it asks what share of total output the public, as represented by its

FIGURE 4.3
Universities: Total operating revenue from MTCU operating grants,
tuition, and mandatory fees, per FTE student, 1987-88 to 2007-08
(constant 2007 dollars)

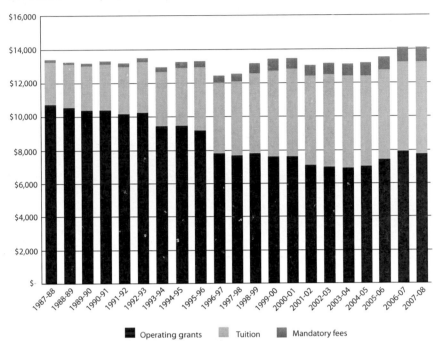

Operating grants ▪ Tuition ▪ Mandatory fees

Source: Operating grants and tuition: Council of Ontario Universities (2007, Table
1.2). Mandatory fees: Calculated from COU COFO Compendium, Table E-3. Data for
2005-06 to 2007-08 from Council of Ontario Universities COFO database. Converted
to 2007 dollars using Statistics Canada Consumer Price Index for Ontario.

government, is prepared to spend on public support for universities and
colleges. It does not explicitly consider changes in enrolments or changes
in students' contribution through tuition and fees. The denominator is
total economic output, so this indicator tends to rise during recessions,
even if there is no change in government operating grants.

This perspective confirms that public support for post-secondary education declined from about 0.9 percent of GDP in the late 1980s to a low of
0.55 percent in 2001-02, and has since partly recovered to about 0.7 percent
in 2007-08, as shown in Figure 4.5. The overall decline is consistent with
the common view that health care and reducing tax rates have been higher
public priorities during this period. The partial recovery since 2001-02
suggests that these priorities are not absolute and that higher education
can benefit from changing political circumstances.

FIGURE 4.4
Colleges: Total operating revenue from MTCU operating grants,
tuition, and mandatory fees, per FTE student, 1987-88 to 2007-08
(constant 2007 dollars)

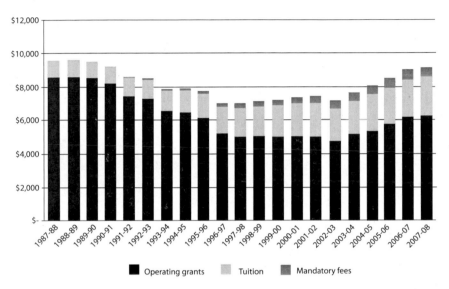

Source: Colleges Ontario (2008, 58; 2005, 93). Adjusted to include revenue from
deregulated fees and mandatory ancillary fees, both from MTCU. Converted to 2007
dollars using Statistics Canada Consumer Price Index for Ontario.

The proportionate loss from the late 1980s to 2001-02 was about the
same for the college and university sectors. The partial recovery since
2001-02 has been somewhat stronger for the university sector, reflecting
government efforts to respond to stronger enrolment pressures in the
universities.

The Federal Government's Role

An important backdrop to this analysis of provincial funding is the
shifting level of federal transfer payments to the provinces for post-
secondary education. From 1967 to 1977 the federal government encouraged the growth of post-secondary education across Canada by
paying provinces an amount equal to 50 percent of all operating costs.
The decision of the federal government in 1977 to roll together federal
transfers for post-secondary education, hospital insurance, and medical
care into a single transfer payment, based on population and economic

FIGURE 4.5
Operating grants to universities and colleges as a share of GDP,
1986-87 to 2007-08 (percent)

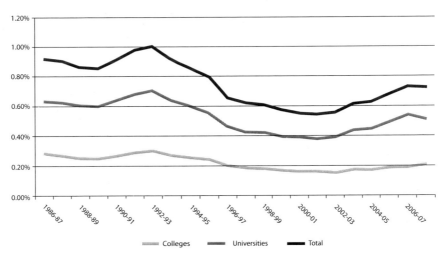

growth rates, had the effect of distancing the federal government from actual program costs, removing the distortions inherent in cost-sharing, and transferring to the provincial level most of the debate about funding adequacy.

Provincial governments were free to spend the new transfer payment—known as Established Programs Financing (EPF)—as they wished, subject to certain conditions under the 1984 *Canada Health Act*. This continued to be the case with EPF's successors, the Canada Health and Social Transfer and the Canada Social Transfer. For this reason, these transfers should be seen as a backdrop; they are suggestive of the level of federal support for post-secondary education, but there was no automatic linkage between changes in federal support and actual provincial grants to universities and colleges.

Table 4.1 shows the level of federal cash transfers to Ontario notionally provided for post-secondary education from 1985-86 to 2007-08. For most of this period the federal government took no position on what share of the transfer payment was intended to support the cost of post-secondary education, and so analysts may differ on how to calculate this share. It is clear from the expenditure pattern that federal transfers for higher education are closely related to federal fiscal capacity and not to program costs. In constant dollars, they have fallen by about one-third. During this same 22-year period, higher education enrolments in Ontario have grown by more than 60 percent.

TABLE 4.1

Federal cash transfer payments to Ontario
for post-secondary education, 1985-86 to 2007-08

	$ million	$ million (constant 2007)	Index 2007 = 100
1985-86	792.3	1,420.5	146.7
1986-87	805.0	1,380.7	142.6
1987-88	782.0	1,278.0	132.0
1988-89	775.9	1,210.8	125.1
1989-90	790.2	1,165.8	120.4
1990-91	824.9	1,161.4	120.0
1991-92	923.9	1,242.3	128.3
1992-93	985.0	1,311.8	135.5
1993-04	990.2	1,295.3	133.8
1994-95	960.3	1,256.2	129.8
1995-96	916.0	1,169.3	120.8
1996-97	567.0	712.3	73.6
1997-98	311.1	383.9	39.7
1998-99	242.9	297.1	30.7
1999-2000	383.2	459.5	47.5
2000-01	439.1	511.6	52.9
2001-02	772.2	873.1	90.2
2002-03	860.4	953.3	98.5
2003-04	860.3	928.2	95.9
2004-05	728.0	771.2	79.7
2005-06	831.0	861.3	89.0
2006-07	869.5	885.5	91.5
2007-08	968.0	968.0	100.0

Notes: (1) EPF and transfers under the Canada Assistance Program were merged into the CHST in 1996-97. The method used in this table to apportion the CHST among health care, social assistance, and post-secondary education is to pro-rate the total CHST in the same proportion as the CAP and EPF in 1995-96. (2) CHST was divided into the Canada Health Transfer and Canada Social Transfer in 2004-05. In 2007 the federal government announced that 25 percent of the CST would be earmarked for post-secondary education. (2007 Budget, Annex 4) The method used in this table is to apply this 25 percent rule to all years beginning in 2004-05.

Source: 1985-86 to 2002-03: COU (1997), Table 2, and COU (2004b), Table 1.3. 2003-04 to 2007-08: Authors' calculations based on Ontario Budget documents.

Total Canada Social Transfer cash levels have been set in legislation up to 2013-14 and will grow by 3 percent annually, effective 2009-10. These adjustments notwithstanding, federal funding has not increased to support the move from a mass to a universal system of higher education, and there is little prospect that it will do so in the future. Instead, increased federal funding over the past decade has been tied to research activities, infrastructure, and financial aid to students.

GOVERNMENT PURPOSES AND FUNDING FORMULAS

The ability of universities and colleges to respond to changing public demands depends on both the volume of funds available to them and the conditions governing the funds. The primary means by which the government has attached conditions to funding has been through the funding formulas for the college and university sector. Within each sector, the formula sets the rules of the game by which institutions can attract more funding, and it creates incentives for behaviour.

Universities

The university funding formula was introduced in 1967 and, with many amendments, remains in place to this day. It embodied the decision of the provincial government in the mid-1960s to reduce its involvement in the internal financial decisions of universities. At the same time—given the government's reluctance to impose new regulations or legislation on universities—the funding formula has proved to be the largest single instrument through which the government carries out its policy towards universities. The formula has supported the commitment of the government to access; it has provided a means for the government to impose fiscal restraint on universities; and it has permitted the government to encourage universities to respond to new government priorities through the awarding of special-purpose grants.

The lion's share of funding is distributed based on each university's enrolments, with adjustments for differences in the mix of program offerings at each university. Funding is provided as a block grant to support all university operating activities, including instruction, research, academic support services, libraries, computing, student services, public service, administration, and plant maintenance (OCUA, 1995, 262). A much smaller share of funding—about one-tenth of the total in most years—is distributed to reflect the special needs of Northern universities and universities offering French-language programming, and to fund special priorities set by government.

The basic features of the formula have been described as follows:

> [P]ublic support for operating purposes would [beginning in 1967] be based on the number of students registered at each institution. In order to reflect the variations in the costs of different programs, the subsidies would be weighted according to costs per student. For example, the support of an agricultural student was deemed to be about twice as expensive, and that of a medical student five times as expensive, as the support of an undergraduate student in the first year of general arts. Moreover, other private or public income that an institution might receive, with the exception of tuition fees, would not be deducted from government subsidies. Finally, extra-formula grants would be instituted to cover the higher operating costs of emerging post-secondary institutions and French-language learning programs. (Commission on Post-secondary Education in Ontario, 1972, 139)

The formula provides equal revenue per student at every university for students in similar programs. The weighting of programs—expressed by counting each student as a certain number of Basic Income Units (BIUs), depending on his or her program—has provided significant revenues for universities with high concentrations of graduate and professional programs. The weights established in 1967 remain in place today, with some program additions and some upward revisions in small programs. Table 4.2 shows the government grant per student in 2007-08 for major programs.

The authors of the university formula were aware that the introduction of a formula would not ensure any specific level of funding to the universities. Even in the heyday of university funding growth, they recognized the inevitable tension between the funding ambitions of universities and the willingness of governments to pay:

> It is frequently pointed out that universities are spending institutions and that there is no upper limit, within reason, to what they can usefully spend on improved teaching, more extensive research and the facilities which these things involve. These comments are made in order to emphasize that while a formula will ensure equitable distribution of moneys, it will not, in itself, ensure an adequate level of support. (Ontario Minister of University Affairs, 1967)

Rather than setting out the level of funding required to achieve a desired level of quality in teaching and research with a desired level of efficiency in operations, the authors of the funding formula simply argued that, "within reason," there is "no upper limit" to what universities can

TABLE 4.2

MTCU operating grant per student for selected university programs, 2007-08

Funding weight	Programs (examples)	Grant per FTE student
1	1st year Arts and Science General Arts and Science	$3,100
1.5	Upper-year Honours Arts Commerce Fine Arts Law	$5,800
2	Applied Science and Engineering Architecture	$8,300
2	Upper-year Honours Science Education Nursing Pharmacy Master of Business Administration	$8,500
3	Master of Arts	$12,700
4	Master of Science	$18,200
5	Medicine Dentistry	$24,200
6	Doctoral	$29,100

Notes: Grant assumes three terms for master's and doctoral students and two terms for others. There are time limits on funding for master's and doctoral students.

The funding weight is applied to income from the MTCU grant and a portion of students' tuition fees. For this reason, the resultant MTCU grant per FTE student is not directly proportional to the funding weight.

Source: Estimated by the authors based on MTCU data.

"usefully" spend.[18] This has left the level of total funding per student to be politically negotiated by governments over time.

The largest single change in the university formula was the introduction of so-called corridor funding in 1987, under which each university's

---

[18] This observation is not unique to Ontario. Howard Bowen, a former university president and scholar in the field of the economics of higher education, formulated "the revenue theory of unit costs in higher education" (Bowen, 1980, 15-19). This theory holds that revenue is the main determinant of cost in higher education, because universities aim to raise as much money as they can, and spend as much money as they can raise. One of the real-world observations that this theory helps to explain is the enormous variation among institutions in expenditures per student. All institutions face similar production functions, but they differ enormously in their ability to raise revenue.

share of total operating funding would remain constant provided that its enrolment remained at a fixed level, plus or minus three percent. The introduction of corridor funding formally authorized universities that so chose to exempt themselves from planning for any future enrolment growth. However, the potential significance of this policy shift was quickly mitigated by an unexpected rise in applications from prospective students. In the majority of the years since 1987, the government has made available additional funding to universities that would agree to accept more students. The offer of this funding, in years when little or no funding was available to cover inflation, has meant that the incentives for universities have been similar to those in the period before the 1987 change.

From its inception, one of the purposes of the formula has been to give universities independence to decide how general-purpose funds are spent (Ontario Minister of University Affairs, 1967, 98). In particular, the formula gives the provincial government no direct means of shaping the balance between teaching, research, and other activities at each university. A proposal from the Ontario Council on University Affairs to introduce a formula that would have done exactly that was rejected by the government in 1996 following vigorous opposition from university administrations, faculty associations, and student groups.

While there have been frequent adjustments to the formula, governments have been highly reluctant to revise the formula without the agreement of the universities. The formula began as a joint project of the government and the universities, and the universities have watched it closely to ensure their interests were protected.

Colleges

In the college sector, a formula based on many of the same principles as the university formula was introduced in 1981. The college formula remained in place until 2006-07, when significant interim changes were introduced, followed by the introduction of a new formula in 2009.

The college formula was used to distribute approximately 70 percent of the college operating grant. Like the university formula, it was based on the principle of equal funding per student, weighted by program. This funding was provided as a block grant to give colleges flexibility in its use. In contrast to the university formula, the college formula has not employed a corridor system; instead each college received a share of the general purpose operating grant based on its share of weighted enrolments. In addition to the general purpose operating grant, the ministry provided a wide range of special grants to support specific objectives.

Another contrast to the university formula is that program weightings in the college formula have taken into account a range of detailed operational factors, such as classroom hours per term and costs for instructional equipment. The weightings in the college formula are narrower than in the university formula, and so the variation in funding per student is less (although a few programs are outliers). Average funding levels are shown in Table 4.3. As in the university sector, the formula does not explicitly recognize rising costs, and so the level of total funding per student has been politically negotiated by governments over time.

TABLE 4.3
MTCU operating grant per student for college programs, 2007-08

Program	Grant per FTE student
Post-secondary certificate and diploma programs (mean)	$5,500
Applied baccalaureate degree programs (median)	$5,000

Source: Estimated based on MTCU data and Colleges Ontario (2008, 58).

THE RELATIONSHIP OF FUNDING TO COSTS

To say that total funding per student in the middle of the current decade was approximately equal to funding in the mid-1980s, adjusted for consumer price inflation, is a limited claim. It is not a claim about how funding compared to the period when most of the current universities and colleges were established. (Funding per student declined substantially in both sectors between 1970 and the mid-1980s.) It is not a claim about whether funding was competitive with other provinces or other countries. (Ontario's government grants per student were among the lowest of the ten provinces during most of this period, and regulated university tuition fees by the end of the period were among the highest.) It is not a claim that funding was adequate. Indeed, throughout the past two decades governments and higher education institutions have been unable to agree whether institutions did or did not have enough funding to do the job that was expected of them.

A salient feature of Ontario's funding arrangements is that there is no explicit discussion of what the cost is, or should be, of educating a student or carrying out the other functions of a university or college. This practice is in contrast to jurisdictions where annual funding increases are directly related to the cost of inputs and are disaggregated into an increase for the continuing costs of current operations and a separate increase to accommodate higher enrolments and other new priorities.

A corollary is that Ontario's funding arrangements incorporate no explicit discussion of inflation. Anxious to protect their fiscal flexibility, governments have sometimes appeared to take the position that inflation is so low as to be negligible, readily within the range of what universities and colleges could accommodate through improved productivity.

For their part, university and college administrators have often asserted that inflation at their institutions was 2-4 points above CPI inflation and would continue at this rate for the indefinite future, for reasons outside the institutions' control. For example, in 2006 the Council of Ontario Universities estimated the multi-year inflation rate for universities at 4.6 percent, and it projected that the rate would continue at this level through at least 2009-10. COU cited long-term trends in faculty salaries (3.7 percent annual increase), non-academic salaries (3.1 percent), employee benefits (14.2 percent), and non-payroll costs (3.6 percent) (Council of Ontario Universities, 2006a and 2006b.) By comparison, the actual increase in Ontario CPI averaged 2.0 percent in the period 2004 to 2006.

Inflation and compensation costs

We have defined inflation as change in the Ontario Consumer Price Index. Salaries, wages, and benefits account for about three-quarters of university and college operating expenditures. The Consumer Price Index is used on the premise that the living standards of higher education employees, as a group, should reasonably be expected to keep pace with inflation and to reflect any productivity improvements in the higher education sector.

Alternatively, one can argue that the living standards of higher education employees, as a group, should keep pace with those of other public sector employees. This means measuring inflation against a benchmark such as the change in Ontario public sector wage settlements for unionized employees. Using this measure makes little difference to the overall change from 1985 to the mid-2000s, but it changes the timing of some of the peaks and valleys in the intervening years. Public sector wage settlements outpaced inflation in the late 1980s and early 1990s, and lagged inflation in the mid-1990s. By 1996 these two effects had balanced out, and so from 1996 onwards there is little difference between the two measures.

Three other arguments are sometimes made to show that cost inflation in universities or colleges should be expected to be higher than that in the general economy. The first is that, as faculty members' average number of years of experience increases, salaries will tend to rise more quickly than CPI inflation. As in many fields of employment, full-time faculty receive increases based on a salary grid as well as increases for inflation. This phenomenon is time-limited in the sense that average faculty years of experience cannot rise in perpetuity: eventually the average stabilizes or declines. If the distribution of faculty on the grid is uniform, then the cost of progression through the grid is self-funding, as senior faculty retire and are replaced by junior faculty. Nevertheless, it is important to note that the combination of faculty demographics and long-term salary commitments may cause some universities and colleges to experience supranormal salary inflation that must be funded by seeking higher revenues or by reducing other expenditures.

A second argument is that unit costs of production in a service industry with limited access to technology gains will rise more quickly than unit costs in the economy as a whole, since the industry must pay competitive wages even though its rate of productivity improvement is lower than that of the economy as a whole. This phenomenon—known as "Baumol's disease"—was first described with respect to the performing arts (Baumol and Bowen, 1966; Baumol, 1996). In the classic case, Baumol and his colleague Bowen noted that salaries in symphony orchestras tend to rise with salaries in the rest of the economy, even though the performance of a Beethoven string quartet requires the same number of workers and the same amount of time as it did in 1800. This observation raises the question of the extent to which productivity improvements in higher education—meaning increases in the volume of instruction, research and service outputs, taking quality into account—are possible over time.

A third argument is that in recent years demand from private firms, seeking gains from new technologies and improved management, has caused a permanent upward shift in the wages of knowledge workers relative to those of other workers, driving up post-secondary institutions' costs more than those of other employers. This argument requires careful specification of the relevant labour market (or markets). Some faculty are highly mobile geographically and are in high demand from private-sector employers, while others are less so.

There is evidence to support all of these arguments. All are layered on top of the cultural norm of equity among faculty, which is supported and carried forward through the collective bargaining process. From a public policy perspective, the tradition of collective and equity-driven remuneration is a strange and uncomfortable bedfellow of the performance-based remuneration associated with the competition of the market place.

University administrations and faculty unions (or associations) have both argued that the recruitment and retention of the very best faculty requires competitive salaries. This argument is relatively new to the academic world where, in earlier generations, compensation was thought to flow primarily from the academic life itself, and it was generally accepted that financial remuneration would not reach levels attainable in other professional domains. The notion of merit-based or performance-based salaries was regarded by many as foreign to the academic world and contrary to its values. However, annual merit components and market-based adjustments are now included in many university union agreements.

In the past two decades, movement across national borders has become more common. Fears of a "brain-drain," especially in universities, fuelled arguments for greater flexibility to attract and retain the best faculty and, indeed, to attract Canadian expatriates and foreign nationals to this country's universities. Although some cross-border competition was driving these changes, much of the competition has in fact been between

For example, every institution feels the need to actively market its programs to prospective students; the consequence of not doing so is to have too few students, or to have only those students who were not accepted by other institutions. Competition has raised the bar for recruitment publications, events, advertisements, and electronic media, each of which brings its own higher costs.

Most universities also feel obliged to offer merit scholarships to attract well-qualified students who might otherwise attend another institution. A university that failed to attract students with high marks would be left only with students who are average or below-average—lowering both faculty morale and national rankings, and creating a self-perpetuating cycle for future years. A recent study found that 55 percent of incoming students at the Ontario universities responding to a survey received entrance scholarships based on merit, and the large majority of these scholarships were based solely on high school marks. The majority of these awards were funded from general operating budgets and were not targeted to underrepresented demographic groups. Further, the amounts involved have been increasing over time. The study speculated on whether Ontario universities are engaged in a merit awards "arms race" whose effect was to drain university funds without substantially affecting students' choices (Education Policy Institute, 2008). This situation is different from the 1960s, when the provincial government banned universities from using their operating resources to offer financial incentives for enrolment (Fleming 1971, 70).

We noted in Chapter 3 that every university feels the need to have an office devoted to advancing the institution's research mission, so as not to miss out on potentially tens of millions of dollars in competitively-awarded funding from federal and provincial research programs, as well as funding from private partners. Closely related to this is the need to have full-time executives, typically at the level of vice president, to pursue donations and raise the institution's corporate profile. "Friend-raising" has become a professionalized function, and institutions have adopted strategies to raise their public profiles in ways that might produce un-defined benefits in the long term. Institutions outside of Toronto, feeling disadvantaged in the province's largest media market, have become regular advertisers in Toronto newspapers in the hope of winning the attention of decision-makers, donors, and prospective students. New graduates from many MBA programs can expect to see their photographs in full-page newspaper ads, although to date it is rare that the achievements of students in other programs are similarly heralded.

The outcome of competition is not necessarily zero-sum. Competition has caused institutions to sharpen their research priorities, offer academic programs that respond to students' interests, and woo donors who might otherwise not have given to public causes. Some forms of competition bring net new revenues to the institution. But the shift from a culture of entitlement to a culture of competition has created costs that go beyond normal inflationary increases. The escalation of these costs is beyond the control of any single institution, since the price of not competing is to fall behind.

Consequence: No choice but to grow

The fact that costs per student have tended to rise more quickly than government funding and tuition revenue has had an important effect in shaping university and college growth strategies. A primary device by which universities have accommodated inflation has been to enrol additional students. They have done so in the expectation that the marginal revenue from these students will exceed the marginal costs and so leave a surplus to cover inflationary costs that would otherwise be unfunded. An institution that might have wanted to remain a constant size over the long term would have faced unsupportable challenges in managing its budget.

This circumstance accounts for the similarity in university enrolment strategies over the past two decades. Regardless of their professed commitment to differentiation, all universities have expanded their undergraduate enrolments to take advantage of targeted government funding and students' tuition fees. This has been true for both general-purpose expansions (such as the enrolment funding associated with the double cohort) and special-purpose expansions such as those for engineering and teaching.

The most successful universities have timed their expansions to meet the availability of additional government grants and deregulated tuition fees—growing when there was funding support to do so, and holding back on growth in other years. The absence of an inflationary funding mechanism makes careful, highly contingent decision-making crucial for each institution. After two decades of such a system, it is apparent that many universities have been remarkably adept at walking this tightrope.

The college sector has faced similar financial pressures to grow in order to cover inflation. These pressures were exacerbated by the reductions in total funding per student (adjusted for CPI) that colleges experienced in the 1990s. The pattern of enrolment growth is more variable among the colleges than among the universities, but this is primarily because college enrolments depend more heavily on local population growth.

As with the universities, colleges received additional funding from time to time for general or program-specific enrolment growth. Colleges' behaviour was heavily shaped by the growth incentives embedded in the funding formula in place until 2006. Each college's government funding depended on whether it was growing at least as quickly as the other colleges (rather than depending on whether it was growing at all). The prospect of increased tuition revenue also encouraged growth, although tuition per student remained much lower than in the university sector.

The behaviour of the colleges and universities raises the question whether governments have unintentionally taught institutions to respond to the incentives of government funding, rather than responding directly to changes in student demand. It also suggests that, in practice, an institution has limited autonomy to determine its own size and to offer a distinctive mix of academic programs. While each university and college is expected to set its own strategy, constrained funding has pushed all universities and all colleges to adopt similar strategies in order to survive financially.

THE PROFESSORIATE TRANSFORMED

Enrolment growth by itself has not been enough to allow universities to make ends meet. Universities have faced strong incentives to expand their research activities. These incentives arise in the first instance from the strong cultural imperative within the academy to emphasize research rather than teaching as a measure of a faculty member's performance. The incentive has been strengthened with the creation of the Canada Foundation for Innovation and related programs since 1997. The conflicting pressures to teach more students and to win more research grants have transformed the nature of the full-time faculty. Undergraduate teaching loads—measured as the average number of courses taught by a full-time faculty member per year—have declined. Average class sizes have increased. The share of undergraduate teaching performed by temporary and part-time faculty has risen and is now reported by some universities to be in the range of half of all instruction in the largest undergraduate teaching faculties. If current trends in per-student funding and expenditures continue, it is reasonable to expect that average class sizes and the share of teaching performed by instructors who are not permanent faculty will continue to rise indefinitely into the future.

Full-time faculty, teaching, and research

At the heart of any North American research-intensive university and, in fact, all of Ontario's universities, lies the cherished principle that undergraduate students should be taught by instructors who also engage in discovery research and scholarship. As we discussed in Chapter 1, from this principle arise the strong commitments to the complementary relationship between teaching and research, as well as associated arguments against accepting the possibility of a second category of university instructor whose responsibilities would not include traditional research and discovery scholarship. It is, however, inconceivable that the numbers of tenured and tenure-track faculty, constrained by available resources, could themselves have accommodated the increased enrolment and the substantial broadening of research responsibilities described above. The number of FTE students per full-time faculty member at universities has increased from 17 in 1987 to 25 in 2007, as shown in Figure 4.6—a 45 percent increase in two decades.

Universities have adjusted by changing the way teaching is done. Most obviously, average class sizes have increased, even though relatively smaller classes continue to make up a substantial part of the course offerings, especially in some disciplines, and at the advanced and graduate levels. (It is simply not possible, even if the pedagogical issues are ignored, to teach laboratory sections, languages, and courses with intensive writing and participation requirements in large classes.) Evidence of large class sizes is especially pronounced for first-year students at universities with enrolments of over 10,000, which account for about 90 percent of all first-year students. At eight of these large universities, 30 percent or more of first-year courses have more than 100 students, as shown in Table 4.4.

Increasing class sizes has increased the teaching productivity of full-time faculty, but this has been offset in whole or in part by another contemporaneous trend. The average number of classes taught by an individual tenured or probationary member of faculty has diminished. This decrease is a function in part of a general tendency to reduce undergraduate teaching class load in recognition of increased graduate and research responsibilities.

FIGURE 4.6
University FTE enrolment per full-time faculty, 1987-88 to 2007-08

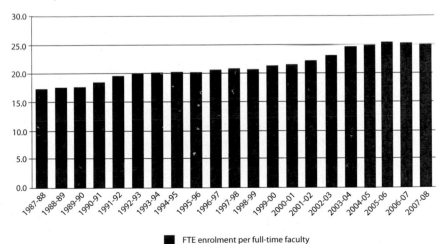

FTE enrolment per full-time faculty

Note: Full-time faculty counts include all teaching ranks, and medical and dental teaching staff. 2005-06 to 2007-08: Common University Data Ontario.

Source: 1987-88 to 2004-05: Council of Ontario Universities (2007, Table 8.1).

TABLE 4.4
Incidence of large class sizes (100+ students) for first and second year
Ontario university students, Fall 2007

	Universities with 20,000 or more undergraduate students:		Universities with 10,000-20,000 undergraduate students:		Universities with under 10,000 undergraduate students:	
	First year	*Second year*	*First year*	*Second year*	*First year*	*Second year*
Share of classes with over 100 students	Number of universities	Number of universities	Number of universities	Number of universities	Number of universities	Number of universities
Over 30%	4	-	4	-	1	-
20-30%	1	2	1	1	1	1
10-20%	-	3	2	6	1	-
Under 10%	-	-	-	-	3	5

Source: Common University Data Ontario, 2008. One university not reporting.

Universities do not publish comprehensive data on teaching loads, which vary by university, department, and individual faculty member. Teaching loads are usually determined by customary practice rather than by collective agreements. We examined teaching loads in thirty departments and programs, collectively representing ten Ontario universities, using administrative documents made public by each university.[19] The most common teaching load in these departments and programs is four one-term courses per year per faculty member; the second most common is five such courses. Many individual faculty are reported to have a teaching load below these norms due to their responsibilities for research, graduate supervision, or administration. A few have higher teaching loads for reasons that are not explained. These findings, while incomplete, suggest that Nossal's survey of the situation in political science reflects a broader trend:

> Since [the 1970s] ... we have seen large-scale reduction in undergraduate course teaching in Canadian political science departments. First, the nominal teaching load in many departments has been reduced, driven by the widespread adoption in the 1970s of a 2+2 load by American political science departments—down from the standard 3+2 load in the 1960s. Today, all but a

---

[19] In most cases these documents were applications to the Ontario Council on Graduate Studies, seeking approval for new graduate programs or re-approval of existing programs. For this reason the sample may be biased toward departments that have master's or doctoral programs. The ten universities include a variety of sizes and research profiles.

couple of Canadian political science departments offering the doctorate—and several MA departments—have a 2+2 load. More recently, some departments with a 3+3 load have sought to reduce it to 3+2, a function of the increased importance of research in "primarily undergraduate" universities, as SSHRC has noted. (Nossal, 2006, 742)[20]

The general reduction in teaching loads has been compounded by specific factors that include a proliferation of research-promoting teaching reduction programs, teaching relief for junior members of faculty, and teaching relief for more senior faculty granted in recognition of demanding administrative responsibilities of a variety of kinds. The Canada Research Chairs program expects (but does not require) universities to reduce the teaching loads of faculty who receive support from the program. In many departments it is accepted practice for a faculty member with a large research program to buy out a portion of his or her teaching responsibilities by paying the university the cost of hiring a replacement instructor.

The reduction in teaching loads does not mean that faculty are less than fully occupied—quite the contrary. The reduction is a rational response to the time demands of seeking competitive research funding and carrying out the expanded research role. In some cases it is also a response to the burden of teaching larger classes, supervising the research of increased numbers of graduate students, or participating in the administration of increasingly complex institutions.

How have universities dealt with the shortfall of class instructors resulting from increased enrolment and expanding research commitment? A large part of the answer can be found in a growing reliance on full-time faculty with no, or very limited, research responsibilities, and on part-time faculty who are not involved in such scholarship. The ability of universities to increase the scale of their activities in all areas of their function over the past decade or more has in no small part been fuelled by an increased reliance on temporary, part-time, and teaching-only professors. The change represents a *de facto* transformation of the university and a functional acceptance of the teaching of undergraduates by those who are not also discovery researchers.

Temporary and part-time faculty: From the margins to the centre

The increased reliance on temporary, part-time, and teaching-only members of faculty is driven by the fact that teaching by these instructors is less costly; more students can be taught for fewer dollars. This assertion holds, first, for classes taught by full-time teaching-only members of faculty with teaching loads that are higher and salaries that are, on average,

---

[20] The expression 2+2 means teaching two courses in each of two terms.

considerably lower than those for regular faculty. Many universities have formally established such teaching-only full-time instructor posts in recent years with appropriate professional and career development policies and practises. Eight of the thirteen Ontario universities responding to our survey on this subject confirmed that they have full-time teaching-only positions. The number of such positions at each university ranges from fewer than ten to more than 300. Teaching-only faculty typically have course loads that are 1.6 to 2.0 times the course loads of regular full-time faculty (i.e., they may teach eight one-term courses per year rather than four or five, although there are exceptions). The number of such positions is in some institutions tightly controlled by collective agreements. Several universities without such positions reported that faculty unions had opposed their creation. An analysis by the Ontario Confederation of University Faculty Associations reached similar conclusions, finding that half of Ontario's universities have full-time teaching-only positions. The OCUFA study reported that the teaching loads of these positions are between six and ten one-term courses per year, compared with four one-term courses for faculty who have responsibilities for both teaching and research (OCUFA 2008, 2, 15). In only three of the universities cited in the OCUFA study are the full-time teaching positions in the tenure-stream, and they are confined to specific program areas, such as languages, and limited in number.

The vast majority of teaching by non-tenured members of faculty, especially in the arts, humanities, and social sciences, is performed by part-time instructors who typically are remunerated on a course-by-course basis. Part-time instructors include a wide range of individuals: pre-doctoral graduate students, qualified professionals in the community with other full-time or part-time employment, and those who earn a living from teaching multiple courses at one or more institutions.

Data on universities' reliance on part-time faculty is not systematically gathered, but the Council of Ontario Universities has reported that the number of part-time faculty (expressed as full-time equivalents) grew from 1,780 in 1987-88 to 2,153 in 2002-03—the last year that COU surveyed its members on this matter. More recently universities have reported that their use of part-time faculty was about 3,900 full-time equivalents in each of the years 2005, 2006, and 2007; this figure excludes faculty at five large universities that do not disclose this data. While there are challenges in defining part-time faculty, the growth rate for part-time faculty has clearly outstripped that for full-time faculty, whose numbers have increased by only 9 percent in this twenty-year period, to 14,300 (COU 2007, Table 8.1; Common University Data Ontario, 2006, 2007 and 2008).

The presence of part-time faculty in the classroom is even stronger than these figures would suggest because part-timers have few or no responsibilities for research or service. At one large comprehensive university, the union representing part-time and temporary faculty has said that its members do 54 percent of the teaching. Data from a doctoral/medical university suggest that only approximately 45 percent of its undergraduate classes in arts and humanities are taught by full-time members of faculty. The figure is 59 percent in social science. Even in the faculty of science, where qualified part-time instructors are less readily available, 26 percent of classes are taught by part-time members of faculty at this university. Given that part-time faculty often teach larger, junior level courses, the percentage of teaching performed by part-time faculty would be considerably higher if expressed in terms of students taught.

Costs of full-time vs. part-time faculty: A hypothetical model

The savings associated with teaching by part-time instructors are considerable. In order to illustrate some of the issues pertaining to the deployment of academic staff in Canadian universities, consider the following hypothetical example illustrated in Table 4.5. The example uses simplified assumptions; it is easily possible to vary the parameters and trace the implications. Assume a typical associate professor with an annual salary of $100,000 who teaches four one-term courses per year (on average, taking into account sabbatical years and other reductions in teaching load). The professor's employee benefits amount to 30 percent of salary, including mandatory payroll taxes and other benefits such as pension, group life insurance, long term disability, dental insurance, extended health care, and tuition remission. Also assume a part-time instructor who earns a flat fee of $6,000 per course taught, plus benefits of 10 percent. Both teach undergraduate students who take ten one-term courses a year and who pay tuition and mandatory fees of $5,500. The government contributes an operating grant of $6,000 per year per student. The university's other operating costs—such as the cost of student academic services, information technology, university-funded student assistance, building operations, utilities, administration, and the like—average about $5,500 per student per year. (This figure does not include costs paid by other sources of funding, such as fees for food and residences, externally-funded research, capital grants, and endowments.) Assume the university wants to offer average class sizes of 35 students—comparable to what a student would have experienced in secondary school.

These figures will vary from one university to another, but one conclusion is clear. At current funding and cost levels, and with class sizes of about 35 students, a university staffed entirely by full-time faculty who all have substantial responsibilities for research as well as teaching could not pay its bills.

The university in our hypothetical model would have several options for reaching financial sustainability. As one option, it could increase average class sizes. In our hypothetical case, the university would cover its costs if it increased average class sizes to 55 students. Many universities

TABLE 4.5
The economics of full-time and part-time faculty

	Full-time faculty with research and teaching responsibilities	Part-time faculty— teaching only
Assumed class size	35	same
Average student course load per year	10	same
Government operating grant per student	$6,000	same
Tuition and mandatory fees per student	$5,500	same
Total operating revenue to the university, per student per course	$1,150	same
Total operating revenue to the university, per course taught	**$40,250**	**same**
Instructor's annual salary	$100,000	Not applicable
Number of one-term courses taught annually (average, taking into account sabbatical years and other reductions in teaching load)	4	Not applicable
Instructor's salary per course	$25,000	$6,000
Benefits	30 percent	10 percent
Instructor's salary and benefits per course	**$31,250**	**$6,600**
Surplus available to cover all operating costs other than instructor salary and benefits, per course taught	**$7,750**	**$33,650**
Average of all operating costs other than instructor salary and benefits, per student per course	$550	same
Average of all operating costs other than instructor salary and benefits, per course taught	$19,250	same
Operating surplus (deficit), per course taught	**($11,500)**	**$14,400**

have found this to be a partial solution to financial problems, since faculty have been more concerned about reducing the number of courses they each teach than about maintaining class sizes. But, as we have already seen, some courses involve modes of teaching that make a large class size impossible. Other courses, especially in the students' upper years, are too specialized to attract a large number of students. In practice, implementing this option would mean creating many large lecture courses of more than one hundred students, and narrowing course options to eliminate uneconomical courses.

Another option is to increase faculty teaching responsibilities. In our hypothetical case, the university would cover its costs if every faculty member taught six or seven one-term courses per year. But this would substantially reduce the university's research output. It would also be a very major revision to faculty terms of employment and long-term career paths. Faculty who were hired in the expectation of dividing their efforts equally between teaching and research would rightly feel unfairly treated.

Another option would be to increase revenues from the government, students, or other sources. In our hypothetical case, the university would cover its costs if it increased revenues by about $3,300 per student. This raises the political problem of how to persuade either the government or the students of the merits of this option. If tuition is raised, the government would face additional costs to provide financial assistance to low-income students. At present about 30 percent of university students receive government financial assistance; the number of recipients and their financial need would both rise if tuition was sharply increased. Donations and non-government grants for general operating purposes currently amount to about $200 per student per year, so even a large percentage increase would not contribute much to the amount required. Many universities have succeeded in increasing grants and contracts for research, but it is difficult to get research to pay for itself, let alone to support teaching. For the most part, revenue from other sources tends to be matched by the additional costs of the activities that generate it, and the pursuit of these revenues diverts attention and effort away from core academic activities.

Another option would be to reduce costs other than faculty salaries and benefits. In our hypothetical case, the university would cover its costs if it reduced these other costs by about 60 percent. While it is popular among some faculty to complain about excessive overheads and the proliferation of administrators, non-teaching staff provide services that faculty and students want or need, and in many cases that faculty have actively sought. As well, a large share of these costs is for hard-to-reduce items like building operations and student financial assistance.

With so many unpalatable options, it is little wonder that universities turn to part-time instructors for some of their teaching. All other factors held constant, our hypothetical university would need to have part-time instructors doing about 45 percent of its teaching in order to break even financially.

No matter how a university chooses to close the gap between revenue and expenditures, it still faces the ongoing problem of how to increase per-student revenues every year in order to match universities' level of inflation. If revenue per student grows by 2 percent annually and costs per student grow by 4-5 percent annually, the budget problem would re-appear every year.

The impact of teaching loads on class size

Another way to look at the effect of the teacher-researcher faculty model is to consider the economics of class size. Suppose a university hires well-regarded professors with salaries of $150,000 who teach two courses in each of two terms per year (a 2 + 2 teaching load). All other financial assumptions are the same as in the hypothetical case we just examined including the student course load of five courses each term. The university will cover its costs if such professors' classes average 75 students each.[21]

But suppose the university has a policy that all students should have at least one one-term class each year with only 20 students, to allow greater engagement with the professor and other students. In order to provide for one such course each year, the other nine courses must average 107 students. In order to provide one 20-student class in each of the two terms, the other eight courses would have to average 240 students.

Let us further suppose that the professors win large research grants and have their teaching loads reduced by half, to two one-term courses each year. Bear in mind that government research grants in Canada do not contribute to the professor's salary, only to the additional costs associated with the research. In this case, the professors' courses must average 150 students each in order to cover the university's costs. In order to provide

---

[21] The required class-size numbers are derived from a simplified model that assumes that each class requires one faculty member and the classes are either in large lecture format (Format A) or small seminar format (Format B). The faculty cost of sections in a given format = number of sections of this format x faculty compensation / teaching load. The revenues from operating grant plus tuition are required to equal the costs which are taken to be the fixed cost per student x number of students + cost of A sections + cost of B sections. This produces the following formula: $N = ((c-b)(1+e)S/t)/(R-rR-b(1+e)S/nt)$ where N is the number of students in A sections, n is the number of students in B sections, b is the number of courses in B format, c is the course load for each student, t is the teaching load for each faculty member, R is the revenue per student from operating grant plus tuition, S is the faculty salary, e is faculty benefits as a fraction of salary, and r is the fraction of the operating grant plus tuition that goes to costs other than faculty compensation.

a single one-term course per year with 20 students, the other nine courses must have 540 students. If the university wanted to provide for two such courses in a year, it would have to subsidize the professors' salaries from other sources.

Compare this case to professors who earn $150,000 annually, but teach eight one-term courses annually and are not expected to do original research. The university will cover its costs if such professors teach all their courses with 38 students each, or one course with 20 students and nine with 42 students, or two courses with 20 students and eight with 48 students.

Finally, consider faculty members who earn $75,000 and teach eight one-term courses annually. The university will cover its costs if such professors teach classes with only 19 students. These four cases are summarized in Table 4.6.

These cases show the dramatic impact that teaching loads and faculty salaries have on average class sizes. It is not financially possible to hire outstanding teacher-researchers, keep their teaching loads low, offer students at least one small class, and keep other classes to a moderate size. The solution is normally to increase class sizes, hire faculty who do little original research, or both.

TABLE 4.6
The economics of class size

	Case 1	Case 2	Case 3	Case 4
Teaching load	2+2	2+0	4+4	4+4
Instructor's annual salary	$150,000	$150,000	$150,000	$75,000
One-term courses taught annually	4	2	8	8
Class size needed with all courses taught in same size format	75	150	38	19
Class size needed to have 1 one-term course per year in 20-student seminar format	107	540	42	n/a
Class size needed to have 1 one-term course per term in 20-student seminar format	240	not possible	48	n/a

The retreat of the teacher-researcher model

The expansion of Ontario's university system since the Second World War has been based on the premise that every undergraduate student should be taught by faculty who are also deeply engaged in discovery research. The significance of the increase in teaching-only and part-time instructors in recent years is that the teacher-researcher model is in retreat, and the vision of a university system where almost all students are taught by teacher-researchers is no longer with us. As Ontario moves from a mass system to a near-universal system of higher education, we need to plan for a system where the majority of undergraduate teaching will be conducted by faculty who are not engaged in their own original research. This phenomenon will be driven by the continuation of the long-term expansion of higher education and the tendency of per-student costs in higher education to grow more quickly than ordinary CPI inflation. While greater resources—from government, student tuition, or both—are highly desirable, there is no reason to think they will be adequate to fund normal university inflation and future enrolment growth based exclusively on the teacher-researcher model. Instructors not engaged in discovery research have grown from being a relative rarity in the 1960s to being responsible for half or more of all undergraduate teaching in some of the largest university faculties today. Under any reasonable funding scenario, their share of undergraduate teaching will continue to grow in the future.

The weight of available evidence suggests that instructors who are not active researchers are no more or less effective in the lecture hall or classroom than their tenured colleagues (see, for example, Hoffman and Oreopoulos, 2009). While it is widely claimed that faculty who are engaged in research are in a better position to be effective teachers, a recent survey of the literature on this question highlighted several studies showing that there was no correlation (positive or negative) between faculty research and teaching effectiveness. The survey concluded that "productive linkages between [teaching and research] have to be designed and nurtured; they are not created or sustained by chance" (Halliwell, 2008, 13).

There are, however, many implications of expanding the role of teaching-only instructors. To the extent that they are part-time, they are generally less available for duties that require a presence on campus, such as meetings with students, professional development and departmental meetings. To the extent that they do not hold permanent appointments, they are not required or expected to participate in the self-government of the university. The burdens and privileges of self-government fall almost entirely on full-time permanent faculty. Lacking security of employment or other protections, part-time and temporary faculty are increasingly likely to adopt an industrial model of labour relations.

It seems increasingly likely that this contingent workforce will become regularized, with greater security of employment, a more respected role within the university, and salary levels that reduce the current financial benefit to the university of hiring part-time instructors. There is a substantial public interest in ensuring that this transition takes place without lengthy disruptions in students' education, and without moving to a universal teacher-researcher model that is financially unsupportable in a near-universal system of higher education. We return to these themes in Chapter 7.

Colleges: The sustainability challenge

The pressures on the professoriate in the colleges differ from those in the universities because they are not shaped by the increased expectation of research. Colleges never adopted the teacher-researcher model that is prized in universities. While some colleges are developing a role in applied research, colleges have so far been relatively small players in the national and provincial research strategies.

Yet the rise in faculty-student ratios at colleges over the past two decades has been even more severe than at universities. College FTE enrolments per full-time academic staff have nearly doubled—from 14.4 in 1987-88 to 27.5 in 2007-08, as shown in Figure 4.7.

The reasons for this increase are intrinsic to the pattern of funding and enrolment growth colleges have experienced. Colleges were affected simultaneously by government funding cuts and sharp enrolment growth in the early and mid-1990s. College tuition increased modestly in the 1990s and so did not make up for lost government revenue per FTE. Operating funding per FTE from government grants and student tuition and fees,

FIGURE 4.7
College FTE enrolment per full-time academic staff

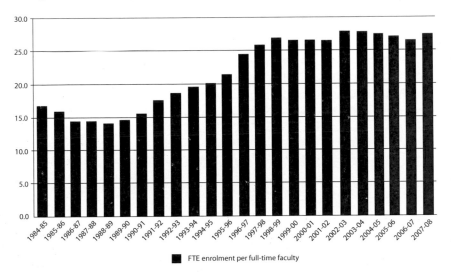

FTE enrolment per full-time faculty

Source: College Compensation and Appointments Council (2008), and authors' calculations.

adjusted for CPI, is now recovering after a long downturn. Yet even as of 2007-08, the number of full-time academic staff stood at about 7,000, which is 1,500 fewer than in 1991-92.

Colleges have fewer options than universities for managing the reduction in full-time staff, primarily because of workload provisions in the colleges' province-wide collective agreement. There is anecdotal evidence of increased class sizes, but this option is constrained because full-time faculty are allotted time to mark assignments based on the number of students in their classes—so a faculty member who teaches a large class has fewer hours available to teach other courses.[22] Colleges do not have master's and doctoral students, and so have not adopted the common university practice of employing graduate students to mark papers and lead tutorial groups. The most common strategy for managing within constrained resources has been to use part-time instructors, although there is no accepted set of data to document this trend. The union representing college faculty has estimated that colleges employ 6,000 faculty who teach credit courses for six hours or fewer per week, 2,000 faculty who teach non-credit continuing education courses, and 750 "sessionals" who teach more than 12 hours a week but who have not worked more than 12 months of the last 24. (Organization of Part-time and Sessional Employees of the Colleges of Applied Arts and Technology, 2007) The collective agreement with full-time faculty makes provision for a union local at a college to make representations about the assignment of work to part-time instructors, and these matters are the subject of regular grievances at some colleges.

The colleges' financial situation will be difficult to sustain in the medium term. Colleges do not publish an estimate of their own inflation rate, but the most recent faculty collective agreement—which provided a salary increase for the most experienced faculty of 15.33 percent over four years (CAAT Academic Negotiating Team, 2006)—suggests that colleges' overall inflation in compensation and non-compensation costs is higher than CPI inflation. A 1975 statute that barred part-time instructors at colleges from unionizing was replaced in 2008. At this writing the process of unionization is underway, providing potentially another financial pressure. The current economic recession is causing a larger number of laid-off workers

---

[22] The collective agreement limits college full-time faculty to 44 hours of work per week, including a maximum of 18 hours of instruction per week for a 36-week academic year. In practice, it is difficult for a college to assign 18 hours to any faculty member, because the formula allots time each week for preparation, marking, attending meetings, and other assigned activities, plus a minimum of six hours per week for out-of-class assistance to individual students and administrative tasks. The remaining work-weeks of the calendar year are reserved for "complementary functions and professional development" that may be proposed by either the instructor or the college.

to enrol at colleges, and there is evidence that these students are more likely than other students to require preparation in literacy, numeracy, and computer technology skills, making them more expensive to serve. For both colleges and universities, the cost of moving to a near-universal system of post-secondary education is proving to be higher than what governments and students have been prepared to pay.

THE IMPACT OF THE GLOBAL ECONOMIC RECESSION

The global recession began with the financial crisis and stock-market losses that spread from Wall Street to other financial centres in 2008, and was accompanied by sharp contractions in economic activity in most parts of the world, including Canada and Ontario. The full extent of the impacts on the post-secondary education system is not clear at the time of writing, but it is obvious that the impacts will be substantial and some of them are already apparent. They make the financial pressures in higher education more urgent. Universities and colleges can expect lower-than-planned revenues and higher-than-planned expenditures.[23]

Decreasing institutional revenues

Universities that have been receiving revenue from endowment funds face the sudden loss of this revenue. These effects will be highly variable by institution; some universities have large endowments relative to their size, while others do not. In the medium-term, all universities and colleges can expect to feel the pinch of constrained government funding, as governments will face pressures to bring their finances back into balance.

Increasing institutional costs

The largest single portion of higher education costs—the salaries and benefits of faculty and staff—is difficult to constrain in the short- to medium-term. Education is inherently labour-intensive. Public sector salaries have historically been slow to respond to lower-than-expected public sector revenues. The environment for retirement has also changed. This is the first recession since the passage of legislation outlawing mandatory retirement. Faculty and staff who have lost a portion of their retirement savings will be less likely to retire—increasing the net experience level of the institution, but reducing flexibility to lower costs through the hiring of more junior replacements or by restructuring operations. Universities

---

[23] This section draws on an important study by Usher and Dunn (2009) and on other sources.

with defined-benefit pension plans face immediate pressure from regulators to make contributions that will ensure the plans' solvency.

Shifting enrolment pressures

Historically, recessions have had little apparent effect on university undergraduate enrolments since students' decision to attend has often been made over a period of years. In universities, the greatest effect of recessions is in master's programs, especially those that lead to a professional or career-related degree, where applications tend to increase. Colleges are typically much more affected by recessions, as students use the economic slowdown as an opportunity to pursue a diploma or certificate. College apprenticeship programs are an exception, since their capacity is limited by employers' willingness to take on new apprentices.

Student aid

The need for student aid rises sharply during recessions. During the last recession, the number of students receiving aid from the Ontario government more than doubled, from 100,000 in 1989-90 to 214,000 in 1996-97. This increase coincided with high government deficits, triggering the policy shift from a grant-first program to a program that relies heavily on repayable loans. The current recession is the first recession since the Ontario government adopted an explicit policy of requiring universities and colleges to devote a portion of revenues to needs-based student aid. Institutions will face pressures to maintain these programs, and the government will face pressure to protect students where institutions are unable to do so.

Implications for government

Although the Ontario government has not been active in system design since the 1960s, the crisis has made many of the underlying problems more apparent, and perhaps easier to act on. Perceived necessity has driven governments around the world to intervene in sectors such as banking and manufacturing in ways that would have been unimaginable before the crisis.

We will suggest a number of possible substantive system changes in our concluding chapter, but first we will deal with the broader question of the methods by which governments, and the institutions themselves, attempt to assess, measure and control for quality in post-secondary education, and how these measures affect the responsiveness of the system to societal priorities.

5

THE IMPACT OF QUALITY AND ACCOUNTABILITY MEASURES ON SYSTEM RESPONSIVENESS

With the expansion of higher education and the increase in the scale of public funds going to universities and colleges that began in the 1960s, interest grew in the performance of higher education systems. This interest has given rise to two distinct but related spheres of practice and associated discourses that are dominated by different stakeholders, one connoted by the term, "quality," the other by the term, "accountability." The latter is the broader of the two terms and could be viewed as including quality. However, historically, the discourse and practices associated with quality developed earlier than those that are associated with accountability, and the two concepts have spawned distinct bodies of literature. In addition to these two spheres of practice, accreditation, which is related to both, has also been the focus of sufficient attention to warrant some discussion on its own.

The processes and measures associated with quality and accountability likely have some influence on institutional behaviour. Indeed these processes and measures were developed in order to enhance quality and advance accountability as these terms were understood by those who developed and implemented the associated practices and measures. It is thus important to inquire into how these processes and measures may affect the responsiveness of the higher education system to the kinds of pressures and expectations that have been discussed in earlier chapters. While the empirical literature on the impact of quality and accountability processes and measures on institutional behaviour is somewhat limited,

Academic Transformation: The Forces Reshaping Higher Education in Ontario, I.D. Clark, G. Moran, M.L. Skolnik, and D. Trick. Montreal and Kingston: McGill-Queen's University Press, Queen's Policy Studies Series.

we can also examine the extent to which these measures are aligned with espoused societal goals for higher education. The purpose of this chapter is to explore the alignment of quality and accountability measures with societal goals for higher education in Ontario, and to consider the influence of these measures on institutional behaviour.

While the focus of this chapter is on the structures and arrangements for accountability and quality assurance, it is important to keep in mind that the reason for the existence of these structures and arrangements is so that the government responsible for post-secondary education, the public, and the stakeholders can tell whether students are getting a good education. Although it is not our objective in this chapter to attempt to answer this question, we will report some related findings based upon a recently employed data source in Ontario that has been getting considerable attention.[24]

THE EMERGENCE OF QUALITY AND ACCOUNTABILITY DISCOURSES AND PRACTICES

Quality first emerged as an important concern in Canadian higher education in the late 1960s and 1970s. The discourse on quality in those years was initiated by the university community, primarily by university administrators, and they controlled the quality agenda. There were three reasons why initiating a discourse on quality in higher education was in the interest of university administration. First, university administrators anticipated that increased attempts by government to monitor and perhaps even control universities in the name of public accountability would inevitably follow the increased funding that government was providing. University administrators wanted to preempt government and thereby shape both the accountability discourse and the instruments of accountability in ways that protected the academic values that they held dear. By making quality the focus of attention, they were able to head off, for a few decades at least, moves to make universities more broadly accountable to agencies and groups outside the university and to control how quality was defined.

In the 1970s and 1980s, university administrators defined quality primarily in terms of the resources they had available, referring to such indicators as the faculty-student ratio, operating expenditures per student, the value of library acquisitions, and the amount of capital expenditures (Skolnik, 1986). Thus, they could argue in their briefs to the government

---

[24] For a comprehensive examination of what is known about the quality of post-secondary education in Ontario, see the Second Annual Review and Research Plan of the Higher Education Quality Council of Ontario (HEQCO, 2009).

that quality would be placed in jeopardy if the government did not provide sufficient funding (e.g., Council of Ontario Universities, 1984). That this argument was not often very successful in gaining more funding for the universities did not keep them from continuing to make it, often with increased stridency.

Another potential benefit for the publicly supported universities of focusing on quality and taking the lead in defining quality might have been protection from competition. If other institutions came along that offered to educate students at a lower cost, for example by relying mainly on distance education or employing only faculty who did not do research, the public universities could argue that such competitors would not provide an acceptable level of quality as they defined it. Historically, the argument that competition might result in a reduction of quality had been used in the western provinces of Canada to limit the number of universities (Harris, 1976, 224-226). The argument proved to be of limited value to Ontario universities in the 1970s and 1980s, as governments of all parties were opposed in principle then to the idea of private universities, although allowing some out-of-province universities to operate satellite campuses in Ontario nonetheless. It was not until much later, in 2000, that legislation was finally enacted to allow private universities to operate in Ontario—though to date only a few have come along to take advantage of the legislation.

By the 1990s, governments were no longer so willing to leave accountability to the universities' own interpretations of quality and their processes of quality assurance. Pressures arose for both a broader conceptualization of accountability and for the provision of information on university performance to the government and external stakeholders. A few unrelated issues were catalysts in the accountability movement in Ontario. One was the concern that had been growing in many jurisdictions besides Ontario about the quality of undergraduate education (Smith, 1991). Ontario universities had a well developed process for assessing the quality of graduate programs, but nothing comparable pertaining to undergraduate programs. Nor was any systematic data available on learning outcomes of undergraduate students. Around the same time, there was a somewhat technical-legal dispute concerning the jurisdiction of the Provincial Auditor over the publicly supported universities, and the Standing Committee on Public Accounts of the Ontario Legislature took the side of the Auditor (Task Force on University Accountability, 1993; Skolnik, 1994). These concerns set in motion a chain of events that resulted in Ontario universities and colleges providing information on a number of performance dimensions, and ultimately in the government linking a portion of institutional funding to a set of performance indicators. The performance measures developed in the 1990s included several that went beyond those commonly associated with quality and provided some indications of outcomes.

The third concept related to the performance of post-secondary education institutions is accreditation, a formal recognition by a duly constituted agency that a post-secondary institution or program meets a certain standard. Institutional accreditation was developed more than a hundred years ago in the United States. With regulation of post-secondary education being nonexistent or inconsistent across the country at the time, institutional accreditation was a way for institutions to demonstrate to potential students that they met at least minimum standards. Universities and colleges in the United States may now seek accreditation from a regional agency, or from a specialized accreditation body that covers particular groups of institutions such as proprietary or distance education institutions. What is commonly called institutional accreditation is intended to cover all the programs that an institution offers. When an institution develops a new program, it is supposed to notify its accreditation agency and seek a corresponding modification in its accreditation status. In addition to agencies that accredit institutions, there are also agencies that concentrate on accrediting programs, for example professional programs such as engineering.

Because entry into the realm of degree-granting has been so stringently controlled and the appearance of new degree granting institutions normally so infrequent in Canada, it was not felt that there was a need for institutional accreditation. However, with the extension of degree granting to new types of institutions in recent years, primarily colleges and proprietary institutions, interest in institutional accreditation has emerged. For example, within the past few years, both the Association of Canadian Community Colleges and the Canadian Society for the Study of Higher Education have sponsored national conferences that focused on accreditation. The newer, non-traditional providers of degree programs hope that through a national system of accreditation in which all providers of degree programs are members, they will be able to gain recognition for their degree programs as equivalent to those of the older institutions.

Support for a national system of institutional accreditation was voiced also in a 1993 report of the Canadian Association of University Teachers (CAUT), but for a different reason than that which had earned accreditation the support of some new providers of degree programs (Canadian Association of University Teachers, 1993). The CAUT report recognized the need for universities to show that they are accountable, and concluded that instituting a national system of institutional accreditation would be the most benign arrangement for providing accountability. However, this was too little, too late. By 1993, governments would no longer be satisfied with an accreditation system that was run by academics and employed a narrow definition of academic quality as a surrogate for accountability. While there is still no institutional accreditation of the public universities and colleges in Canada, some of the professional programs of these institutions are accredited by specialized accreditation bodies. Also a few Canadian institutions have sought accreditation from accrediting agencies in the United States.

The three concepts discussed here—quality, accountability, and accreditation—are highly interrelated. Quality is one of the major focuses of interest in most accountability regimes, and is the main, and often the exclusive focus, of accreditation processes. In principle, there are two key distinctions between quality assessment and accreditation, but in practice the terms are often nearly synonymous. One difference is that accreditation, by definition, involves the judgment of an agent that is *external* to the institution seeking accreditation, whereas quality assessments can be conducted internally or externally. The other difference is that the focus of accreditation is whether the institution or program seeking accreditation meets minimum standards. In contrast, quality assessments can result in conclusions about the level of quality of the institution or program being assessed.

Another practice in the area of performance assessment that has emerged in recent years is auditing. The term "audit" signals a blend of external and internal responsibility in the quality assurance process. Typically, an external body does a check (i.e., an audit) to ensure that an institution has a quality assurance process in place and that the process meets certain conditions pertaining to such matters as the frequency of assessments and the types of data examined. Subject to meeting the audit conditions, the institution conducts the quality assessment itself, though it may utilize external appraisers in the assessment. There are three possible benefits of the audit model in comparison to an external assessment model. The audit model may require less in the way of an external bureaucracy for oversight; it enables faculty to get more involved in program assessment in contrast with the standard quality assessment process that has been held to marginalize faculty (Harley, 2002; Anderson, 2006); and it intrudes less on institutional autonomy. The downside of the audit approach is that the external standards body is one step removed from the actual review and thus is less able to protect the public interest in post-secondary education.

The next section of this chapter elaborates on the concept of quality in higher education since this concept is central to almost any type of performance assessment. We also offer some general observations about the practice of quality assessment, because it is through these practices that the concept of quality is operationalized. The section that follows describes the principal arrangements that exist for accountability, quality assurance, and accreditation in Ontario. In the final section we make observations about the implications of these concepts and practices for addressing the challenges of accessibility, knowledge production, and financial restraint in Ontario higher education.

THE CONCEPT OF QUALITY IN HIGHER EDUCATION AND THE PRACTICE OF QUALITY ASSESSMENT

There is not universal agreement on how to define quality in higher education and on what the most important dimensions of quality are. Several observers who have studied the matter have concluded that quality is a highly subjective concept. For example, Ratcliff argued that ideas about quality are personal and social constructions that vary from stakeholder to stakeholder (Ratcliff, 2003). Anderson noted that many analysts do not regard quality assurance as neutral or value-free, but as a process that reflects a particular power-knowledge regime (Anderson, 2006). Likewise, Morely asserted that "quality assurance is a socially constructed domain of power" (Morely, 2003, 164).

The literature on quality in higher education reveals several distinct ways of conceptualizing quality (Astin, 1980; Skolnik, 1989). Until just recently, the main ones have been in terms of inputs, educational processes, outcomes, and value added. During the first decade of the 21st century another one that has been receiving some attention is the student experience. Within the input model, because the qualifications and abilities of incoming students are so different from other inputs, this category is sometimes broken down into two: admissions selectivity and resources. Value added can be viewed as a refinement of outcome measurement. It refers to the changes in the knowledge, competencies, and attitudes of students between the time of entry and graduation.

Until recently, the overwhelming emphasis in quality assessment has been on admissions selectivity, resources, and educational processes. The tendency, as reflected for example, in international ranking lists of universities, has been to regard as the highest quality institutions those that admit the smallest proportion of applicants, have the greatest volume of resources per student, and employ traditional processes of education. These conventional views of quality have persisted in spite of frequent criticisms. Astin pointed out that data on the high school grades or test scores of incoming students does not provide any information at all about the performance of the universities that admit them, i.e., the effect that the university has on the learning and development of its students (Astin, 1985). A focus on inputs also tends to lead to the equation of quality with doing things the way that they have been done in the past, a position that has been criticized as discouraging innovation and the search for improved educational practices (Commission on Nontraditional Study, 1973). Very detailed research conducted in the 1980s showed that there was little correlation between measures of resources and measures of outcomes (Anderson, 1983), and there is still no compelling evidence of such a correlation. One of the input indicators which plays the most central role in many quality assessment processes is the quality of faculty as measured by faculty publications and research grants. The logic of using the volume of faculty research activity as an indicator of the quality of education programs has frequently been questioned (Skolnik, 1989, 2000; Barzun, 1991; Lucas, 1996), and in some jurisdictions the assessment of research has been separated from the assessment of instructional programs.

One of the most significant developments in the discourse on quality in the past 15 years has been the emergence of a controversy over the place of student learning outcomes in the quality assessment process. The movement to give greater attention to student outcomes in quality assessment has coincided with the emergence of what we referred to earlier as the accountability movement in post-secondary education. Governments were no longer content with relying upon university controlled quality assurance processes, which they saw as having three undesirable consequences: these practices provided a barrier to innovation, particularly to the development of new forms of higher education that might be cheaper and/or more efficient; the processes identified the level of funding from government as the chief determinant of quality, and thus provided a basis for constant criticism of government for not providing more funding; and they enabled the universities to avoid accounting for what they do with the resources that they are given. These themes are evident in the controversy in the United States over the recommendations of a commission appointed by the Secretary of Education that aimed to change the criteria used in accreditation reviews. The commission recommended that higher education change its approach to accreditation from "a system primarily based on reputation to one based on performance" (Commission Appointed by Secretary of Education, 2006, 21). The recommendation that evoked a particularly strong reaction from the academic community was that accreditation agencies should make student learning outcomes the core of their assessments, and these be given a priority over inputs and processes (25).

Another recent development in quality assessment has been more systematic examination of the student experience. The most prominent vehicle for examining the student experience is the National Survey of Student Engagement (NSSE, n.d.). The NSSE was developed in the United States in 1998-99 and first administered in 2000. In 2006, 31 Canadian universities, including all 19 in Ontario, were among the 557 institutions that participated in the survey (HEQCO, 2009, 66).[25] The NSSE is based upon research which has shown that certain types of student behaviour and institutional practices are associated with higher levels of student

---

[25] The counterpart to NSSE in the community college sector in the United States is the Community College Survey of Student Engagement (CCSSE). This survey has been used by only two Canadian colleges. The *Pan-Canadian Survey of College Students* provided data on student engagement in Canadian colleges in 2005. There is now an Ontario College Student Engagement Survey (OCSES).

learning and personal development (Kuh, 2003). In particular this research has shown that the more time and effort that students put into educationally useful activities, the better their learning and development. Examples of such activities are writing papers, asking questions in class, and discussing assignments with instructors. Thus, many of the questions in the survey of students are about the frequency with which students engage in what are thought to be desirable behaviours. Other questions elicit student perceptions of the campus environment, for example, about the quality of their relationships with their peers. Questions are grouped into five categories which enable results to be reported for five corresponding benchmarks: level of academic challenge, active and collaborative learning, student-faculty interaction, enriching educational experiences, and supportive campus environment. Although the NSSE has become quite popular among post-secondary administrators and policy makers in the past few years, it is important to remember that it is still but one of many diverse elements of quality assessment. Student experience has not replaced the older conceptions of quality, some of which, in particular resources and admissions selectivity, still dominate some formal quality assurance processes.

If quality is as subjective as some observers maintain, and if there are wide differences of opinion about what factors should be given the most weight in making judgments about quality, then the composition of the bodies that judge quality should matter a great deal. Typically, quality assessment and accreditation bodies have been dominated by academics, usually academic administrators and senior academics, often disproportionately from the older, mainstream disciplines. Such skewed representation on quality assessment bodies tends to exclude or marginalize many participants and stakeholders (Guba and Lincoln, 1989; Harley and Lee, 1997; Harley, 2002; Skolnik, 1989). Guba and Lincoln have suggested that the subjective and political nature of assessment makes it important to ensure that all legitimate stakeholders are represented in the process (Guba and Lincoln, 1989). While there has been some shift from quality to accountability in recent years, and a corresponding increase of government influence in performance assessment, the "responsive" model of assessment, advocated by Guba and Lincoln, that recognizes and attempts to balance the interests of different stakeholders in the assessment process, has yet to be adopted.

While quality is but one of several elements in the accountability framework for post-secondary education, most academics would view it as preeminent. This is not an unreasonable position, because no matter how responsive it may be to societal needs, a program that is below the threshold of acceptable quality would not be worthwhile to offer. In short, concern for quality is likely to play at least a modest inhibiting role in regard to system responsiveness. However, quality should be allowed to trump other goals for post-secondary education only if the process for assessing quality is sufficiently transparent and reflects the inherent subjectivity in judging quality and the differences among stakeholders regarding what constitutes quality.

ACCOUNTABILITY, QUALITY ASSURANCE, AND ACCREDITATION PRACTICES IN ONTARIO

The oldest formal quality assurance process in Ontario higher education is the system of appraisal of graduate programs in Ontario universities which dates back to 1967. This process is run by the Ontario Council on Graduate Studies (OCGS). The appraisals are conducted by an appraisals committee that consists entirely of faculty members of Ontario universities who are appointed by deans of graduate studies. Programs are appraised when they are started and periodically from then on. This appraisals process fits the accreditation model in that the thrust of the process is to determine whether a program meets the minimum standard as described in OCGS by-laws. In the criteria used for making quality judgments in the OCGS process, the predominant emphasis is on resources and educational processes.

There was no system of quality assurance for undergraduate programs in Ontario universities until 1997 when the universities decided to establish an agency and process for this purpose. The Undergraduate Program Review and Audit Committee (UPRAC), was established under the auspices of the Council of Ontario Universities through one of its constituent subgroups, the Ontario Council of Academic Vice-Presidents (OCAV). Rather than conducting program appraisals itself like the OCGS does, the UPRAC oversees an audit procedure that examines the processes followed by each university in conducting its own assessments of its undergraduate programs. Since the process for review of undergraduate programs is typically highly decentralized even within a given university, it is difficult to generalize about the criteria that are employed in making the judgments about program quality. The model employed in the UPRAC program review process could be described as that of goal-based evaluation. The emphasis is on ensuring that a program has the appropriate educational processes and resources necessary to achieve its goals which are expected to be specified in terms of learning outcomes (Council of Ontario Universities, 2006c). The factors that assessors are asked to examine include the following: admission requirements; program structure and curriculum; mode of program delivery; methods of evaluation of student progress; and human, physical, and financial resources, including number and quality of faculty.

Following the recommendations in the report of the Vision 2000 review of the mandate of the colleges in 1990, the Ontario Government established the College Standards and Accreditation Council (CSAC) in 1993. The purpose of the CSAC was to establish learning outcome standards for all college programs and assess each program to determine whether it met the standards. The CSAC model differed from the approach to quality assessment that was developed and followed in the university sector in two ways. First, the focus of the program reviews was to be exclusively on learning outcomes. How colleges delivered the programs, and even the specific content of the programs, were not of concern to the Council. In this respect there was an explicit attempt to respect institutional (and program) autonomy and diversity, values that are endangered by the quality assurance model followed in the university sector (Skolnik, 1989). Second, in contrast to the university model, CSAC had broad membership from diverse stakeholder groups, and thus was closer to the responsive model of evaluation advocated by Guba and Lincoln. Before CSAC had been able to develop standards in many areas, it fell victim to government austerity measures and was shut down in 1996. The government took over the task of developing program standards and more than 200 program standard documents have been developed, approved, and disseminated to date. However, little progress has been made on the accreditation side of the original CSAC mandate.

Between 2003 and 2005, the colleges, working in cooperation with the Ministry of Training, Colleges and Universities, developed a new quality assurance process, known as the Program Quality Assurance Process Audit (PQAPA). Following a number of pilot projects, the PQAPA process was approved by the Committee of Presidents of the colleges for full implementation in January 2007 (Ontario College Quality Assurance Service, 2007). The PQAPA is a process that involves the review of each college's program quality assurance processes. In addition, the colleges developed the Credentials Validation Service (CVS), which ensures that programs leading to an Ontario College credential conform to the Ministry-approved Ontario Credentials Framework. The goal of the CVS is to ensure consistency and accuracy of nomenclature of college programs. The PQAPA process is there to ensure the quality of programs. These combined efforts are known as the *Ontario College Quality Assurance Service.*

Another quality assurance process for post-secondary education in Ontario was established under legislation in 2000. The *Post-secondary Education Choice and Excellence Act* required the establishment of the Post-secondary Education Quality Assessment Board (PEQAB). The mandate of the PEQAB is to review degree program proposals of the colleges, of Ontario based institutions which do not have legislative authority to offer degree programs, and of out-of-province institutions that seek to offer programs in Ontario. The PEQAB is the only governmentally established quality assurance body for post-secondary education in the province, and judges whether programs meet the quality standard for such programs in Ontario. It thus functions as an accreditation body for programs that fall under its jurisdiction.

The PEQAB has developed very comprehensive and detailed quality standards to guide the assessment panels that it appoints for the review of programs. The PEQAB quality standards, which are highly prescriptive, contain several references to outcomes, but the strongest emphasis in the standards is on educational processes and the policies of applicant institutions. The PEQAB standards tend to concentrate on institutional and program characteristics that are connoted by the term quality and to exclude those that reflect broader accountability concerns. Quality, as judged by the PEQAB, is a major but not the only consideration in the decision of the Minister as to whether to approve an application for a degree program from an institution in one of the categories that requires a review by the PEQAB. The Minister may decide, on the basis of broader criteria than just quality, not to approve a program that is recommended by the PEQAB.

When the PEQAB standards were developed they contained standards for degree level that were among the most detailed in existence anywhere. Through consultation with the Council of Ontario Universities and officials in other provinces, the PEQAB now has the same degree level standards as the Council of Ontario Universities, and the same as those adopted by the Council of Ministers of Education, Canada. Moreover, almost all program assessment panels established by the PEQAB include a member or members who are faculty or academic administrators in Ontario universities. Thus, programs that are recommended by the PEQAB meet the degree level standards of the Ontario universities and normally have the endorsement of one or two academic staff of Ontario universities. Nevertheless, Ontario universities do not necessarily consider graduates of baccalaureate programs that have been recommended by the PEQAB and approved by the government eligible for admission to graduate and professional programs.

The Higher Education Quality Council of Ontario is unique among agencies in Ontario that are concerned with quality of university education in Ontario in having advocated the value added paradigm (Higher Education Quality Council, 2007). In HEQCO's value added conception,[26] which is explained in its *First Annual Review and Research Plan*, the determination of quality of learning would require information on four stages as follows:

- "the characteristics of students entering the post-secondary system, such as their aptitudes, knowledge and skills from secondary school,"

---

[26] The HEQCO paper notes that its approach draws on the work of numerous recent research, including Finnie and Usher (2005), Lang (2005), and Kuh et al. (2006).

- "the resources devoted to learning, such as full-time and contractual faculty, physical plant, libraries, laboratories and so forth,"
- "what students actually learned by the time they left higher education. Learning includes general skills such as critical thinking, problem-solving and communication; softer skills such as being able to work with others; and technical and disciplinary skills," and
- "students' final outcomes after leaving higher education" (HEQCO, 2007, 23).

The quality of a learning experience is judged by the value it adds for students. The greater the difference between the students' initial characteristics and the final outcomes, the higher the quality of the learning experience. Regarding the reference to resources in the second point, the document notes that "[I]nput measures alone are not a measure of quality, but information on how changes in inputs affect quality would be highly useful for policymakers and administrators" (25). Perhaps reflecting its evolving understanding of quality, in its *Second Annual Review and Research Plan*, HEQCO takes a broader view of quality, and devotes considerable attention to the student experience and the results of the NSSE (HEQCO, 2009). These results are summarized in the next section.

HEQCO is not on the operational front line in the process of quality assurance, and its views pertaining to quality are not likely to have as much impact as those of the agencies that are more directly involved in performance evaluation at the program level. As we have suggested, the quality assurance practices of those other agencies tend to give the most weight to the resources, educational practices, and admissions selectivity conceptions of quality. There is thus a discrepancy between the messages that the higher education system is getting from different agencies regarding quality. The agencies that are in a position to reward or punish institutions have one notion of what constitutes quality, while the agency whose job it is to monitor quality at the provincial level and advise the government on related policies is adopting a quite different conceptualization of quality.

NSSE Results for Ontario Universities

Using data from the 2006 NSSE survey, it is possible to compare the results for Ontario universities with those of other universities in Canada and the United States. On average, the scores for Ontario universities are on par with the scores for the rest of Canada and the United States. But a different picture emerges when one looks just at scores for the large research-intensive (as measured by research expenditures) universities, for example the six Ontario members of the G-13 group of Canadian research universities. HEQCO reports that the average benchmark score for first-year students in Ontario G-13 universities was higher than those for other Canadian G-13 universities in three of five categories (level of academic challenge, enriching educational experience, and supportive campus environment). The score was identical in a fourth instance (student-faculty interaction) and was behind in a fifth (active and collaborative learning). In four instances, Ontario's scores for first-year students were lower than those for comparable American universities. The Ontario scores were higher only for the enriching educational experience category. A similar pattern was found for fourth-year students (HEQCO, 2009, 67). Insofar as the NSSE survey provides an accurate indicator of the quality of education, the conclusion from these data is that the large research universities in Ontario do not do as good a job with undergraduates as their counterparts in the United States

Further, the most research-intensive universities in Ontario do not do as well as other, smaller, Ontario universities. Actually, this is a Canada-wide phenomenon. For example, on student-faculty interaction, which is considered one of the most important benchmarks, the five lowest scoring institutions in Canada are members of G-13; and no G-13 member is in the top 26 institutions. On the level of academic challenge benchmark, one G-13 member (from Ontario) is ninth, and another is fifteenth, the only ones in the top 20 (*Maclean's On Campus*, 2009). Given that Ontario's six G-13 universities account for about half of undergraduate education in the province, this should be cause for concern. Moreover, if it is true that many other universities in Ontario strive to be like the G-13 institutions, it does not bode well for the future of undergraduate education in the province.

THE USE OF PERFORMANCE INDICATORS

Until the mid-1990s, government accountability requirements for the provincial universities focused almost exclusively on verifying enrolments. In addition, each university was required by statute to publish audited financial statements. When the government decided to adopt accountability measures for the provincial universities that went beyond these reporting requirements as well as a university-controlled quality review process, it started by requiring institutions to publish indicators of institutional performance. This requirement evolved into reporting on a set of performance indicators, which the universities must now report publicly: graduation rate, employment rate six months and twenty-four months after graduation, and default rates on Ontario Student Assistance Program (OSAP) loans. A relatively small proportion of a university's funding is based upon the first three of these indicators. In the college sector, the indicators required, which are referred to as Key Performance Indicators (KPIs), are graduate employment rate, graduate satisfaction, employer satisfaction, student satisfaction, and graduation rate. About 2 percent of a college's funding is based upon the first three indicators.

Several concerns have been expressed about these indicators. One is that some of them show quite little variation among institutions, so that a very small difference in indicator values between two institutions can be associated with a disproportionately larger difference in performance funding. There is also a concern about the validity of some of the indicators, arising from problems of definition and measurement. Yet another concern is how well these indicators reflect the most important institutional and government objectives for post-secondary education. For example, none of these indicators relate directly to accessibility, and only the college sector has an indicator pertaining to student satisfaction with the quality of the learning experience. However, even the latter indicator is of limited usefulness since it is not tied to any specific factors over which institutions have some control, e.g., institutional practices, academic policies, or resources.

A feature of these indicators, perhaps too obvious to have been noted in the dialogue about performance measurement in Ontario post-secondary education, is that the overwhelming emphasis is on *institutional* indicators.[27] One of the most fundamental questions in designing an accountability framework for post-secondary education is what should be the unit of accountability. Specifically, should it be the individual post-secondary institution, the sector, or the system as a whole? Presently in Ontario the focus of accountability is only the institution.[28] Provincial indicators can be obtained by aggregating or averaging institutional indicators, but this is not the same as setting out to establish appropriate provincial indicators. Moreover, such judgments as are made on the basis of the indicators, for example in allocation of funding, are based upon

---

[27] Much of the information from which the institutional performance indicators are derived is also available at the program level. Also the questionnaires used in the data collection address other matters besides the five performance indicators for which data are published. For example, there are questions about the number of graduates working part-time, the number working in a job related to their field of study, and their starting salaries. The information from the performance indicator surveys can be used for program management, for example in examining how well a program is meeting labour market needs.

[28] In its submission on accountability to the Rae Review, the Council of Ontario Universities used the term "system-level performance indicators" to refer to a set of *institutional* indicators that *all* institutions are required to report on publicly (Council of Ontario Universities, 2004). The Council submission did not recommend the use of such indicators, though it did suggest some principles to guide their use if they were to continue to be required. Nonetheless, these are still indicators of institutional performance rather than of system performance.

institutional data. No benchmarks have been established for provincial values of these indicators.

Though institutional accountability is clearly important, there is some question as to whether that is sufficient by itself. It is conceivable that each institution could be performing well in relation to its own goals, and yet because of an inappropriate mix of institutions or problems in the interrelationships among them, the system fails to achieve its goals. In the next chapter, we consider how the design of the post-secondary education system may influence the overall performance of the system. Insofar as the overall performance of the higher education system—its quality, productivity, or effectiveness—is a function of both institutional performance and system design, restricting quality assessment or accountability to the level of the institution provides an incomplete picture of how well the post-secondary system serves society.

Another reason why it may be useful to consider accountability at the level of the system relates to the way that post-secondary education receives its basic operating funding. The major decision that the government makes in regard to operating funding is the global amount to be provided to each sector. The allocation of these sums among institutions in each sector is a second order decision. Restricting the focus of accountability to the institution level would be more defensible if the funding process were the reverse, i.e., the first order funding decisions were how much to provide to each institution, and the global amount was simply the sum of the amounts that each institution received.

A system accountability framework would include institutional accountability indicators, but it would also include measures of overall system performance. Examples of indicators of system performance are the provincial participation rate, in aggregate and for particular groups, the college to university transfer rate, and the proportion of undergraduates in the province that are on campuses where graduate enrolment is less than x percent of total enrolment. The rationale for the latter indicator is that the nature and quality of the undergraduate experience might vary with the emphasis on graduate studies on the campus (Leslie, 1980). To date, however, the provincial government has not shown interest in indicators of system performance. In contrast, the Government of Canada has made a considerable effort to develop indicators of performance for the national system of post-secondary education (Canadian Council on Learning, 2007; see also Council of the Federation, 2006).

In recognition of the limitations of the existing indicators of institutional performance, the government developed an additional approach for institutional accountability, a multi-year accountability agreement (MYAA) between each institution and the MTCU. In these agreements, the institution indicates its strategies, programs, and appropriate performance targets in regard to various goals set by the Ministry and its own goals. Then the institution subsequently reports on its performance corresponding to the goals, such as increased participation of underrepresented groups or availability of learning technology. There is considerable scope within the MYAA process for making universities and colleges accountable for addressing any identified societal needs. The present set of government goals for post-secondary education was drawn from a 2005 Ontario Budget document which was informed by the Rae Review (Ontario Ministry of Finance, 2005). Through the goal setting and review process, the government is able to exercise a degree of control over post-secondary institutions that did not exist before the MYAA process. Although there has been consultation with each sector in developing the MYAA system, the process through which system and sectoral goals are formulated could be more transparent. In addition, there may be reason for concern as to how the values served by institutional autonomy are balanced with those served by institutional accountability within the MYAA process.

THE INFLUENCE OF PERFORMANCE ASSESSMENT ON THE BEHAVIOUR OF POST-SECONDARY INSTITUTIONS

Performance assessment regimes are intended to have a steering influence on institutional behaviour. The impact of such regimes may not always be strong enough to overcome the influence of other factors such as market forces, the pressures of funding systems, and institutional cultures; moreover, assessment regimes may have unanticipated side effects. Thus, it is important to ask what the likely influence of a performance assessment regime would be with respect to desired goals.

Values emphasized in quality assurance processes

The predominant values underlying the quality assurance regimes for Ontario universities reflect the resources, educational process, and selectivity conceptions of quality. As a result, other things being equal, these regimes are not likely to promote accessibility, and in fact, they are more likely to discourage it. There are a few arguments that support this assertion.

It is inherent in the resources conceptualization of quality that quality and accessibility are inversely related. This was in fact the thrust of an argument that was made by the Council of Ontario Universities in a 1982 report entitled, *Squeezing the Triangle* (Council of Ontario Universities, 1982). This document suggested that quality, funding, and accessibility could be pictured as apexes of a triangle that depicts policy choices by alternative points within the triangle that correspond to different combinations of the three parameters. The three parameters are connected in such a way that if one of them were altered, at least one of the others must necessarily be altered also. If enrolment were to be increased while funding was held constant, then deterioration of quality would be an inevitable result. Or if funding were to be increased while enrolment was held constant, then quality would increase. The implications are that universities should not be expected, or pressured, to increase enrolment without a simultaneous increase in funding, and that the only way to increase quality is to increase funding faster than enrolment.

As long as quality is conceptualized in a way that makes it a scarce commodity, it will be possible to purchase more accessibility only at the expense of quality. Scarcity is not just a function of the amount of money available for higher education. If the quality of faculty is defined by the number of publications, then all professors with less than the average number of publications are, by definition, of less than average quality. The same holds true for student admissions. Not all universities can admit only students in the highest quintile of secondary school grades and test scores. If quality is deemed to be a function of admissions selectivity, it is impossible for all institutions to be of equal quality. Insofar as secondary school grades are correlated with socioeconomic status, an institution pursues a policy of socioeconomic egalitarianism at its own peril—if its quality is judged at least in part on the basis of the average secondary school grades of the students that it admits.

One of the motivations of those who developed the value added conception of quality in higher education was to avoid the dysfunctional effects of an admissions selectivity conception of quality. If quality is defined in terms of value added, then it is possible for an institution that, for whatever reasons, admits many students whose prior academic performance is less than average to reach the highest level of institutional quality. It all depends upon what impact the institution has on its students. As Astin has argued, if quality is conceptualized in terms of value added, then there need not be a conflict between quality and accessibility or equity (1985). Moreover, if quality were to be measured by value added, it might make sense to put resources disproportionately into programs for the educationally disadvantaged because there would be so much potential for adding value.

However, the jury is still out on the promise of the value added conception of quality for increasing equity in higher education. There has not been much research on the amount and type of resources that are needed to produce value added for students with various academic backgrounds in different educational settings. Many educational institutions likely anticipate that they would need to devote substantial resources to students with weaker academic backgrounds in order to produce much value added for them, and this concern likely makes them more reluctant to admit such students. For these institutions, a safer strategy is to admit students who they assume will need little if any help from the institution, and who can succeed after graduation no matter how much or how little value their education adds.

Thus far we have commented on the implications of the admissions selectivity and resources conceptions of quality. Another conception of quality that is very strongly reflected in practices in Ontario is quality as adherence to established educational processes, which include the organization of programs into discrete classes, the number of class contact hours required for graduation, and certification requirements for post-secondary teachers and ideas about their qualifications. Few, if any, of these process requirements can be justified on the basis of empirical evidence of their influence on student outcomes, because the research on most of these relationships has not been done. Rather, subscription to these practices constitutes statements of educational values in and of themselves.

If quality is seen as synonymous with constancy of educational processes, i.e., "doing things the way that they have always been done," then by definition it will be impossible for the post-secondary sector to adapt to changing demands and conditions without impairing quality. Over thirty years ago, Trow warned that in the transition from elite to mass higher education there would necessarily be many changes in the forms of higher education, and that academics would likely be of divided opinion as to whether quality would be diminished by these changes (1973). As Trow predicted, there are considerable differences of opinion over the extent to which quality may have been impaired (or enhanced) by many of the changes that have occurred over the past three decades, e.g., awarding credit for experience, use of internet based courses, extensive use of part-time faculty, relaxation of residence requirements for doctoral programs, and abandonment of core course requirements for bachelor's degrees.

Where traditional ideas about educational practice are being put to a particularly severe test is over the question of what are the essential characteristics of an institution that awards degrees. As will be discussed further in Chapter 6, many new institutions that had not previously awarded degrees in Canada have recently begun to do so. These include community colleges, for-profit institutions, and internet-based institutions. As Trow anticipated, these institutions are quite different in form than the universities that traditionally have been the only institutions in Canada allowed to award degrees.

Although these institutions differ from Canadian universities in many ways, one difference that has been the subject of particular attention pertains to faculty role in research. In many of these institutions, faculty who teach in the degree programs have little, if any, involvement in research. Accordingly, a question that has arisen in conjunction with these institutions is whether it is possible to have a quality baccalaureate program delivered by faculty who do not do research, or who spend considerably less time on research than on teaching. The relationship between teaching and research has been the subject of a great deal of research (Hattie and March, 1996; Halliwell, 2008). This research does not support the view that substantial conduct of research by faculty is essential to good undergraduate teaching, and suggests that research and teaching are either independent of one another or, as Newman maintained, they are competitive rather than complementary functions.

For example, based upon a meta-analysis of 58 studies of the relationship between teaching effectiveness and research productivity, Hattie and March found the correlation between these phenomena to be zero. They concluded that "the common belief that research and teaching are inextricably entwined is an enduring myth" (1996, 529). Crimmel offered an explanation for the persistence of this myth, namely that it serves "to justify existing interests and institutions" (1984, 192).

This whole body of empirical literature has been criticized, however, for limitations of the measures that are commonly used and the way that the research questions are formulated. Most studies have used student evaluations to measure teaching effectiveness, although some have used peer ratings or faculty self-evaluations. Research productivity is normally measured by numbers of publications, citations, grants, and peer assessments. The unit of analysis is typically the individual faculty member. Thus, the questions addressed in this body of research are whether the best teachers are also the best researchers, and whether a professor must attain at least a certain level of research productivity in order to be an effective teacher. In this body of literature, the answer to the latter question was found to be "no."

Studies that use other variables to measure teaching effectiveness, and that use a different unit of analysis are the exception. One such study, Volkwein and Carbone (1994), takes the academic department as the unit of study and explores the correlations between the strength of departmental teaching and research orientations, on the one hand, and various self-ratings of students' intellectual growth on the other. The data for the study came from a single university. For most combinations of high, medium, and low departmental research and teaching orientations respectively, the correlations are not statistically significant. However, for two of the intellectual growth ratings, the associations were statistically significant for departments that ranked high on both teaching and research, and for those that ranked low on both, with the growth ratings for the former exceeding those of the latter. There was one other statistically significant, but weak, association for one outcome measure, between departments with a high research and low teaching orientation and students' intellectual growth. Noting the exploratory nature of their study and the limitations of their data, the authors were cautious in their claims. They suggested that their results show a "probable" impact of departmental research and teaching climates on undergraduate education, but indicated that this impact was small. This finding was further qualified by the fact that the authors found no correlation between their research and teaching climate variables, which suggests that these two spheres of activity were unrelated. Further they found "congruence" between their analysis and earlier studies of the relationship between teaching and research at the level of individual faculty (162). Although providing only limited and qualified support for an influence of research on undergraduate learning, the Volkwein and Carbone study was cited—and it was the only study on the relationship between teaching and research cited—in many of the university community responses to the 1994 OCUA Discussion Paper referred to Chapter 1 that raised the question of whether funding for research should be separated from funding for teaching. Citing just this single study out of the whole body of literature on the relationship between teaching and research perhaps indicates the attachment of the university community to the belief—or as Crimmel and Hattie and March would have it, the myth—that research productivity is a necessary condition for effective teaching.

Attachment to this belief is one of the major reasons why many Ontario universities are skeptical about the quality of baccalaureate programs in colleges, and are reluctant to admit graduates of college baccalaureate programs to master's programs. There are two striking ironies here. First, as noted earlier, the college baccalaureate programs undergo an *external* quality review that is both rigorous and transparent, and is based upon the same degree level standards as have been adopted by the provincial universities, while the undergraduate programs of Ontario universities do not undergo such a review. Second, as detailed in several other points in this discourse, the reality today is that contract instructors, who—like most college faculty—are not engaged in research, conduct a very substantial proportion of the teaching at Ontario's universities.

Innovations in educational processes, like distance education and the delivery of degree programs by different types of institutions, can help increase accessibility, especially in terms of including members of groups previously underrepresented in higher education. On the other hand, while it is easy to criticize universities for their conservatism in regard to new educational practices that increase accessibility, a certain amount of caution in regard to adopting radically new practices is prudent. The challenge is how to avoid rejecting newer forms of higher education out of hand simply because they are new. This is a difficult challenge because quality is so subjective, and ideas about quality are so connected to forms and practices that have been used in the past.

Values reflected in performance indicators

Turning from quality to accountability, earlier we described the performance indicators that were developed to satisfy the government's demand for the higher education system to be more accountable. In view of the attention that governments have given to accessibility over the past two decades, a curious thing about these indicators is that none of them pertain to accessibility. Graduation rates and employment rates may be useful indicators for some purposes, but they don't reveal anything about accessibility. In fact, if universities and colleges expect that persons with weaker academic backgrounds are more likely to drop out, then these performance indicators introduce a bias against accessibility, particularly for members of historically underrepresented groups.

Some of the best indicators of accessibility are system level statistics, like participation rates, but there are also measures of institutional performance that could shed some light on accessibility, such as the annual percentage increase in enrolment, admission rates for persons from educationally disadvantaged groups, and the amount of credit given to transfer students. Although the performance indicators that institutions are required to report do not include any specifically related to accessibility, the Ministry has introduced accessibility considerations into the Multi-Year Accountability Agreement process by getting institutions to set targets and report on progress with respect to admission of students from underrepresented groups. There is thus a curious disparity between the indicators that are emphasized in these two distinct accountability arenas.

In addition, of course, the funding mechanism provides an inducement to increase enrolment. This is most clearly the case with regard to the highly enrolment-sensitive formula used in the college sector. In the university sector, the corridor funding model was originally introduced at a time when tuition was stringently controlled, and thus, appeared destined to remove any substantial financial inducement to increase enrolment. However, as discussed in Chapter 4, during the more than two decades since the introduction of the corridor funding system, almost all new funding has been the product of traditional enrolment-driven envelopes. Also, tuition fees now constitute a larger proportion of total operating revenue than they did twenty years ago. As a result, the university funding system has provided a strong incentive to increase enrolment. Thus, it appears that of the four systems that influence the behaviour of universities, two—the funding system and the MYAA process—promote accessibility; one—the required performance indicator reporting system— is neutral with respect to accessibility and contains a modest disincentive to making admission more equitable; and the other—the quality assurance system—discourages accessibility. It is difficult to say what the net effect of these four systems is with respect to encouraging or discouraging accessibility. Most likely, the quality assurance and funding systems are the dominant ones, and these give conflicting messages. Quality assessors tend to be concerned about too high a student-faculty ratio, whereas funding mechanisms encourage higher ratios. In addition to formal quality assessment processes, institutional behaviour may be influenced also by rankings that are produced by magazines and newspapers, such as the *Maclean's* rankings of Canadian universities or the *Business Week* rankings of business schools. Such rankings are based almost entirely on inputs, although *Maclean's* has given attention recently to student engagement data from NSSE and some years ago provided companion data on value added—that showed an inverse correlation between ranking by inputs and reputation and ranking by value added.

Thus far in drawing conclusions about the influence of performance assessment measures, we have commented mostly about the influences on the university sector. The influence of the MYA process and of the performance indicator system would be about the same in the college sector as in the university sector. The present system for quality assurance in the college sector is too new to support conclusions based upon experience. However, insofar as the underlying quality paradigm in the college sector is that of learning outcomes, the college sector would be spared the consequences of the admissions selectivity, resources, and educational practices paradigms that we have described for the universities. Moreover, accessibility is a cornerstone of the mission of the college sector. Along with providing skilled workers for Ontario industry, the other reason for establishing the colleges was to extend the opportunity for post-secondary education to people who would not otherwise have had that opportunity.[29]

For much of their history, the colleges were kept quite separate from the universities. However, as colleges have more interactions with universities, and possibly are more influenced by the university culture, for example though offering baccalaureate programs, they may adopt university attitudes towards admissions selectivity and constancy of educational processes. Moreover, demand exceeds capacity in many college programs, particularly some of the ones whose graduates are in greatest demand. Although the selection process for these programs has been the subject of some controversy, there has been a tendency to base decisions at least in part on the academic qualifications of applicants. Thus admissions selectivity is hardly foreign to the colleges. Still, it would take a very substantial change in the way that quality is conceptualized in the college sector for quality assurance practices in that sector to exert a constraining influence on accessibility that is anywhere near what it is in the university sector.

Finally, our discussion of the influence of performance measurement regimes on higher education has concentrated on the implications for accessibility, but what about the implications of these regimes for higher education's knowledge production role? It is noteworthy that none of the

---

[29] It is possible that making colleges more accountable for graduation rates could push them to be more selective in admissions, but it is more in keeping with the mission of the colleges to try to improve graduation rates by providing greater support for at risk students than by being more selective in admissions.

major performance indicators on which universities are required to report, and on which a small portion of their funding (about 1 percent) is based, pertain at all to their research function, either pure research or commercially driven research. Also, as noted earlier, quality assurance practices in Ontario do not include a separate assessment of research performance like the Research Assessment Exercise in the United Kingdom. Research performance is brought into the quality assessment process mainly for the purpose of assessing the quality of faculty. While from the perspective of some observers, there may be too much emphasis on faculty research and publication for the purpose of assessing degree programs, there is not enough, or the right kind of, emphasis for the purpose of assessing the performance of research in the universities. Nonetheless, it has been observed that there is significantly more peer assessment of research than of teaching within the academy. This assessment occurs mainly in spheres of refereed publications and conference presentations, and in the awarding of research grants. If these two spheres are considered to be part of the quality assurance system broadly construed, then there is a substantial amount of assessment of research. However, assessment of research in this manner lacks the comprehensiveness of program quality assessment and accreditation systems.

Perhaps Ontario should have a more comprehensive, structured system for the assessment of research. Yet another question that arises, however, in the context of this chapter is whether the existing mechanisms for assessment of research encourage, discourage, or are neutral with respect to the research activities that are connoted by the term knowledge production within the new research paradigm explored in Chapter 3. Aside from the difficulties involved in obtaining the data that would be necessary to determine what types of research related activity are most rewarded, there are also major conceptual issues in addressing this question. These involve distinguishing between research that is motivated by the prospect of it being able to be transformed into something of commercial value and that which is not so motivated.

As noted earlier, governments have been encouraging universities to devote more effort to commercially driven research and development, and collaboration with industry, and have been providing considerable inducements to move in this direction. The response of universities to these incentives and opportunities has been so great that now there is concern, as discussed in Chapter 3, that the tide of commercialization may place core academic values in jeopardy (Bok, 2003). Insofar as this concern is actually warranted, it is important to ask whether there are, or could be, any countervailing force to check the tide of commercialization and help to maintain a balance between curiosity and commercially driven research. Perhaps the system of quality assurance could rein in unbridled commercialism in research as it has served to rein in unbridled enrolment expansion.

SUMMARY

This chapter has shown that there are several different quality assurance and accountability systems operating in Ontario. They are based upon different assumptions and values pertaining to academic quality, use different methods and types of data, and provide institutions with conflicting incentives, rewards, and penalties. The challenge of getting consistent and effective processes of quality assurance will become more difficult if there is greater diversity in the types of providers of baccalaureate education. The literature on quality assurance emphasizes the superiority of the outcomes, value added, and student experience conceptualizations of quality, and accordingly institutions and provincial agencies would be well advised to embrace these rather than the resources and admissions selectivity notions of quality. The use of NSSE, and NSSE type instruments developed locally, looks like a promising direction, but more research needs to be done on the validity and implications associated with such a move. Early results of NSSE surveys in Canada support the conclusion that it would be healthy if a greater proportion of undergraduate education were provided in other types of institutions than large research universities.

6

THE DESIGN OF ONTARIO'S SYSTEM OF POST-SECONDARY EDUCATION

The challenges facing Ontario's post-secondary education system can be addressed through modifications of the behaviour of the individual institutions that comprise the system and through modifications in the design of the system itself. In this chapter, we explain how modifications in the design of Ontario's post-secondary system could enable the system to address the challenges that it faces more effectively. The present design, which dates back to the late 1960s, is characterized by relatively little institutional differentiation. Institutional differentiation is an important property of post-secondary education systems: in general, it can result in more access, better quality, and lower costs. However, left to their own devices, degree granting institutions—not just in Ontario—will gravitate toward the same model of emphasizing research and having light teaching loads. Experience around the world has demonstrated that the only way to avoid the march toward institutional homogeneity in this regard is through government action. Governments can specify the mandates of different institutions within the publicly funded system of post-secondary education, set boundaries, and be vigilant in preventing mission creep. They can also provide rewards for doing an institution's mission well, rewards that do not include expanding the institution's mission. Institutions should be given autonomy with respect to how they carry out their missions, e.g., how they perform their teaching and research functions, but specifying the missions of the post-secondary institutions that it funds is a proper and responsible function of government.

The chapter begins by explaining briefly what post-secondary system design means and giving some examples of different designs and of modifications in system design that some jurisdictions have made in order

Academic Transformation: The Forces Reshaping Higher Education in Ontario, I.D. Clark, G. Moran, M.L. Skolnik, and D. Trick. Montreal and Kingston: McGill-Queen's University Press, Queen's Policy Studies Series.

to cope with the same issues that confront post-secondary education in Ontario. Then the chapter describes the present design characteristics of Ontario's post-secondary system and their origins, and discusses some of the important implications of the present design. The chapter concludes by identifying six issues in the present design for which possible modifications are discussed in the following and final chapter.

The Design of Post-secondary Education Systems

The design of a post-secondary education system refers to the mix of institutions by mission, type, and major characteristics such as highest academic credential awarded, their relationships with one another, and the arrangements through which the system is governed. Although all systems of post-secondary education perform essentially the same functions, there are substantial differences from one jurisdiction to another in the way that these functions are distributed among different types of post-secondary institutions. These differences in the configuration of institutions and division of functions among them reflect different design choices.

The most fundamental design choice concerns the extent and nature of institutional differentiation. What this choice involves can be illustrated by considering the extreme points along a continuum of institutional differentiation. At one end of the continuum is the situation where every post-secondary institution offers the full range of programs, credentials, and functions, and has the same mission. This might be termed the Homogeneity Model. The only source of institutional differentiation in this model would be location, which could give rise to some differences in the distribution of enrolment by program reflecting local needs and tastes. The other end of the continuum, the Heterogeneity Model, would be characterized by having institutions that are highly specialized—and hence differentiated from one another—by program area, function, credential awarded, and targeted clientele. For example, in the Heterogeneity Model, each industrial sector may have a post-secondary institution that is dedicated to training workers and conducting research related specifically, and exclusively, to that sector.

In practice, no jurisdictions have elected to occupy the extreme ends of the differentiation continuum, though at times, the post-secondary systems of France, the former Soviet Union, and China have been rather far toward the Heterogeneity end of the continuum. For example, these systems have included a number of post-secondary institutions that specialize in meeting the needs of particular industrial sectors. Most jurisdictions have designed their post-secondary systems to be near the middle of continuum, avoiding both extreme homogeneity as well as heterogeneity. As we have argued earlier, and will elaborate in this chapter, Ontario's post-secondary system is relatively far toward the homogeneity end of the system design continuum.

The reason why most jurisdictions have sought to find a healthy midpoint along this continuum is that there are both benefits and drawbacks of institutional differentiation. The chief benefits of institutional differentiation are associated with specialization and division of functions among institutions. Other things being equal, an institution that specializes in certain functions can perform those functions more efficiently and with a higher level excellence than an institution that tries to cover all functions. It was based on this principle that most American states and some Canadian provinces decided to establish or expand community colleges in order to handle the large increase in the demand for undergraduate education in the 1960s that included many students with weaker academic backgrounds than had been the norm previously. These jurisdictions believed that the needs of these students could be met more effectively and efficiently if they did their first two years of undergraduate study in newer institutions that were created expressly for this purpose than by the existing universities. This example fits the observation often encountered in the literature on system design that institutional differentiation enables a post-secondary system to provide both elite and mass higher education (e.g., Birnbaum, 1983).

The downsides of institutional differentiation are associated with separation and isolation. While there are some benefits of grouping students of similar ability levels and interests who are pursuing similar fields, there are also benefits for students of interacting with others who have different characteristics in these regards. Where institutional differentiation takes the form of hierarchical stratification, the prestige and labour market value of credentials earned in different institutions may vary substantially. Also in a post-secondary system that has more institutional differentiation, some levels and fields of study may be offered in fewer locations than in a system that has less differentiation. As a consequence, some students may find that the program they want to pursue is not available in their community.

Because institutional differentiation has both upsides and downsides, there is no "right" amount or pattern of differentiation. However, the prevailing view in the literature on system design is that post-secondary education systems that exhibit a considerable extent of institutional differentiation can respond more efficiently and effectively than can very homogeneous systems to variety and change in the demands on higher education (Birnbaum, 1983; Huisman, 1998; Meek et al., 1996).

Thus far, we have discussed institutional differentiation as a general property of post-secondary education systems. However, post-secondary institutions may be differentiated from one another (or not) in regard to many different characteristics, and any judgment about institutional differentiation is dependent upon which specific institutional characteristics are under consideration. For example, institutions may be undifferentiated by function (i.e., all do both teaching and research), yet highly differentiated by program (many may concentrate on particular fields of study).

One of the most basic design choices—and hence characteristics by which institutions may be differentiated—concerns the academic credentials that institutions award. Should all institutions award all types of credentials, or should institutions specialize in different types of credentials (and the types of programs that are associated with the credentials)? In the binary designs that were adopted by many jurisdictions in the 1960s, post-secondary institutions were divided into two sets: one set of institutions concentrated on bachelor's and higher degrees, and the other on sub-baccalaureate credentials such as associate's degrees, diplomas, and certificates. In some jurisdictions, these two main categories were further divided into sub-sets. For example, one sub-set of non-degree institutions might concentrate on programs of at least one year's duration for students who have a secondary school diploma or the equivalent, and the other sub-sector would concentrate on adult upgrading and short term vocational training. Within the degree sector, some institutions would award only bachelor's, or bachelor's and master's degrees, while other institutions would cover all degree levels including doctorates.

Perhaps the best known example of a post-secondary system that is structured on the basis of differences in the highest academic credential that institutions award is the California system. The design of the California post-secondary education system was introduced in the 1960 Master Plan for the state system. The system consists of three sectors: the community colleges, which are restricted to awarding two-year degrees; the campuses of California State University, which are restricted to the bachelor's and master's level; and the campuses of the University of California, which are authorized to award bachelor's, master's, and doctoral degrees.

Another design choice involves the functions of teaching and research. In some jurisdictions, it was decided to concentrate much research, particularly advanced research, in research institutes that are separate from universities, and so many of the latter concentrate on teaching. In systems where institutions are differentiated by academic credential awarded, generally the faculty in the institutions that concentrate on bachelor's degrees are not expected to devote as much time to research as are the faculty in the institutions that award doctoral degrees.

An important aspect of system design pertains to the relationships between institutions, particularly the way that these relationships enable students to move from one institution to another. If every post-secondary institution offered all possible programs, students would need to change institution only if, for some other reason, they had to change the location of their residence. However, in practice, there is considerable variation among institutions in regard to credentials awarded, disciplines offered, and in educational philosophies and types of learning environment. In general, the greater the differentiation among institutions, the greater is the need to make provision for student mobility. The problem is that where institutional differentiation is greater it is also more difficult to build effective pathways between institutions. For example, institutions that are highly differentiated from one another often find it difficult to award academic credit for courses from other institutions because of differences in curriculum structures, types of programs, and educational philosophies.

The third element of system design is governance. There are two principal design choices pertaining to governance. One is how broadly to group institutions for administrative and financial allocation purposes. Most commonly, institutions with similar mandates are grouped together in sectors that operate within a common administrative and financial framework. This may facilitate the development of institutional identity and sense of purpose, foster public understanding of the mission of the institutions in the sector and the needs that they serve, and make it easier to provide consistent governmental oversight of the institutions. However, the segmentation of post-secondary education into separate sectors makes it more difficult to foster student mobility and alter resource allocation patterns in response to changing needs. For these reasons, some jurisdictions have opted instead to place all institutions under a single governance structure.

Another major design choice with respect to governance is how far to decentralize authority toward the campus level. One option is to place all institutions in a sector under a single governing board which has the authority for financial, managerial, and other corporate affairs. An alternative is to vest this authority with campus level governing boards, with or without some agency that tries to coordinate the activities of the individual campuses. Governing boards and coordinating boards can be sector or jurisdiction wide in scope.

The design choices that we have summarized in this section pertain to public post-secondary systems. A larger system design choice is whether to allow private post-secondary institutions, and if so how much to rely on the private sector to meet the jurisdiction's needs for post-secondary education. From his study of private post-secondary education in different countries, Geiger concluded that the main determinant of the scale and role of private post-secondary sectors is the scale and shape of public post-secondary systems (1986). In other words, the private sector exists largely to address the demands that are not met by the public sector. Some countries have made the decision to create public systems that meet only a portion of the demand for post-secondary education and only certain needs, and leave the balance to private institutions to address. Other countries, including Canada, have tried to develop universal public systems of post-secondary education, leaving only certain specialized niches for private sector activity.

EXAMPLES OF MODIFICATIONS IN SYSTEM DESIGN IN OTHER JURISDICTIONS

The issues described in earlier chapters that confront post-secondary education in Ontario are faced, to varying extents, by other jurisdictions as well. One of the common themes in reforms of post-secondary education in many countries has been reducing the reliance on research universities for meeting the increasing demand for undergraduate education. In general, two main strategies have been employed to achieve this objective: (1) establishing new degree granting institutions whose mission is predominantly that of teaching, and in which it is understood faculty will devote a substantially greater proportion of their time to teaching than to research; and (2) expanding the role of non-university post-secondary institutions in degree granting and making those degrees as comparable as possible to the degrees awarded by universities (Taylor et al., 2008). Having had neither community college type institutions to relieve universities of some of the burden of first and second year students, nor private universities to relieve the public treasury of some of the financial burden of mass higher education, many European nations established or upgraded alternative degree granting post-secondary sectors to help meet the demand for places in baccalaureate programs, especially for programs of a more applied nature. Generally, these sectors operate on less funding per student, largely because their involvement in research is much less than that of the universities.

For example, faced with increasing student numbers, over-crowding and underfunding of universities, Austria created a *fachhochschule* sector in the early 1990s (Hackl, 2008). These institutions offer degree programs of a more applied nature than the universities. Finland created a sector of degree granting polytechnic institutions in the early 1990s as an economical way of expanding higher education thereby increasing student choice, particularly for programs of a professional nature, and putting considerable effort into the improvement of teaching in these institutions (Valimaa and Neuvonen-Rauhala, 2008).

In Germany, *fachhochschulen* have existed since the early 1970s, but, since the 1990s, these institutions have become more like universities in some ways, while retaining their distinctness in other (Klumpp and Teichler, 2008). *Fachhochschulen* now may offer degrees with the same nomenclature as universities, for example the Diplom-Ingenieur. The *fachhochschulen* refer to themselves in English as universities of applied sciences, but they stop short of referring to themselves as universities in German (Klumpp and Teichler, 2008, 114).

In recent years, over 30 percent of new entrants to post-secondary education have been in the *fachhochschulen* sector, and half of the new entrants in the *fachhochschulen* have the qualifications for admission to a university. The normal teaching load in the *fachhochschulen* is 18 hours per week for 34 weeks, compared to eight hours per week for 30 weeks in the universities, and the average faculty salary is 20 percent less in the *fachhochschulen* than in the universities (Klumpp and Teichler, 2008, 103). On the surface it looks as if the cost per student is substantially less in the *fachhochschulen* than in the universities. Indeed, Klumpp and Teichler reported that the average basic funding per student in the *fachhochschulen* was about half what it was in the universities. However, by assuming that 90 percent of the resources of the *fachhochschulen* are used for teaching, while only 50 percent of the resources of the universities are used for teaching, they suggested that one could argue that the actual costs of teaching are almost the same in the two sectors (Klumpp and Teichler, 2008, 104). The difference between the total costs per student and the teaching costs per student is of course due to the substantially greater amount of research in the universities than in the *fachhochschulen*. Thus, apart from the other differences between the two types of post-secondary institutions, such as emphasis on teaching and applied studies, the decision about whether to accommodate additional enrolment expansion by expanding one sector or the other could depend in large part on the perceived value of funding a corresponding expansion of research.

In theory, another route to having some degree granting institutions that concentrate less on research would be to modify the role of some existing universities. A question that arises in jurisdictions like Ontario and many European countries that do not have formal stratification in their university sectors is whether to concentrate graduate studies and research in a limited number of universities. Germany moved in this direction in 2006 with the naming of three institutions as elite universities which will receive special funding. The president of one of the newly designated universities noted that such concentration of funding might help a German university to make it into the top 50 worldwide (*Deutsche Welle Online*, 2006). Along the same line, a 2008 report on the future of universities' intellectual property in the United Kingdom recommended that research funding be concentrated so that the U.K. has no more than 30 or so institutions specializing in postgraduate research (Feam, 2008). The report suggested that by 2020 each region should have no more than one or two major graduate schools. Critics of the report objected strongly to the recommendation and accused its author of wanting to stop many academics from doing research. In a review of the impact of globalization on higher education, Zha reported that several countries in Asia, Europe, and Latin America have moved to increase the concentration of funding for research and graduate studies to a small number of universities or are giving serious consideration to doing so (Zha, 2009).

Even with the traditions of community college transfer and private universities in the United States, there has been much concern in the past decade about whether the American post-secondary system is doing a good enough job of addressing its accessibility needs. This concern has been driven in part by awareness of the decline in the proportion of the US population with a college degree relative to other nations, and the gap between its rate of college participation and completion (National Center for Public Policy and Higher Education, 2006). One response to this concern has been the authorization in a number of states for community colleges to provide complete baccalaureate programs (Floyd, Skolnik, and Walker, 2005). Floyd and Walker reported that in 2009, community colleges in 11 states (or in 16 if a wider definition of a community college baccalaureate were employed) had gained the authority to award baccalaureate degrees. The numbers of baccalaureate programs provided by colleges, however, remains rather modest except in Florida (Floyd and Walker, 2009). The states in which community colleges have been allowed to award baccalaureates tend to be those that have a limited range of private universities and less stratified public university sectors, e.g., California is not one of these states.

Allowing community colleges to award baccalaureates enables many individuals to complete a degree who might not otherwise be able to do so due to a variety of factors: being place-bound, facing financial barriers, not being able to find the desired program at a local university, and inflexible admission requirements of universities (Floyd, Skolnik, and Walker, 2005). Almost all of the community college baccalaureate programs in the United States are job-oriented, often geared to meeting local labour market needs, and delivered in a learner-centered paradigm by faculty whose sole or major responsibility is teaching. Florida, the state with the largest enrolment in community college baccalaureate programs, moved further in this direction in 2008 with the establishment of a new system of state colleges that consists of former community colleges that are authorized to offer associate's and baccalaureate degrees, but not graduate degrees (Floyd, Garcia-Falconetti, and Hrabak, 2009). This initiative is seen as a way of increasing access to, and success in, baccalaureate programs in an economical way and thus improving Florida's historically low baccalaureate attainment rate. Allegedly, one of the factors that led the state to move in this direction was the perceived preoccupation of its universities with graduate studies. Between 1993 and 2003, production of master's degrees increased by 59 percent, and doctorates by 56 percent, while baccalaureates increased by only 42 percent (Inside Higher Education, 2008). Changes in system design of the type described here have been made also in British Columbia and Alberta, and they are described later in this chapter.

The most important point to bear in mind from our description of principal variations in the design of post-secondary education systems and examples from other jurisdictions is that there are many different ways of organizing a system of post-secondary education. Attention to system design is an important part of policy-making for higher education (Skolnik, 2005b). In many jurisdictions, ongoing monitoring of the effectiveness of their system design and making modifications in the design as the external and internal environment of higher education changes are considered to be a core responsibility of those who oversee the higher education system. Thus, system design is integrally linked with system governance. The next parts of this chapter, which describe the Ontario post-secondary system, reveal the design choices that have been made in this province. The discussion of the design of Ontario's post-secondary system begins by identifying the components of the system.

THE NATIONAL CONTEXT OF ONTARIO POST-SECONDARY EDUCATION

Ontario's universities and colleges operate within a national post-secondary educational context. Some important dimensions of that national context include the following: the flow of students and resources between Ontario and other provinces; the influence of policies of the federal government in some areas of post-secondary education, such as research funding, student financial assistance, and workforce training; and the role of Ontario post-secondary institutions in serving national as well as provincial needs. As outlined in Chapter 3, the shift over the past two decades in federal government support for higher education from unconditional transfers to the provinces to direct funding for specific programs and projects has substantially altered the financial environment, particularly for universities.

Given the extent to which post-secondary education operates in a national milieu and is vital to the nation's prosperity and well-being, some observers have suggested that there is a need for national coordination of post-secondary education. For example, in its 2007 report on the state of post-secondary education in Canada, the Canadian Council on Learning urged the development of a national strategy for post-secondary education, and former Ontario Premier Davis endorsed this idea (Canadian Council on Learning, 2007, 22-24; Davis, 2008). However, it is hard to see how Ontario could participate in the development of a national strategy for post-secondary education when, as will be noted later in this chapter, it does not have a provincial strategy for post-secondary education.

While there is no national agency with a responsibility for overseeing and coordinating the whole of post-secondary education in Canada, there are a number of bodies through which different stakeholders may voluntarily coordinate some aspects of their activities. For example, even in the absence of a national accreditation mechanism, at least rough comparability of standards of university education has been attained through the participation of all universities in the Association of Universities and Colleges of Canada.[30] The sharing of information about practices through scholarly societies and various national associations concerned with teaching or research also helps to foster common terminology, definitions, and understandings. Nevertheless, there continue to be very substantial differences in the way that post-secondary education is organized and governed across Canada, particularly within the non-university sectors and in the relationships between the two sectors. These differences offer an opportunity to examine the implications of different ways of organizing post-secondary education.

It is important to appreciate that the composition of the post-secondary system is not fixed for all time. Over time, new institutions appear and others may change their form or status. The process of institutional entry, merger, or transformation is difficult, and the paths through which such changes to the system can occur are not well defined. Yet changes in the institutional composition of the post-secondary system can be an important element in how systems respond to changes in their environment and societal needs. In the next section we describe in some detail the current design of the post-secondary system.

THE DESIGN OF ONTARIO'S POST-SECONDARY EDUCATION SYSTEM

The institutions that comprise Ontario's post-secondary education are primarily the 19 publicly assisted universities that are members of the Council of Ontario Universities and the 24 colleges of applied arts and technology (CAATs). Although the focus of this chapter is on these universities and colleges, there are other institutions in Ontario that also provide programs and courses of post-secondary education.

Institutions other than Ontario publicly assisted universities and colleges providing post-secondary education in the province

Other institutions also provide post-secondary education: a few public post-secondary institutions that have special missions; private post-secondary institutions based in Ontario that offer degree programs, all but two of which are religious institutions; post-secondary institutions based outside Ontario that offer degree programs in Ontario under a Ministerial

---

[30] In 2007, the Council of Ministers of Education, Canada issued a Ministerial Statement on Quality Assurance of Degree Education in Canada (Council of Ministers of Education). This statement includes a Canadian degree qualifications framework to which the governments of the provinces and territories have agreed.

Consent; private vocational/career colleges offering non-degree programs often similar to those of the Ontario colleges; and a variety of institutions and organizations providing post-secondary programs and courses to Ontario residents over the internet. We shall refer to all these providers of post-secondary education collectively as "other providers" in order to distinguish them from the public universities and colleges. One reason why the other providers of post-secondary education are relevant to our study is that competition or potential competition from them may influence the behaviour of universities and colleges. A second reason is that recognition of the extent to which other providers meet certain needs of Ontario residents may have implications for how universities and colleges do, or should, direct their efforts and resources.

The only other public degree granting institutions besides the provincially assisted universities are the Royal Military College of Canada and the Ontario College of Art and Design, both of which are associate members of the Council of Ontario Universities. While there is no public post-secondary institution that offers programs of two or more years like the colleges, the Michener Institute for Applied Health Sciences—which was founded by a group of hospitals—is a quasi-public institution in that it receives the bulk of its operating funding from the Ministry of Health and Long Term Care.

Post-secondary institutions based outside Ontario may apply to the Ministry of Training, Colleges and Universities for a Ministerial Consent to offer degree programs in Ontario. Under the conditions set forth in the *Post-secondary Education Choice and Excellence* Act, 2000, the Minister may grant consents to applicants after their application is assessed by the Post-secondary Education Quality Assessment Board. Similarly the Minister may grant approval to Ontario based institutions that do not have a degree-granting charter, enabling them to offer a degree program for a specified period of time. As of April 2009, only two Ontario-based private institutions other than religious ones had consents, one a chiropractic college, the other a small technical college. The nine out-of-province institutions with Ministerial Consents included four offering Master of Education programs, one highly specialized program in technology at the bachelor's level and one at the master's level, and three individual bachelor's programs in business, education, and nursing (Post-secondary Education Quality Assessment Board, 2009). A chronic excess demand for places in Master of Education programs in Ontario is suggested by the presence of four out-of-province institutions currently offering M.Ed. programs, as well as by other out-of-province institutions having offered similar programs in the recent past and by some American institutions on the Ontario border actively recruiting Ontario students into their M.Ed. programs.

A few of the programs of out-of-province institutions give special attention to the needs of students who want to transfer from a college in order to complete a bachelor's degree, suggesting one other area where the demand from Ontario students has not been met by Ontario universities. From a public policy perspective, these instances raise the question of whether the Ontario post-secondary system should aim to fully meet all demands for post-secondary education, or leave some types of demands to be met by other post-secondary institutions.

It is more difficult to identify all the other providers of non-degree post-secondary education that provide programs and courses similar to those of the colleges, both because the regulation of the non-degree sector is less stringent and pervasive and because the educational activities of the colleges are so varied (Skolnik, 2004). There are a number of private career colleges that offer programs that require a year or more of full-time study in some of the fields in which the CAATs offer programs, particularly business and technology. What differentiates the CAATs from the private colleges is more emphasis on general education and extra-curricular activity and lower tuition fees, though the latter may be at least partially offset by the fact that students in the private colleges often can finish their programs and get into the workforce more quickly than students in comparable programs in the CAATs. In the realm of short term training activities, the CAATs have many competitors including community agencies, school boards, and private training firms; and a challenge for public policy is for the CAATs to concentrate their resources on activities where they can meet needs that others cannot meet or cannot meet as effectively or efficiently as the CAATs.

Ontario's binary structure of publicly assisted post-secondary education institutions

The most visible and pervasive type of institutional differentiation in Ontario post-secondary education is the partitioning of the system into a binary structure consisting of two sectors, universities and colleges. Before discussing the nature of Ontario's binary structure of post-secondary education and the issues that arise in the relationship between the sectors, we shall outline briefly some of the key characteristics of the institutions in each sector.

THE UNIVERSITY SECTOR

Each of the 19 universities is an autonomous, not-for-profit corporation that has its own establishing act. Typically, the establishing act vests financial and administrative control of the institution in a governing board, and delegates responsibility for academic matters to an academic senate.

In every university there is a faculty association that has been recognized by the governing board as the exclusive bargaining agent for faculty.

The majority of faculty associations have been certified as unions by the Ontario Labour Relations Board, but even those that are not certified have collective agreements that cover similar areas of terms of employment and working conditions (except that those that are not certified do not have the right to strike).

In almost all cases the acts give the university authority to award any and all degrees in all branches of learning, a factor which it has been suggested has militated against institutional differentiation (Monahan, 2004, 120). Most of the university acts describe the mandates and general objectives for their institutions in similar ways. In addition, the acts of some of the most recently established or recently designated universities contain clauses which describe a special mission or unique characteristic of the institution.

The *Ryerson University Act* refers to its role in regard to "the advancement of applied knowledge and research in response to existing and emerging societal needs ... of Ontario," and to the provision of programs that "provide a balance between theory and application" (*Ryerson University Act*, 1977 (Amended)). The *University of Ontario Institute of Technology Act* states that the university should be responsive to "the market-driven needs of employers," have a particular focus on the needs of the county in which the university is located, and "facilitate" student movement between college and university programs (*University of Ontario Institute of Technology Act*, 2002). In spite of the institution's name however, the UOIT Act neither restricts the institution to, nor directs it to concentrate on, technology related programs.

The *Nipissing University Act*, 1992 assigns a somewhat special role to that institution. After stating that the objects of the university are "the pursuit of learning through scholarship, teaching and research within a spirit of free enquiry and expression," the act states that it shall be the special mission of the university to "be a teaching-oriented institution that offers programs in education and in liberal arts and science and programs that specifically address the needs of northern Ontario." However, the teaching-oriented part of its mission statement in the original act was somewhat neutralized by a 2001 amendment of the section of the act that describes the institution's degree granting authority. Like other Ontario universities, Nipissing now has the authority to grant any and all degrees in all branches of learning. The university offers master's programs in Education and in History, and its web site indicates its intention to expand graduate programming. In the original 1992 act, Nipissing was restricted to offering bachelor's degrees and master of education degrees. In the absence of a provincial policy to maintain a sector of undergraduate, teaching-oriented institutions, there has been no basis for denying a newer university the same broad unlimited degree granting authority as its older peers have.

Another newly established university looks likely to follow a path similar to that which Nipissing followed. The 2008 *Algoma University Act* makes it able to operate as an independent university rather than as an affiliate of Laurentian University which, like Nipissing, it had been previously. Besides providing a general mandate as a university, the act assigns the institution a special mission that includes being "a teaching-oriented university," with programs primarily at the undergraduate level and with a "particular focus on the needs of northern Ontario," and having a responsibility to "cultivate cross-cultural learning between aboriginal communities and other communities" (*Algoma University Act*, 2008). Initially, Algoma University is limited to awarding bachelor's degrees in arts and sciences. However, a clause in the act gives the cabinet discretionary authority to replace the initial degree granting authority with the same broad degree granting powers as the other universities have, which would include the ability to award graduate degrees. Thus, although established as a primarily undergraduate teaching institution, the act makes provision for the institution at some later date to become more like its peer institutions. Indeed, one may infer from the act that progression to broad unlimited degree granting authority is the government's expectation for all Ontario universities.

Apart from the exceptions just cited, some of which are likely to be only temporary, a striking feature of the Ontario university system in comparison with other public systems of comparable size has been the lack of mandated institutional differentiation by mission, function, areas of study, educational philosophy, or approach to program delivery. For example, all the universities have statutory authorization to offer graduate programs, which they all do, and all but two offer doctoral programs. There are differences in the numbers of graduate programs among the universities, related mainly to the size and age of the institutions. There are also differences in program mix among institutions; indeed, this is the main type of differentiation within the university sector. Of course there are differences among the universities in character, traditions, and institutional culture reflecting their individual histories and adaptations to local environments. This is no doubt the case in all jurisdictions, but in addition to these differences, university systems in many jurisdictions also display differences in mission and role that are the result of deliberate public policy decisions.

Each university is committed to both teaching and research, and the teacher-scholar is the faculty ideal. This is reflected in the widespread expectation that faculty will normally devote approximately the same proportion of their time to research as to teaching. This stands in contrast to some American states, such as California, where the expectation about the balance between teaching and research varies by type of institution within the university sector.

It is understood that both in their teaching and research functions, Ontario universities are committed both to the pursuit of knowledge for its own sake and to the search for, and transmission of, knowledge that will improve the material well-being of the community and that will provide graduates with marketable skills. Expressed in different terms, all the universities have a substantial role in both pure and applied research; and their educational programs are intended to facilitate the development of intellect and character, and help individuals better understand themselves and the world around them, as well as make productive contributions in society as workers and citizens.

How universities balance their different roles—teaching with research, or economic goals with broader intellectual, social and cultural goals—has frequently, if not always, been a major challenge for them. Often there has been criticism from the outside world that they are too committed to the pursuit of knowledge for its own sake, and from within the university community that they are too much oriented toward meeting external demands for marketable products and skills. Although it is difficult to make judgments about such broad and imprecise tendencies, it does seem that the concerns expressed about vocationalism and instrumentalism in Canadian universities within the past two decades are unprecedented. During this era of globalization, higher education has faced what may be an historically unique combination of pressure to seek external funding *and* opportunities to capitalize materially on the knowledge that it produces. Higher education occupies a central role in the knowledge economy and in government policies to make Canada more economically innovative, productive, and competitive (Cameron, 2002; Prichard, 2000). As discussed in Chapter 3, the expectations and funding opportunities related to this role have stimulated considerable controversy about how universities should, and can, reconcile the increased demand for knowledge production in the service of economic ends with the other goals of the university (Jones, McCarney, and Skolnik, 2005).

With the sole exception of Algoma University until its broader charter provisions are invoked, Ontario does not have a university that is limited to offering undergraduate programs, nor any that concentrate mainly on teaching. Except for the Ontario College of Art and Design, it does not have a degree granting institution that concentrates on a particular field of study, for example engineering and technology. Another type of post-secondary institution missing in Ontario, that has been increasing in number in the United States and has been established elsewhere in Canada and in other countries, is one controlled by aboriginal people that concentrates on meeting their educational needs and advancing indigenous knowledge.

Among degree granting institutions, perhaps one of the largest gaps in Ontario post-secondary education is the absence of an institution that plays the role of an open university. While the term "open university" may be synonymous with online education for many people, it is its educational philosophy, rather than its technology, that defines such an institution. An open university is committed to open admissions and to providing the flexibility that enables learners to utilize its resources and infrastructure in ways that will best meet the learner's needs. This may involve taking courses at an open university that can be used for credit in the learner's home institution, or enabling learners to combine its own courses with some from other institutions in pursuit of a degree from the open university that best meets their learning goals. The flexibility and affordability that an open university provides make it a valuable component of a post-secondary system, especially for individuals who find it impossible to access a conventional degree program due to work and family responsibilities, mobility constraints, inflexible admission requirements of conventional universities, or a mismatch between their educational needs and the programs available at their local university.

An indication of the interest that Ontario residents have in the opportunity that such institutions provide is that about a third of those registered at Athabasca University in Alberta, which describes itself as "Canada's open university," are residents of Ontario. In Athabasca University's submission to the Rae Review, it noted that in the period of 1994-2004, the university admitted 29,274 Ontario students (Athabasca University, 2005). It was noted also that in 2003-04, 6,689 persons in Ontario were registered at Athabasca, and the annual growth rate of course registrations by Ontario residents exceeded 15 percent. Baccalaureate completion for graduates of Ontario colleges is one of the prevalent needs that Athabasca is meeting.

THE COLLEGE SECTOR

Unlike universities, colleges do not have their own charters, but are established—and thus may be altered—by regulation under the *Ontario Colleges of Applied Arts and Technology Act* (S.O. 2002, Chapter 8, Schedule F). Each college has its own board of governors, and although these boards do not have the same statutory authority as do university governing boards, in practice there may not be much difference in the authority wielded by the boards in the two sectors. A much greater difference in governance arrangements between the two sectors involves the role of faculty. Unlike university senates, academic councils in the colleges have limited responsibility for academic matters and are authorized only to make recommendations to the president.

College faculty and support staff are represented by the Ontario Public Service Employees Union, which also represents civil service employees and a wide range of public sector employees. Faculty in all colleges are covered by a single province-wide collective agreement negotiated on behalf of all colleges and all faculty. There is a long history of confrontational labour relations in the college sector that has included three province-wide strikes by faculty.

Preparation for employment is the predominant function of the colleges. Employment preparation programs range from four-year applied baccalaureates to two and three year diploma and certificate programs, and to short term occupational training and retraining programs as well as to apprenticeship programs. In addition, the colleges have substantial involvement in adult upgrading, remediation, general interest courses and community education, contract training for industry, international education, and special programs for specific clientele such as small business, aboriginal groups, and immigrants. Applied research is a recognized function of the colleges, and several have received grants for it, including grants from the Canada Foundation for Innovation, and contracts from industry. Although these grants are small compared to the amounts that most universities receive, and constitute a small amount of college revenue, they are a noteworthy new source of revenue for the colleges.

While the sweeping authority given to the minister under the *Colleges Act* could be used to effect considerable differentiation among the colleges, little use has been made of this power to that end. For the most part, such differentiation as does exist within the college sector is the result of each college responding to the demands and opportunities of its local environment and pursuing its own developmental strategies. The fact that there is a single province-wide collective agreement for faculty has militated somewhat against differentiation among colleges.

When the colleges were created, the goal was to replicate the same institutional model in different communities across the province. The homogenous approach that Ontario took in the design of its college sector stood in sharp contrast to the more heterogeneous approach adopted in other jurisdictions, as can be seen, for example, when comparing the situation in Toronto with that in Edmonton. The province of Alberta established three quite different non-university institutions in Edmonton: a community college that combined a substantial transfer role in arts and sciences with a number of career programs mainly in applied arts and business, an institute of technology that combined long and short term technology oriented programs with apprenticeship programs, and a vocational college that concentrated on adult upgrading and short term occupational training. In contrast, Metro Toronto was given four colleges, and the GTA six colleges, each of which incorporated all the functions that were divided among the Edmonton colleges except the transfer function.

It was not until early in the 21st century that the Ontario government undertook to create deliberate differentiation within the college sector with the conferring of the status of Institute of Technology and Advanced Learning (ITAL) on five colleges, four of them in the GTA. The significance of the ITAL status is that institutions so designated are permitted to have up to 15 percent of their activity in baccalaureate programs, whereas the limit for other colleges is 5 percent.[31]

The standards developed by the Post-secondary Education Quality Assessment Board and approved by the Minster require that all baccalaureate programs offered by the colleges consist of eight terms of on-campus study plus at least one paid work term of at least 14 weeks. According to data obtained from the Ontario College Application Service (OCAS), there were 11,778 applications to college baccalaureate programs in 2008, and enrolment in these programs totalled 4,363 for 2007. The OCAS data show that in Fall 2008, 52 baccalaureate programs were being offered by 12 colleges. The only colleges that offered more than one or two programs were ITALs. Humber offered the most, 21; followed by Seneca, 9; Sheridan, 5; and George Brown, 3.

The addition of baccalaureate granting to the functions of community colleges in Ontario reflects a recent development that has occurred in several American states and two other Canadian provinces (Floyd, Skolnik, and Walker, 2005). The main objectives of giving colleges the authority to award baccalaureates are to expand access—often in a way that governments expect will be more economical than relying upon universities to provide them, and/or to provide a new type of baccalaureate program that some proponents believe will meet emerging labour market needs (Skolnik, 2005c).

The idea of colleges awarding baccalaureates has raised several issues. One is whether the baccalaureate is an appropriate designation for the credential earned in a program that has such a strong applied orientation as many college programs do. Those who support this new development note both how elastic the idea of the baccalaureate and what it represents has been over time, and the increasing presence of programs of an applied nature in the universities. Another issue that has been the subject of considerable concern is whether offering bachelor's programs might divert colleges' resources and attention away from their heretofore core activities. Owing to this latter concern among supporters of the colleges, there has probably been more opposition to the community college baccalaureate movement within the college sector itself than from the university sector. A third question arising from the movement of colleges into baccalaureate programming is whether it will, or should, lead to increased differentiation among colleges by possibly altering the stature and identity of colleges that offer a substantial number of bachelor's programs.

---

[31] Conestoga, Humber, and Sheridan Colleges have incorporated the ITAL designation into their institutional names. George Brown and Seneca Colleges have obtained the status of an ITAL, but have chosen not to use that designation in their names.

An example of how a college system, indeed a whole post-secondary system, might be modified as a result of some colleges moving substantially to offer baccalaureates is provided by the new classification of post-secondary institutions announced by the Government of Alberta (Alberta Advanced Education and Technology, 2007). Two colleges, in Edmonton and Calgary, were designated "baccalaureate and applied studies institutions." These institutions were authorized to award "regular" baccalaureate degrees in addition to the applied degrees that all Alberta colleges have been allowed to offer since 1996, as well as transfer, diploma, and certificate programs. The applied degree programs in Alberta colleges consist of six terms of on-campus study plus two terms of paid work experience. The applied degrees were intended to serve primarily a vocational purpose, and the government indicated that students should not expect the degrees to facilitate admission to graduate programs. Although some graduates of Alberta's applied degree programs have been accepted into master's programs in Canadian universities, these degrees are not generally considered to be equivalent to university bachelor's degrees. Besides the baccalaureate and applied studies institutions, another new category of post-secondary institutions in Alberta is that of polytechnic institutions. The two provincial institutes of technology have been so designated, and these institutions also may now offer baccalaureate degree as well as applied degree programs.

In April 2008, the Government of British Columbia introduced legislation to convert the remaining three university colleges and one community college into "special purpose, teaching universities" (BC Ministry of Advanced Education, 2008). Under this legislation, special purpose teaching universities will be expected to offer adult upgrading, technical and trade programs, and diplomas and certificates, as well as bachelor's and master's programs. The university colleges had been created in the mid 1990s by empowering five colleges to offer four-year baccalaureate programs in addition to the kinds of college programs that they had been offering. Before 2008, one of the university colleges had been converted into a university and another had become a campus of the University of British Columbia.

As noted earlier, in the same year as the university college experiment in British Columbia was terminated, the government of Florida created a system of state colleges that consists of nine former community colleges that are now authorized to award four-year degrees in addition to the two-year degrees that they had been awarding, but not graduate degrees (Florida Laws, 2008).

As the examples just cited show, jurisdictions that have opened the door to modification of the mandate of colleges to award baccalaureate degrees have differentiated among colleges in the way that this new authority has been granted. In turn, colleges on their own have made decisions that have resulted in considerable differentiation in regard to involvement in baccalaureate activity. Only about half the colleges are offering baccalaureate programs at all;[32] most of those that are offering programs could be considered "niche providers," delivering one or two programs in areas of unique expertise and high labour market demand; and just a few could be considered general providers of baccalaureate education.

THE RELATIONSHIP BETWEEN POST-SECONDARY SECTORS

In the binary structures that many jurisdictions developed during the 20th century, the non-university sectors were functionally differentiated from the university sector in one or both of two ways which could be depicted as horizontal and vertical differentiation. In the horizontal differentiation model, the non-university institutions offer programs of a vocational nature that are conceived as an alternative to the academic programs offered by universities. In the vertical differentiation model, the non-university institutions offer the lower level courses in the same fields that are offered by the universities, mainly arts and sciences, but possibly including some professional fields like teacher education. While some provinces opted to have both types of functional differentiation—though not necessarily within every college—the original design of the Ontario colleges included *only* horizontal differentiation from the universities. Over the years, many colleges have added small General Arts and Science (G.A.S.) programs in which they aim to offer the first year or two of courses in some of the arts and science subjects that the universities offer. However, enrolment in G.A.S. programs constitutes only about 2 percent of total enrolment in post-secondary programs in the colleges. Moreover, in most cases the major purpose of the G.A.S. programs is not university transfer, but to prepare students for entering one of the college's own career programs. Thus, the differentiation between the sectors is still almost exclusively of the horizontal type.

When the colleges were established, the government described their relationship to the universities as separate but equal. However, the colleges were clearly not equal because they were not empowered to award degrees. In some jurisdictions that have horizontal differentiation, the non-university institutions award baccalaureates, and even graduate degrees, for completion of the applied curricula; for example, this was the case with former polytechnics in the United Kingdom before they became universities. In Ontario, colleges were allowed to award only diplomas

---

[32] We are referring here to colleges offering baccalaureate programs on their own. In the next section we note that colleges also participate in collaborative programs with universities in which the degrees are awarded by the partner university.

or certificates until the year 2000, when they were given the authority to award a limited number of bachelor's degrees in applied areas of study.

Because the baccalaureate programs of the colleges are restricted in number and confined to specific areas, they offer only limited opportunities for students who start post-secondary education in a college to attain a bachelor's degree. Yet according to surveys of incoming students in some colleges, a substantial proportion of college students aspire to a degree. For example, at one college a majority of students in 43 of 67 programs surveyed in the late 1990s said that their goal was to obtain a degree, and in another college 40 percent of all incoming students reported in a 2004 survey that they wanted to obtain a degree. And yet, the proportion of college graduates who enrol in a university in the next year is only about 7 percent (Association of Colleges of Applied Arts and Technology, 2005, 6). This is a much lower rate of transfer from college to university than in Alberta, British Columbia, and many American states.

While many college leaders have tended to blame the low rate of transfer on elitist attitudes of Ontario universities, the major reasons would appear to be structural. In jurisdictions that have both vertical and horizontal differentiation, the bulk of transfer occurs from the college programs that are vertically differentiated from the universities, that is, in the arts and sciences. For example, in British Columbia it is estimated that the transfer rate is over 40 percent for arts and sciences but less than 10 percent for students in career programs (Association of Colleges of Applied Arts and Technology of Ontario, 2005, 17). The rate of transfer from career programs for Ontario is not far below that of other jurisdictions. In the ACAATO study of student mobility, rates for Washington, Alberta, Texas, and Oregon were 5, 6, 6, and 11 percent respectively, compared to 5.6 percent for Ontario. The *overall* transfer rate for Ontario was so much lower than for these other jurisdictions because such a tiny proportion of enrolment in Ontario colleges is in the arts and sciences. Moreover, because there is no provincial policy framework for vertical differentiation, the rate of transfer from G.A.S. programs in Ontario colleges is much lower than for their counterparts in other jurisdictions. However, because these programs make up such a small proportion of total college enrolment, boosting that transfer rate wouldn't have a major impact on the overall transfer rate.

There are two reasons why it has been difficult in all North American jurisdictions to develop effective arrangements for transfer to university from college career programs. One is that most of the courses in the college programs are of a highly specialized nature where there is no corresponding course in the university, so it is difficult to identify course equivalencies for credit. Second, because the college graduate has already taken courses of a highly specialized nature relating to the career field, the main thing that the university has to offer him or her are courses of a more general or foundational nature. However, the idea of proceeding

from specialized to more general courses goes against the prevailing curriculum philosophy of the contemporary university, which assumes just
the opposite type of progression.

In order to deal with these problems, a number of universities in the
United States have recently developed applied baccalaureate programs
whose purpose is to enable students who complete applied associate's
degrees in US community colleges to transfer to universities. A recent
study of this phenomenon defines an applied baccalaureate degree as
"a bachelor's degree designed to incorporate applied associate courses
and degrees once considered as "terminal" or non-baccalaureate level
while providing students with higher-order thinking skills and technical
knowledge and skills so desired in today's job market" (Bragg, Townsend,
and Rudd, 2008, 4). A survey conducted by Bragg, Townsend, and Rudd
showed that 125 "traditional baccalaureate granting" institutions in 39
states offer applied baccalaureate degrees that meet the definition cited
above.

The study identified three types of applied baccalaureate programs.
In the "career ladder" type of program, transferring students take a
substantial number of upper-level courses in the technical major of the
applied associate's degree. In the "upside-down" (Townsend, 2004), or
inverse, degree program, the occupation-focused courses taken in the
associate's degree are accepted by the university as satisfying much of
the specialization requirement for the major, and the emphasis in the
university portion is on general education courses sufficient to meet the
university's general education requirement. The resulting baccalaureate
is typically titled a Bachelor of General Studies, Bachelor of Professional
Studies, or Bachelor of Applied Studies. The "management ladder" type
of program is "designed to provide the degree recipient with the applied
management skills sufficient to prepare for a managerial position" (6).

Other than the universities that have developed these new types of
degree completion programs, technical universities have been the most
hospitable to transfer students from college career programs, because
there is a better fit between such universities and feeder colleges, both in
the nature of curriculum and in educational philosophy. Because Ontario
has lacked the kind of technical university that recognizes the value of
college career courses, many Ontario college graduates have transferred
to such universities in the United States, for example, Northwood University which has campuses in Michigan, Texas, and Florida.

Another type of university that has been particularly amenable to transfers from community colleges is an open university. As was noted earlier
in this chapter, one of the major roles played by Athabasca University
in Ontario is facilitation of degree completion for graduates of Ontario
colleges. A 2001 survey by the Ontario College University Consortium
Council (CUCC, 2002) showed that 19 colleges in Ontario had degree
completion agreements with Athabasca University. There were 190

separate agreements in total covering different subjects in different colleges. No other university in Ontario or elsewhere had degree completion agreements with as many Ontario colleges. Many graduates of diploma and certificate programs in Ontario's colleges continue on to complete a baccalaureate at Athabasca, without actually leaving their homes.

At present there are six major ways in which the colleges are differentiated from universities in Ontario: (1) the relationship between socioeconomic status and participation in post-secondary education; (2) the vocational or applied orientation of the college instructional programs; (3) the emphasis on teaching and learning, and the associated nurturing environment in the colleges; (4) the substantially greater institutional autonomy of the universities relative to the colleges; (5) the significant restrictions on degree granting in the colleges; and (6) the unique role of the universities in regard to basic research.

The participation rate for individuals from the lowest income categories in Canada is about 50 percent greater in colleges than in universities (Drolet, 2005, 30). Moreover, participation in university is highly correlated with parental income, while participation in college is not. Individuals in the highest income category were twice as likely to attend university as were people in the lowest income category. For colleges, the participation rate is almost the same in the highest income category as in the lowest. These data show that colleges play a crucial role in making opportunity for post-secondary education in Canada more equitable. They also suggest that the overall equity of the post-secondary system could be enhanced considerably by significantly improving the opportunities for students who begin their post-secondary education in a college to continue on to a university. In fact, the goal of social equity provides a strong rationale for enhancing opportunities for college to university transfer. Further, creating some types of post-secondary institutions that are particularly amenable to transfers from colleges, such as open and technical universities, could also make opportunity to obtain a baccalaureate more equitable.

While emphasis on applied learning has been one of the fundamental factors that has distinguished colleges from universities since the colleges were created, the extent and the appropriateness of this source of differentiation between the sectors has come under some questioning in recent years. For example, Fisher and Rubenson argued that a blurring of the boundary between universities and community colleges has occurred as Canadian universities have tended to increase the vocational orientation of their programs (1998, 94-95). They buttressed this assertion with some examples, including one of a wood processing program introduced at the University of British Columbia that appears similar in many ways to a program at Conestoga College in Ontario.

Of the new baccalaureate programs in Ontario universities that have been approved over the past six years, about 90 percent have titles that suggest a career orientation. However, this observation does not necessarily confirm the validity of the Fisher and Rubenson assertion. For one thing, preparing people for employment has always been a major function of the university. As historian of higher education, Harold Perkin, noted, what stimulated the growth of the earliest universities was the increasing demand "for trained elites to serve the bureaucracies of church and state and the emerging professions of clergy, law, and medicine" (1991, 171). Programs in the professions have long occupied an important place in the university, and getting a university to offer a program in an emerging or evolving field of practice has often been a significant milestone in gaining professional status for that field.

Something that may be giving the appearance of universities becoming more like colleges is the increasing number of new university programs whose titles pertain to a very specific area of employment. Some examples are: Bachelor of Engineering in Software Engineering and Game Design, Bachelor of Electronic Business Technologies, Bachelor of Applied Science in Business Informatics, and Bachelor of Recreation and Leisure Studies in Community Recreation. Not only do many of these program titles sound like those used in the college sector, but in some cases, there are programs in the colleges with the same or similar titles, for example, programs in recreation and leisure studies, photonics, viticulture, sports management, and informatics. However, the narrow focus suggested by the use of such titles for university programs can also be seen as a manifestation of the tendency toward increased specialization in university studies in areas that are not explicitly oriented toward the labour market, except perhaps for the academic labour market. This tendency is reflected in new degree titles such as a Bachelor of Arts in Social Justice, or a Master of Arts in Globalization Studies. Further, to determine whether new programs with titles that relate to particular areas of practice really do herald a blurring of the boundary between sectors, it would be necessary to compare the actual curricula of college and university programs that have similar sounding titles. In the few cases that we examined, the difference in the approach to the subject taken in the two sectors was noteworthy. The university curricula emphasized the philosophical and theoretical underpinnings, fundamental concepts, and research methodologies, while the college curricula emphasized application. In addition, there are important differences between the environment of a university and college campus, and in the nature and content of courses outside the main field of study.

Regardless of how much movement there has been in the university sector along the applied-theoretical continuum to date, there may be some indication that university bound students would like to see more of this movement. One such indicator is the extent of what has been called reverse transfer, the phenomenon of university graduates subsequently enrolling in a college to acquire a marketable skill for the work force. The number of Ontario students that move from university to college in recent years has been greater than the number that has gone from college to university. For example, it is estimated that about six thousand university graduates registered in colleges in 2004, while about four thousand of those who registered in universities had previously attended a college (Association of Colleges of Applied Arts and Technology of Ontario, 2005, iv).

Another indicator of the interest that university bound students have in obtaining job-ready skills is the popularity of programs offered jointly by universities and colleges. Entrants to such programs, which have increased in number in recent years, usually must meet normal university admission requirements. Besides meeting the university's degree requirements, students take additional courses at the partner college to earn a certificate or diploma in the related career field. The web site for one joint program (University of Toronto Scarborough, 2009) describes it as enabling the student to combine "the solid academic education [of the university] with the technical and practical skills" [of the college]. While such joint programs produce both personal and societal benefits, they have two limitations. First, while they make the expertise and resources of the college available to the university bound student, they do not make the expertise and resources of the university available to the college bound student. Second, it is often quite difficult for universities and colleges to develop and sustain the administrative arrangements that are necessary to make such inter-institutional initiatives successful. There is nothing wrong with encouraging individual colleges and universities to enter into partnerships for specific programs; however, this should not be seen as a substitute for developing systemic arrangements for the more effective use of the combined resources of the two post-secondary sectors. This is especially needed in regard to opportunity for students who complete occupational programs in the colleges to transfer to a related baccalaureate program in a university.

In theory, there are three ways in which the content of these joint programs could be provided: all of it by a university itself; all by a college itself; or, as it is provided presently, with each partner institution contributing a portion. The rationale for universities to provide such programs wholly on their own is that an increasing proportion of those who seek the baccalaureate, particularly males, may prefer this type of education which blends academic and applied knowledge. In a presentation to the Canadian Association of University Business Officers, Clive Keen, former director of enrolment management at the University of Prince Edward Island, argued that offering programs that prepare graduates for specific jobs would help both to attract more male students and contribute to the Canadian economy (Tam, 2007). Some of the fields in which Keen suggested universities should develop programs are computer games and animation, sports marketing, adventure recreation, disaster management, fire safety, exercise and nutrition, and renewable energy. Although he did not say so, presumably in order to make his proposal viable, the curriculum and teaching in the new programs would need to be more like that of the colleges.

The main argument against universities making a substantial move in the direction suggested by Keen is that doing so would divert them from their primary mission and duplicate expertise that presently exists in the colleges. The same article that related Keen's suggestion to the universities also cited criticism of this idea by Côté, a professor of sociology at the University of Western Ontario and co-author of *Ivory Tower Blues* (Côté and Allahar, 2007). Côté argued that universities should leave applied learning to the colleges rather than introduce new programs in order to attract students who would not otherwise attend university. Côté's advice is in the tradition of Flexner who argued that just because an educational activity was worth doing, it did not follow that the university should be the institution to do it. Flexner maintained that universities should concentrate on doing "supremely well what they almost alone can do" (1930, 27).

Colleges have developed applied bachelor's programs in several of the program areas mentioned by Keen in hopes of addressing the interest that students have in preparing for careers in these fields at the baccalaureate level. It is, however, still too soon to tell how well baccalaureate programs delivered wholly by colleges will satisfy this demand. Insofar as many students might prefer both the exposure to a university campus and having the name of a university on their degree, it may be worthwhile for universities and colleges to make greater attempts to overcome the obstacles that stand in the way of inter-institutional initiatives like the joint programs that have been described here.

We conclude this subsection by commenting briefly on the other characteristics that presently differentiate colleges from universities.

While some universities have been giving more attention to teaching and learning in recent years, the emphasis placed on helping students succeed in the community college sector is still unmatched in most if not all universities, except perhaps in their medical schools. Indeed, it is the special expertise and commitment of community college faculty to help large numbers of underprepared and academically at-risk students, many of whom are from lower income groups, that more than any other factor distinguishes community college teachers from their university counterparts (London, 1980, 66). The success that many college students have been able to achieve in the nurturing environment of the college has provided one of the chief rationales for authorizing colleges to offer full bachelor's programs rather than forcing students to transfer to the less nurturing environment of the typical university (Townsend, 2007).

Although the authority to award degrees is no longer a distinguishing characteristic between the sectors, the conditions under which colleges award degrees are vastly different than those for the universities.

Colleges may offer only applied baccalaureates, and there are limits on the number that they may offer. Moreover, unlike for universities, each degree program of a college must have explicit consent from the Minister of Training, Colleges and Universities following an assessment by the Post-secondary Education Quality Assessment Board. The control that the ministry exercises over college degree programs is but one aspect of much greater external control to which the colleges are subject compared to the universities. In the college sector the argument for institutional autonomy, to the extent that it is granted, is based on practical considerations; in the university sector it is based upon principle.

Finally, pure research is a core function of the universities and curiosity-driven research a right of every faculty member. Only recently has applied research been recognized as a legitimate function of the colleges. However, college faculty do not have a right to participate in applied research, and there are only very limited support mechanisms for them to engage in it, even though a similar argument can be made in the colleges to that promoted in the universities for the value of faculty involvement in research to student learning (Skolnik, 2008).

The revolution in the organization of nursing education: An example of college/university cooperation

The field of study in which there have been the most substantial developments in the relationship between universities and colleges in baccalaureate programs in Ontario is nursing. These developments illustrate the difficulties in trying to balance the roles of the two types of post-secondary institutions in the provision of baccalaureate education, and for that reason this experience is worth examining.

When the legislation for the CAATs was introduced in 1965, someone who aspired to become a nurse could enrol at one of six universities or at one of 59 hospital schools of nursing. The university programs accounted for less than 5 percent of total enrolment and less than 2 percent of graduates. In his remarks that introduced the legislation, the Minister of Education had not mentioned nursing or the health sector in the list of fields where it was envisaged that the colleges would offer programs (Davis, 1966). Nevertheless, in September, 1973, after the colleges had been operating for just six years, the 56 hospital schools of nursing that existed at the time were placed under their jurisdiction through a joint decision of the Minister of Health and the Minister of Colleges and Universities. The transfer of the hospital schools of nursing reflected a view within the nursing profession that it was time for the service-oriented model of nursing education to give way to a more education-centered approach. Also, some hospitals were finding these programs too expensive to run, and hospital insurance commissions across Canada were questioning why hospitals should be in the business of education.

For nearly the next three decades, registered nurses in Ontario were trained either in universities or in colleges, with the latter accounting for 80 percent of new entrants to the profession. Graduates of the baccalaureate programs in universities and of the diploma programs in colleges wrote the same qualifying exam for registration and received the same professional credential. The rationale for this unusual situation of parallel provision of professional education by two different types of post-secondary institutions had been provided in a report prepared by Mussallem for the 1965 Royal Commission on Health Services in Canada, chaired by Mr. Justice Emmett Hall, which, of course, had other significant impacts on the delivery of health care in Canada (Mussallem, 1965). In his history of the founding and early years of the CAATs, Fleming attributed the transfer of the hospital schools of nursing to the Hall Royal Commission, and more specifically to the study that Mussallem did for the Commission (Fleming, 1971).

Mussallem maintained that there should be two categories of registered nurse which she termed "professional" and "technical." The technical nurse, who would be trained in a college, would be able to perform all the basic, every day, essential functions of nursing. The other type of nurse would receive training in a university, and that would provide better preparation for assuming a position of leadership, or going into education or research. In Mussallem's view, only a university training would produce nurses with a sound understanding of scientific principles and the capacity to make complex judgments, but, she argued, these were not qualities that were required in the majority of nurses. The idea of formally designating two different types of nurse aroused considerable negative reaction and caused division within the nursing profession.

While Mussallem's vision of two different types of nurses provided one rationale for the parallel structures of nursing education that existed through almost the whole 20th century, it was not the only rationale. Some within the profession were concerned that if nursing education were provided exclusively by universities, there might be an insufficient supply of nurses, and the connection between education and practice might be weakened (Committee on the Healing Arts, 1970). In regard to the latter issue, Greenslade found concern among faculty members of university schools of nursing in Ontario about the limited involvement of nursing teachers in professional practice which they attributed to the university value and reward structure (2003).

Not long after the hospital nursing programs were transferred to the colleges, several organizations that represented nurses in Canada, including the Registered Nurses Association of Ontario (RNAO) in 1980, and the Canadian Nurses' Association (CNA) in 1982, began to advocate that the baccalaureate in nursing should be required for entry to practice (Wood, 2003). In their resolutions, these organizations argued that the *baccalaureate* should be an entry requirement, not necessarily that all new nurses should receive their preparation in a *university*, or at least all of their preparation in a university. For example, a task force on nursing education in Alberta recommended that "by 1990 the minimum educational preparation for professional nursing be the baccalaureate, whatever route to the degree is chosen" (Alberta Department of Advanced Education and Manpower, 1975, 114). An article in the CNA's journal following its resolution also made reference to the need for articulation of diploma with degree programs as a route to the baccalaureate (Kerr, 1982). The Task Force that the RNAO established to develop strategies to achieve its "baccalaureate for entry" goal identified collaborative programs between colleges and universities as one of the ways of achieving the goal (Registered Nurses Association of Ontario, 1986).

After a plethora of committees and task forces within the profession had pressed their case for nearly two decades, in March, 1999, the Ontario Minister of Health and Long-Term Care announced that a four-year baccalaureate in nursing would be mandatory for nursing graduates seeking professional registration as of 1 January 2005. This requirement was enacted through changes to the nursing registration regulations under the Nursing Act on 24 March 2000. The government also made clear that the approach that it preferred for making the baccalaureate the required credential was the development of collaborative programs between universities and colleges. To that end, in April 2000, the Ministry of Training, Colleges and Universities announced funding arrangements that were intended to encourage the development of collaborative programs and guidelines for these programs. In collaborative programs, part of the curriculum is delivered by a university and part by a partner college.

Prior to the April 2000 announcements, there had been a few attempts by colleges and universities to develop collaborative arrangements in nursing, but only one collaborative program, involving one university and three colleges, had actually been implemented. In the aftermath of these announcements, negotiations were initiated (or resumed) between almost all colleges and universities that had nursing programs. Issues of contention in these negotiations were the sharing of revenue and costs, admission requirements, faculty qualifications, and program governance. In most cases these issues were resolved, and by 2005, when the new requirement for nursing registration took effect, 22 colleges were participating with 12 universities in collaborative baccalaureate nursing programs. Only two universities that offered nursing were not involved in a collaborative program with a college; and only one college involved in nursing was not in collaboration with an Ontario university—its collaboration was with a university in another province. Considering that as recently as five years earlier, only one university and three colleges were involved in a collaborative nursing program, and that by 2005 the collaborative program had become the predominant model, it seems that a revolution had occurred in the way that basic nursing education was provided.

To some extent, however, accessibility was a casualty of this revolution. For years the colleges had sought—generally without success—agreements with the universities that would enable a graduate of a three-year college diploma program to obtain a baccalaureate in one additional year of study at a university. Now students can obtain a four-year baccalaureate in four years through a combination of courses taken at a college and a university—but the opportunity to obtain the degree is limited to those who meet university admission requirements from day one. In settling for collaborative programs instead of getting better transfer agreements, colleges have had to exchange their previous more flexible and less stringent admissions requirements for university admission requirements.

Revolutions are sometimes followed by counter-revolutions. One university has withdrawn from its partnership with a near-by college, leaving that college to partner with a university from another part of the province. While some other universities might prefer to offer nursing on their own, a more serious threat to the collaborative model may be the desire of some colleges to offer an applied baccalaureate in nursing on their own. Presently, the regulations in Ontario do not permit an individual whose baccalaureate in nursing is from a college to obtain registration, and thus there would be no point in a college seeking to offer a baccalaureate in nursing. However, there have been calls for a change in these regulations so that colleges could offer a baccalaureate in nursing under the Act that allows them to offer baccalaureates in applied fields of study (Chapman and Kirby, 2008). In British Columbia, the regulations allow colleges to offer applied baccalaureates in nursing, and some colleges there do so, having withdrawn from collaborative programs with universities.[33]

Although issues of money, control, and status are no doubt involved in the desire of some colleges to offer their own baccalaureate programs, this desire is rooted also in a difference over educational philosophy. The college approach to nursing education, like its approach to education in other fields, involves a reciprocal and interactive, rather than linear, relationship between theory and practice, and puts more emphasis on application than the university approach (Paquet, 2006). Recognition of the value of this approach to nursing education has been one of the factors contributing to the decisions of some American states to allow community colleges to award baccalaureates in nursing. In fact, nursing

---

[33] The Ontario regulation was drafted by the College of Nurses of Ontario and approved by Cabinet. It is unusual for Cabinet not to accept the advice of a designated regulatory body for a self-regulating profession. Thus, a change in this regulation is not likely unless the College of Nurses can be persuaded to change its position on the acceptability of a college baccalaureate for entry to practice.

is among the most common fields, along with teacher education, in which community colleges in the United States offer baccalaureates (Floyd, Skolnik, and Walker, 2005).

Chapman and Kirby maintained that allowing the colleges to award applied baccalaureates in nursing would challenge the status of nursing as an academic discipline (Chapman and Kirby, 2008). Even if that happened, there are other issues at stake in the organization of nursing education. Applied baccalaureate programs offered by the colleges would add a valuable element of diversity to the system of nursing education. For some of the same reasons that this book questions the prudence of locating all undergraduate education in research universities, we question the wisdom of leaving the provision of baccalaureates in nursing exclusively to the same group of universities. Permitting the colleges to award applied baccalaureates in nursing may bring benefits to nursing education in terms of accessibility and costs. Nurses who have been trained in institutions that have a different approach to the relationship between theory and practice than do universities might be welcomed by employers and make a valuable contribution to the health care system, complementing the contribution made by graduates of the university programs. Also, allowing the colleges the opportunity to award applied baccalaureates in nursing would place them on more equal footing in negotiating collaborative program arrangements with the universities.

Collaboration between universities and colleges in the baccalaureate made sense when colleges offered diploma programs, but, ironically, only one such case of collaboration existed before the diploma in nursing was abolished. The chief rationale for collaboration now inheres in the resources and expertise that the colleges developed when they were in the business of offering diploma programs. Since only the universities have the statutory authority to award degrees, in collaborative programs the universities are essentially sub-contracting some of the teaching and supervision to the colleges. Without having their own programs for educating nurses, the nursing education resources that the colleges possess now could best be described as vestigial. It may be difficult for the colleges to sustain and replenish resources and expertise now that they are no longer required for the colleges' own diploma programs. It is difficult to sustain over the long run an academic unit whose reason for being is to service the program of another institution. Once the decision was made to require the baccalaureate for entry, the main reason for choosing the collaborative route rather than concentrating all baccalaureate programs in universities was to avoid the transition costs and disruption that would result from transferring everything to the universities. As retirements in the colleges occur, and the academic credentials of those who remain in the colleges increase, the transition costs are likely to diminish to the point where ultimately baccalaureate programs will be concentrated in the universities—unless there is a change in the regulations that makes it possible for the colleges to offer applied baccalaureates in nursing on their own.

Finally, the question arises of whether the experience in nursing education holds any lessons for college-university collaboration in other areas. The circumstances in which the revolution in nursing education occurred are unique in some respects. Professional organization is highly developed within the nursing field, and nursing organizations have been working diligently for many years to make the baccalaureate a requirement. Nursing educators from the two sectors have developed strong relationships with each other through the various educational and professional organizations of which they are members. In few, if any, other occupational fields in which the colleges offer programs, is the level of commitment to the baccalaureate as strong, or the infrastructure of professional organization as well developed, as it is for nursing.

If there is a lesson for other fields in the nursing experience, it is that government intervention is probably necessary for significant change in the role of colleges in baccalaureate education. However, the nursing case also raises a caution for other fields. Achieving full credit from the universities toward a baccalaureate for studies done in a college came at the expense of accessibility, since some individuals who met the admission requirements of the former diploma programs would not be admissible to the new collaborative baccalaureate programs. Were this to happen in a broad range of other college programs, it would fundamentally alter the social role of the community college. To reiterate a point made earlier, as valuable as collaborative programs may be in certain circumstances, they are no substitute for systemic improvements in transfer opportunities for students who start post-secondary education in a college.

PROVINCIAL PLANNING AND COORDINATION OF POST-SECONDARY EDUCATION

Most, if not all, jurisdictions the size of Ontario have agencies responsible for overseeing the development of their post-secondary education system, fostering effective use of resources on a jurisdiction-wide basis, and protecting post-secondary education from political interference. In the United States, where every state has at least one, such agencies fall into three categories: state-wide governing boards with responsibility for managing public institutions, state-wide coordinating boards with oversight over the public institutions, and state planning boards. Some of these boards have jurisdiction over the whole post-secondary system; in other cases different boards have jurisdiction over different segments of the system such as colleges and universities.

One area where the action of a higher education oversight body, or of government itself, is indispensable is in promoting institutional differentiation. As a recent study has concluded, "The lesson from these international experiences is straightforward: in a homogeneous environment the natural tendencies for institutional convergence will prevail in a higher education system unless clear and overt policy intervention is enacted to prevent it" (Codling and Meek, 2006; a similar conclusion was reported earlier by Rhoades, 1990).

Provincial agencies of the type just described have not existed as consistently or continuously in Canada as they have in the United States, and the Canadian ones have generally been relatively weak (Skolnik and Jones, 1992). Presently no such agency exists in Ontario. The Ontario Council on University Affairs, which played a limited advisory and coordination role for about three decades, was abolished in 1996. The Ontario Council of Regents started out performing some planning, management, and coordination functions when it was established with the colleges in the 1960s, but its role became more circumscribed until it was replaced in 2002 with the College Compensation and Appointments Council, the mandate of which is limited to what its name suggests.

From the 1960s into the early 1980s, several commissions examining the operation of the post-secondary system concluded that there was a need for a provincial agency with some authority for planning and coordination of the university if not of the entire post-secondary system.[34] Since the mid 1980s, commissions have tended to recommend that institutional differentiation be achieved by less directive means.

In the absence of a provincial agency for post-secondary education, at least some of the functions that those agencies perform could instead be performed in one or more of three other ways. First, the provincial government could perform some of these functions itself. However, most members of the post-secondary community feel that it is inappropriate for government to get too involved in the affairs of universities and colleges. One area, though, where it does seem appropriate, if not essential, for government to be involved is that of planning, particularly in regard to the evolving structure of the post-secondary system. Governments in Alberta and British Columbia have been active in this respect consistently since the 1960s, modifying and reshaping the design of their post-secondary systems in relation to changes in provincial needs and circumstances. Examples of recent changes in system design implemented recently were

---

[34] Royce (1998) provided an exhaustive review of reports recommending the creation of an agency for system planning and coordination. Probably the most thorough analysis of this issue was a 1970 study that was commissioned jointly by the associations of Canadian universities, university professors, and university students (Hurtubise and Rowat, 1970). This study recommended that provinces with three or more university campuses establish "a coordinating and planning commission with a statutory base, a semi-autonomous status and substantial powers" (111).

given earlier. In contrast, successive Ontario governments, whatever their political party, have largely ignored system planning since the system took its present shape in the 1960s.

The second possible way of accomplishing some functions of system governance is through voluntary cooperation of the institutions. Through the Council of Ontario Universities, the universities have successfully coordinated their activities in several areas (Clark, 2002a; Clark 2002b; Monahan, 2004). However, because of potential conflicts of institutional self-interests, there are significant limits to what can be achieved through voluntary cooperation, particularly in regard to some of the big issues like allocation of programs and resources. For example, after an attempt at system planning for graduate studies collapsed in 1981, Monahan noted that "COU effectively removed itself from any leadership role in system program planning, creating a vacuum that thereafter was never adequately filled" (117).

The third alternative is to rely on the actions of the individual institutions as they react to market forces. It is possible that a higher education system might be more responsive to changing needs if the responses of individual institutions do not have to be mediated through a provincial ministry or intermediary body. Besides constituting an additional layer of decision making, provincial agencies may lack the will or the vision for change. Indeed, Steven Parker, Senior Deputy Vice-Chancellor of Monash University, has suggested that reliance on market forces may be partly a substitute for "policy vision and imagination" (2005, 26).

In order for market forces to be effective in bringing about change in post-secondary education, the system must be relatively free of constraints on the ability of institutions to respond to new opportunities and pressures. Two areas where there are significant constraints on institutional behaviour in Ontario are finances, including the setting of tuition fees, and approval for offering degree programs. A characteristic of competitive industries is the opportunity for new firms to enter the market if the needs of consumers are not being met fully or effectively. This characteristic is largely absent from the Ontario university sector because of very stringent control over new entry into the realm of degree granting activity.[35]

In competitive markets, price plays an important role in signalling changes in supply and demand and in the allocation of resources. Because of stringent government control over tuition fees in most areas of post-secondary education in Ontario, the price mechanism cannot play

---

[35] Although there are provisions for approving degree programs of other institutions under the *Post-secondary Education Choice and Excellence Act*, a number of institutions that have tried to use those provisions have complained about their applications being treated arbitrarily, a claim that a former head of the agency that oversees the process has at least partially agreed with (Lewis, 2007).

the role there that it does in other markets. Interestingly though, in some of the program areas where tuition fees are not controlled there has been noteworthy innovation and differentiation in addressing student demand, for example in Executive MBA programs. In contrast, within the university funding system, universities cannot reap similar financial benefits from offering more innovative approaches to serving the demand for transfer from the colleges. This is not to suggest that universities are responsive to new types of student demand only when they can charge relatively high fees, but additional revenue is very helpful when it comes to developing new programs. Nor do we suggest that the barriers to transfer are primarily financial. Earlier in the chapter we described the cultural and curriculum factors that make many universities, not only those in Ontario, reluctant to go further in accommodating transfer students from the colleges. Still, it must be pointed out that there are some costs and limited, if any, financial benefits for Ontario universities in accepting larger numbers of transfer students from the colleges.

There are pros and cons of either relying more on provincial planning and coordination or more on market forces in order to foster the responsiveness of the post-secondary education system to changing conditions. For example, some have argued that a market-driven system will produce private benefits more than it will serve the public good (Kezar, Chambers, and Burkhardt, 2005; Newman, Couturier, and Scurry, 2004; Texeira et al., 2004). While there are arguments for relying more on one or the other of these approaches, there is no compelling argument for rejecting both approaches. A post-secondary system that has neither a mechanism for jurisdiction-wide planning and coordination nor provision for effective use of market forces could be described as drifting (Skolnik, 1996).

In 2005, the Ontario Government took a step that might better enable it, if it were so inclined, to provide more direction for the post-secondary system, with the creation of the Higher Education Quality Council of Ontario. The council is an arms-length agency of the Government of Ontario whose mandate is to conduct research and provide advice on all aspects of higher education, including "the development and design of various models of post-secondary education" (*The Higher Education Quality Council of Ontario Act, 2005*) The council has neither the executive authority nor the specificity of responsibility for system coordination and direction that is characteristic of the agencies described at the beginning of this section. Thus it remains to be seen to what extent, if any, the council will be invited to fill the vacuum that Monahan referred to in regard to system planning.

Issues in the Present Design that Warrant Consideration

Emerging from the discussion in this chapter, there are six issues pertaining to the design of Ontario's post-secondary education system that warrant consideration in light of the developments and expectations for post-secondary education that were discussed in earlier chapters. These issues are outlined briefly below.

An expensive model for undergraduate education

As a consequence of a design decision made in the 1960s that baccalaureate credit education would be provided exclusively by institutions that were authorized to offer programs at all degree levels and have a substantial role in research, Ontario uses the highest cost institutional model, that of the research university, for educating almost all undergraduate students. While many students who have been fortunate enough to experience this uniquely Ontario approach to the organization of baccalaureate level education have benefited from it, the approach has become increasingly difficult to sustain financially. Besides the perennial complaints of Ontario universities about inadequate funding, the best evidence that this approach to baccalaureate education is not sustainable is the increasing proportion of courses in universities that are taught by part-time and contract instructors who have no time for, or involvement in, research. When the system was designed in the 1960s, perhaps it was not anticipated how such factors as the expansion of knowledge, advances in technology, and unionization of faculty would drive up the costs of the research university. Other than enabling the colleges to offer some baccalaureate programs, provincial governments have done nothing to find other ways of serving some of the demand for undergraduate enrolment that might be less costly than the research university.

Quality may depend upon diversity in the provision of undergraduate education

The exclusive reliance on the research university model for the provision of baccalaureate programs has other consequences besides expense. It means that there is less diversity in the types of environments available to undergraduate students than in many other jurisdictions. It may well be that some undergraduate students thrive in the environment of a research university. However, it is equally likely that there are others who do not do their best in this environment. In the previous chapter we noted that the Canadian institutions that have scored highest on key NSSE benchmarks are the smaller, less research-intensive ones. Although more research is needed on this data source, we can say that a system characterized by more institutional differentiation would provide greater possibilities for optimal matching of individual learning needs with institutional characteristics.

As universities become increasingly involved in graduate studies and focus more on their knowledge creation role, there is a concern that the quality of undergraduate education may suffer, at least for some students.

The relationship between graduate studies and research on the one hand, and the attention to and quality of undergraduate education on the other, is a controversial subject about which there are no definitive conclusions. While the increased emphasis on knowledge creation and commercialization of research in recent years may have resulted in increased opportunities for some undergraduate students, it may also have resulted in less attention being given to others. As we suggested in Chapter 5, intensifying research does not enhance undergraduate teaching unless specific measures are taken to connect the two, which is seldom the case.

Increasing accessibility may depend upon diversity in the provision of undergraduate education

As noted earlier, further increases in accessibility necessitate reaching higher proportions of groups that historically have been underrepresented in universities. There is reason to doubt whether the increasingly research intensive orientation of the university will foster the kind of environment that would be most comfortable or most conducive to learning for many of the new students who are interested in pursuing a bachelor's degree. Students with weak academic backgrounds are likely to prefer a more nurturing, student-centered institutional culture to that of the research university (Walker, 2005).

Absence of pathways for human resource development

As a consequence of designing a post-secondary system that consists of two independent and unconnected silos, the pathways for the optimum development of human resources and the realization of aspirations of learners in Ontario have been inappropriately limited. To some extent, individuals have been able to overcome rigidities in the post-secondary system through their own ingenuity and effort, aided by the determination of isolated educators in both sectors. The absence of effective pathways for human resource development may have serious adverse economic consequences for Ontario in the present era of globalization and the knowledge society.

Dispersal of resources for advanced study and research

It is questionable whether the Ontario university sector is ideally structured to meet the challenges of knowledge production in an increasingly competitive global environment. Some jurisdictions rely considerably on research institutes or academies that are independent of universities for much of their advanced research. Others have designated one of their public universities as the flagship institution of the system, with greater funding as well as privileges and obligations than the rest of the institutions. Some deliberately concentrate graduate studies in particular institutions, sometimes with an associated centre for advanced studies. As we noted earlier in this chapter, the idea of greater concentration of resources for graduate studies and resource-intensive research is getting attention in some European countries. Expression of concern about the dispersal of resources for graduate studies and research in Canada and Ontario pre-dates the present era of globalization and the knowledge society (Leslie, 1980). Having some institutions concentrate more on baccalaureate studies and others concentrate more on graduate studies and research could be a way of enhancing both the learning experience for undergraduates and the contribution of Ontario post-secondary education to knowledge production.

Institutional differentiation in the college sector

As noted earlier, the first mandated institutional differentiation in Ontario's college sector was not attempted until 2002, and was limited to one possible area of college activity, baccalaureate programming. Some other jurisdictions introduced institutional differentiation into their non-university sectors early in the development of those sectors and have moved further in that direction in recent years. These jurisdictions believe that the concentration and specialization that comes with institutional differentiation makes their post-secondary systems more effective. There has been almost no study of whether the effectiveness of Ontario's college sector, or of its post-secondary system as a whole, could be increased by institutional differentiation. Nor has there been any study identifying the extent to which various colleges have attained strengths in particular areas that could provide a foundation for policies aimed at achieving the benefits of formal institutional differentiation.

Summary

In this chapter, we have attempted to explain what is involved in the design of post-secondary systems and how modifications in design can enable them to meet societal needs more effectively. The design modifications seeming to hold particular promise are those that would achieve greater institutional differentiation. In the last part of this chapter we have identified some specific types of institutional differentiation that could foster improvements with respect to accessibility, efficiency, and quality. The six system design issues that were identified here will be discussed further in the final chapter, along with other issues that were identified in earlier chapters.

7

CONCLUSIONS AND IMPLICATIONS FOR THE FUTURE

In the previous chapters we described a number of challenges currently facing Ontario's post-secondary education system that will increasingly need to be addressed in the future. We also described a number of constraints and inhibiting factors that may limit the system's ability to address these challenges effectively. Foremost among these inhibiting factors is Ontario's lack of a tradition of, or a mechanism for, systematic monitoring of the performance of the post-secondary system and an associated policy framework for analyzing how the post-secondary education system can most effectively contribute to the achievement of important societal goals.

Elements of such a mechanism and framework have appeared on the scene from time to time in the form of ad hoc commissions and task forces, and occasional bursts of activity in various provincial agencies. Each such initiative has proved to be short lived and had little if any impact. An apparent exception to this generalization is that of the institutional performance indicators that colleges and universities have been required to publish for more than a decade. However, as noted in Chapter 5, these indicators are not connected to a coherent vision for post-secondary education, its role in society, and provincial goals for this enterprise. In fact, not only do these indicators fail to reflect adequately two of the most cherished values in Ontario related to post-secondary education—accessibility and equity—but, other things being equal, these indicators may be biased against them.

Academic Transformation: The Forces Reshaping Higher Education in Ontario, I.D. Clark, G. Moran, M.L. Skolnik, and D. Trick. Montreal and Kingston: McGill-Queen's University Press, Queen's Policy Studies Series.

AUTONOMY AND EFFICIENCY CONSIDERATIONS IN SYSTEM
REFORM

Like others who have conducted an examination of current and emerging
issues in post-secondary education, we are eager to share the implications
for change that arise from our analysis which is placed within the context of the evolution of Ontario's post-secondary education system over
the past half century. During this period the post-secondary education
system has experienced enormous growth while the social and economic
environment within which it operates has changed markedly. Against
the backdrop of these changes in scale and environment, there has been
remarkably little change in the basic features of the post-secondary system
itself. As described in earlier chapters, the design of the post-secondary
system is virtually unchanged since the 1960s. Similarly, there has been
little change in the conception of what constitutes quality education or
in the ideal profile of faculty work.

Individual freedom and institutional autonomy

Institutional freedom and institutional autonomy are important norms
in higher education. Post-secondary education policy operates through
the choices made by individuals and institutions, and rests upon certain
assumptions and values concerning those choices. One of the cornerstone
values is that individuals should have maximum possible choice concerning post-secondary education. The notion of maximizing personal choice
has both an ethical and an instrumental element; such choice is a good
thing in and of itself, and it is believed that innovation and productivity
in society are enhanced when opportunities are increased for individuals
to exercise personal initiative and invest in their own futures. This applies
both to students and to faculty, and is the basis of the concept of academic
freedom, which by extension applies to institutions, where it becomes the
basis for the concept of institutional autonomy.

However, the freedom of one individual or group to make their own
choices pertaining to post-secondary education must take account of the
freedom of other individuals and groups to make their choices. In higher
education, a major issue is how to reconcile the needs and desires for autonomy of different participants. Unlimited freedom for professors would
limit the freedom of students, and vice-versa. Similarly, the autonomy
of one group of faculty (such as full-time faculty) may limit that of other
groups of faculty (such as part-time faculty), and the autonomy of one
post-secondary sector may limit that of another. Individual freedom and
institutional autonomy must also be balanced with other ethical norms
such as quality and reputation. This is seen in the regulation of degree
granting. Individuals and groups in Ontario have considerable freedom
to engage in educational activities except for those activities that lead to

the awarding of a degree. Offering courses that lead to a degree without approval from the government contravenes the statute that pertains to degree granting in Ontario. The restriction of non-approved provision of degree related education can be justified on the basis of the protection it affords for students who invest their time and money in obtaining a degree. Control of degree granting also deals with the externalities that may result from such activity, particularly the concern that this could result in the devaluation of degrees awarded by those institutions deemed to have appropriate status for awarding degrees. With the privilege of granting degrees comes the obligation to exercise this power in the public interest, which includes making the opportunity for individuals to obtain a degree appropriately accessible.

Efficiency and innovation

The second key value in system reform is efficiency—getting the most individual and societal benefit for the dollars expended. Efficient systems capture economies of scale and specialization, avoid duplication, take account of user demands, minimize the cost of inputs, control overheads, price outputs appropriately, and respond innovatively to changes in technology and the business environment.

Impressive efforts have been made over the years to capture economies of scale in the Ontario university and college sectors, and to reduce overlap and duplication. Although it has been suggested from time to time that amalgamation of institutions could reduce costs, given that most Ontario institutions are larger than what is considered the minimum size for efficient operation at an institutional level, and that some may be beyond the size where diseconomies of scale are encountered, there may be relatively little scope for savings here.[36] On the other hand, in

---

[36] Measuring the relationship between institutional size and efficiency is fraught with methodological difficulties in large part owing to the problems of measuring efficiency. Lewis and Dunbar have noted that a particular problem in these studies arises from the inability to control for quality of students as enrolment increases (1998). Schumacher (1983) concluded that the optimum size of a university is between 1,500 and 4,000 students. In a review of studies of economies of scale in higher education, Patterson concluded that supporters and advocates of institutional "mergers and other growth strategies do tend to overestimate and emphasize the benefits and underplay the cost" (2000, 267-268). Her findings called into question the beliefs "that small institutions are inefficient, that large institutions are the most efficient, and that institutions should have a broad array of educational offerings" (268). Citing Odum (1992), Patterson suggested that some notions of complexity theory may apply in higher education, for example that as systems become larger and more complex more of their available energy is required simply for maintenance.

spite of impressive efforts at voluntary coordination among institutions within (but not as much between) sectors, patterns of resource allocation and program rationalization may not be as efficient in Ontario as in other jurisdictions that have consolidated governing boards for some sectors or groupings of institutions. For example, in several large metropolitan areas in the United States, colleges are under a single governing board, and in about half the states, the public universities are under a single governing board. The latter approach has been recommended for Ontario in some reports, for example, by the Spinks Commission (1966). Of course, the extent to which efficiencies would result from such arrangements would depend upon the policies that such agencies pursued. But the fact is that deference to institutional autonomy has been so strong in Ontario that options for more effective system or sectoral coordination have never been given serious consideration.

One of the major questions is whether the system adequately encourages specialization. This was examined in Chapter 6 where it was noted that in comparison with other jurisdictions, one of the striking characteristics of the Ontario system is the absence of almost any form of institutional specialization. At this stage in their development, the ethos of existing institutions may work so strongly against specialization that it could be argued that little can be done to move any of them toward specialization. While we do not completely accept this proposition, we do suggest that the easiest way to generate system specialization would be to create new institutions. Given the lessons of the past, if attempts are made to create specialized institutions in the future, measures should be taken to ensure that specialization is not regarded as a temporary stage on the road to eventually becoming comprehensive institutions like the others.

On the input side, institutions are constrained from optimizing their compensation costs by collective agreements that militate against responding to discipline-specific labour market conditions. Consequently, universities and colleges are paying some faculty more than would be required if collective agreements considered differences in labour market demand for individual disciplines, while having difficulty attracting others whose services are in great demand. The mismatch between institutional salary structures and local labour market and cost of living conditions is particularly pronounced in the colleges due to province-wide bargaining in that sector. Their bargaining structure also tends to reduce the quality of management-faculty relations at all colleges to the lowest common denominator.

When analyzing how to improve efficiency by reducing overheads it is necessary to first consider what constitutes overhead in a modern post-secondary institution, since many functions outside the core operations of teaching and research have been expanding. To what extent is student counseling a core requirement for successful teaching? To what extent should legislatively mandated activities such as those conducted in equity offices and privacy offices be considered overhead? What about marketing, alumni affairs, and government relations?

It is in the area of market pricing that perhaps the most notable efficiency shortcomings can be seen. On the output side, institutions are prevented by government regulation from charging tuition closer to what the market would determine. The rationale for tuition regulation has been debated extensively within the university community and with the government.

Ontario's system has had a mixed record on innovation, particularly where it comes to new institutional forms and new teaching techniques. Although institutions have been very creative in responding to the financial incentives provided by government and in the process have been successful in the first order objective of accommodating the dramatic increase in enrolments, the system as a whole has not provided as much diversity in post-secondary services as can be found in many other jurisdictions. And there has not been a consistent effort to apply the lessons from pedagogical research in the classroom. Also, as noted in Chapter 5, rigid adherence to traditional conceptions of academic quality has militated against innovation. As will be discussed below, government policy could be designed to encourage more diversity of post-secondary offerings. It is less clear what government can productively do to encourage institutions to more rapidly adopt proven technologies and pedagogical theories.

Financial incentives and system reform

There is scope for adding financial incentives (which could, in principle, be negative as well as positive) to support system objectives. For example, college-university transfer is a longstanding stated government priority but the funding system has not been adjusted to give universities an incentive to take on the additional costs that this might require. It may be difficult to make a modification in the system funding formula that would achieve this objective without having adverse side effects, but we will not know if that is the case until a major effort is made to revise the funding formula. It is difficult to see how significant progress on transfer can be made relying solely upon bilateral negotiations. As discussed below, if the government wishes to encourage greater differentiation of institutions, there will have to be both regulatory measures and financial incentives to overcome the tendency to mission uniformity. Another example is the unwillingness of government to recognize the extra costs required to serve underprepared students; this funding stance is clearly inconsistent with its stated accessibility objectives.

CHARACTERISTICS OF AN IDEAL POST-SECONDARY SYSTEM FOR ONTARIO

What additional characteristics, besides the academic and research strengths of existing institutions, would make for an ideal system of post-secondary education in Ontario? In our view the system of colleges and universities would look rather different in several important ways from how it looks now. Our "ideal system" of post-secondary education in Ontario would have:

- More diversity: a greater variety of post-secondary institutions that stretches beyond the current two categories of research universities (including aspirant research universities) and comprehensive colleges of applied arts and technology. For example, our ideal post-secondary education system would include some institutions with entrance standards and faculty-student interactions that can rival those of selective institutions in other countries, as well as some institutions that are among the best in the world in addressing the needs of less able and less motivated students. These institutions would have systematic and well-resourced programs for monitoring the experience of their students and continuously improving teaching and learning (Massy, 2009). Our ideal post-secondary system might have some institutions that concentrate on technology and have programs from apprenticeship to the baccalaureate that are conveniently laddered for student mobility.
- More mission clarity: clearer distinctions in the explicitly described mission of the various component institutions.
- More accessibility: a higher participation rate of traditionally underrepresented groups.
- More nurturing: more institutions that provide a nurturing environment for students for whom the impersonal and demanding environment of big research universities is intimidating.
- More focus on teaching: a higher percentage of post-secondary students taught by faculty who are full-time and who devote a higher fraction of their professional effort to teaching.
- More professional variety: providing rewarding and respected careers for faculty who can be great teachers but whose interests and abilities do not fit the "publish or perish" model of research universities.
- More economical teaching: providing effective teaching for standard undergraduate courses using instructors who devote more of their effort to teaching and who can be compensated differently from faculty who are expected to make substantial research contributions.
- More market-based compensation: making it easier for post-secondary institutions to pay what the market requires, but not more, for teaching and research resources.

- More direct support for high-quality research: providing financial support for research based on its inherent merits and on its contribution to the economic, social, and cultural life of the country, rather than as an add-on to financial support for teaching.
- More cost- and needs-based tuition: students paying tuition that reflects both the real costs of their education and their ability to pay.
- More consistent and appropriate quality assurance: a credible system for assuring the quality of the courses and credentials provided by institutions.
- More sustained capital investment: incentives and funding arrangements to encourage an appropriate fraction of overall expenditures to be devoted to maintaining capital stock.
- More innovation: incentives for innovation in teaching techniques and student support.
- More effective and transparent pathways for students to move between sectors, institutions, and programs: ways to enhance such mobility that build on and recognize prior educational experiences.

There are, of course, good reasons why the current system differs from what we have suggested the ideal system would look like. We do not want to be naïve in our assessment of what could be improved in the real world. There are some features of the current institutions that are likely beyond the capacity of government and institutional leaders to change. This is why it may be important to create some new institutions where the rules of engagement would be clear from the outset and the changes would not require changes in contracts or good faith understandings. We should also not be naïve about the tendency of any new institutions to drift toward the existing institutional models. This is where clear and consistent government policy is required.

A New Teaching-focused University Sector

As we have argued in Chapter 6, some of the changes that are crucial to improve post-secondary education in Ontario are those that would bring about greater differentiation among post-secondary institutions. These include both the establishment, or emergence, of new types of post-secondary institutions, and measures that would lead existing institutions to concentrate more on certain kinds of activities and less on others.

Although a range of types of post-secondary institutions could be imagined that would differ from those now present in Ontario, creating degree granting institutions that are highly focused on undergraduate education is the design change that would do the most to enhance the current system. To be effective, the degree programs offered by such institutions would be solely at the baccalaureate level, and the emphasis of the institution would be teaching rather than research. The responsibilities of faculty, therefore, would be primarily undergraduate education. Although this is not the place to debate details, the normal teaching duties of faculty would be considerably greater than typical in existing universities in Ontario: in the order of 6-8 half course equivalents and without the reductions for research that are common in many departments today. Faculty might spend 10-15 percent of their time in scholarly activities but much of this research would be teaching-related, focused on staying up to date with current knowledge in their discipline and on teaching effectiveness, learning, and the student experience. Although faculty members in these new institutions would not be expected to sustain high levels of discovery research in their teaching disciplines, such scholarship might emerge in the area of post-secondary teaching and learning. As we have noted, British Columbia, Alberta, and Florida have recently established teaching-focused baccalaureate granting institutions, so this seems to be a prominent development in higher education.

There are different ways in which new teaching-focused, baccalaureate granting institutions could be established, and numerous variations on this basic idea. There is no reason why all of these institutions should be precisely the same or established in the same way; indeed, the same argument that leads to the conclusion that a new type of degree-granting institution would be beneficial also implies that variation within that institutional type would be healthy. Such institutions could be newly created or formed by transforming existing institutions. They could concentrate on baccalaureate programs or also offer sub-baccalaureate, vocational, and apprenticeship programs. They could concentrate on career-focused programs, or combine career-focused and liberal arts programs. There are also the questions of how many such institutions are needed and where they should be located. These are important, but are second-order decisions to be made after the primary decision, that the province's post-secondary system needs a layer of four-year, degree granting institutions that concentrate on teaching.

While existing universities and colleges could conceivably be converted into teaching-focused baccalaureate institutions of the type described here, a major issue in making a change of this type in the mission of existing post-secondary institutions is what it would mean for faculty. Earlier we noted that faculty who were hired by universities in the expectation that they would divide their time equally between teaching and research would rightly feel that they were being treated unfairly. The conversion of a college into a baccalaureate-granting institution could also bring significant change in the work situation for many faculty. There might be less need for the services of those who teach in non-degree programs and less status for such teachers compared to those who teach in the baccalaureate programs. Also, faculty in a converted college may be under pressure to pursue postgraduate studies that they did not anticipate when they were hired.

The advantage of creating entirely new institutions would be that they could be designed and staffed to fulfill a new type of mission, unencumbered by their history, institutional culture, and contractual relationships. Although it might seem that creating new institutions would be more costly than converting existing institutions, the latter approach might well include less obvious costs, including conversion of the existing infrastructure and of the disruption of current programs. Any conversion also would need to weigh the consequences of the loss to society of the institutions' present programs of research and education when displaced by the new activity.

One of the major design questions for these new institutions is the balance between largely career-oriented programs, and more general liberal arts and science programs. Conversion of some existing colleges would be the most sensible way of developing institutions emphasizing the first type of programs, although even those colleges would need to have sufficient strength in basic arts and sciences to support their role as baccalaureate granting institutions. Creating new institutions would probably be the most practical way of establishing universities whose focus was in the liberal arts and sciences.

The first of these institutional types, a teaching-focused, baccalaureate granting institution that offers mainly career programs, comes close to fitting the description of a polytechnic institution as that term has been used by Polytechnics Canada. Polytechnics Canada is a national alliance of eight post-secondary institutions that advocates for a model of a post-secondary institution that has the following characteristics:

- providing career-focused and community responsive education developed in partnership with employers,
- committing to a wide range of credentials including bachelor degrees, diplomas, apprenticeships, certificates, post-graduate offerings, continuing education, and corporate training, spanning many fields,
- combining theoretical and applied learning, relevant work experience, and the opportunity to participate in applied research and commercialization projects, and
- offering pathways that allow students to build on their credentials, and recognizing previous learning (Polytechnics Canada, 2009).

The eight members of Polytechnics Canada include the five Ontario colleges that have the status of Institutes of Technology and Advanced Learning (ITAL), plus Algonquin College in Ottawa, SAIT Polytechnic in Alberta, and the British Columbia Institute of Technology. The Ontario members of Polytechnics Canada have urged the Ontario Government to create a new polytechnic sector in the post-secondary system.

The one feature of the polytechnic institute model advocated by Poly-technics Canada that is inconsistent with our notion of a teaching-focused, baccalaureate granting institution is the reference to post-graduate pro-grams in the Polytechnics Canada model. Other than that, a polytechnic institute could be a variant of the type of baccalaureate granting institution that we believe would be a beneficial addition to Ontario's post-secondary education system. There are, however, considerations that argue against following a simple polytechnic model. Some colleges, particularly ITALs, already offer several baccalaureate programs and could be encouraged to expand their baccalaureate offerings without necessitating a formal change of status and role within the Ontario system. That is, in terms of the actual educational opportunities available to students, there may be no substantial difference between polytechnic institutes and ITALs with expanded baccalaureate offerings.[37] On the other hand, a teaching-focused

---

[37] Some colleges have had difficulty attracting students to baccalaureate programs, and in fact, some programs that have received ministerial approval have not been offered because of insufficient student demand. It is possible that the hesitancy of students to enter baccalaureate programs in the colleges—or in some colleges, because other colleges have been able to recruit students—is simply due to the newness of the idea of colleges awarding degrees. One of the arguments made by advocates for a polytechnic sector is that the change of name from college, or ITAL, to polytechnic would make the programs of these institutions more attractive to prospective students. However, the ambiguity of the term polytechnic, and the wide variation in how this term has been used in Canada and elsewhere, makes it difficult to predict how prospective students would react to it. For a discussion of the meaning and history of use of the term polytechnic and comparison with polytechnics in other jurisdictions, see Doern (2008) and Jones and Skolnik (2009). In general, there are two quite different uses of the term *polytechnic*. One is for a type of university that has particular strengths in engineering and technical fields, and offers graduate programs and has strong involvement in research. Often such polytechnic universities are among the most prestigious in their jurisdictions. This is the way that the term is used in the United States and also would include the Écoles Polytechniques in Paris and Montréal. These institutions tend to be very selective and few in number; for example, in the United States there are only about 20. Alternatively, the term polytechnic is used to refer to a non-university institution, the majority of whose enrolment is at the sub-baccalaureate level, and the role of faculty is predominantly teaching. Several European countries have sectors consisting of institutions of this type, some of which in recent years have significantly increased their enrolment in baccalaureate programs and have added some graduate programs. It could be argued that Ontario already has at least three institutions that fit the first usage of polytechnic to varying degrees: Waterloo, Ryerson, and UOIT. The whole col-lege sector could be seen as consistent with the second usage of polytechnic with considerable variation in the extent of institutions' involvement in baccalaureate programming.

baccalaureate institution with substantial arts and sciences offerings would be an entirely new type of post-secondary institution for Ontario.

Whatever their program emphasis, the number and location of teaching-focused, baccalaureate granting institutions should respond to student demand and be informed by careful study of the extent and geographical distribution of this demand. Given the expectation of growth in demand for baccalaureate programs in the Greater Toronto Area as discussed in Chapter 2, the GTA would be the inevitable choice for at least one or two of such new teaching-focused baccalaureate granting institutions. Given that the Ryerson experience provides clear evidence of the challenges involved in maintaining a sector composed of a solitary institution (Smith, 1989), it would be advisable to establish at least two, preferably three, of this new type of institution from the outset and to establish policy that would ensure that all new publicly assisted degree-granting institutions in the province would be of this type for the foreseeable future.

We are mindful of the opposition of some in the university community to the idea of creating institutions whose primary mission is undergraduate teaching on the grounds that quality undergraduate teaching must be done by people who are actively involved in discovery research—the researcher-teacher model. However, as we noted in Chapter 5, the research literature on the relationship between teaching and research does not support this assertion. Moreover, as we have discussed earlier in this book, financial necessity has forced the universities to do exactly what some say should not be done, that is, in effect to create a whole class of teachers in their own institutions who have no research role, and to have an increasing proportion of courses taught by these teachers. Moreover, the majority of these instructors are employed on a course-by-course, part-time basis and have only a very limited stature and presence in the institutions beyond the classroom. The current reality of undergraduate teaching at Ontario's universities, thus, undermines the case against a move to recognize and embrace a role for full-time faculty members whose dominant role is education.

As we have discussed earlier, there are factors other than financial that lead to questioning the principle that degree level education should be provided exclusively by what are in effect research universities. These include: the need to increase the rate of degree attainment and to increase participation in undergraduate programs by members of groups that historically have been underrepresented in Ontario's universities; the expectation that universities will devote increasingly more of their resources and effort to the production of knowledge that has commercial value and will enhance the province's productivity and economic competitiveness; concerns—for which NSSE data give some support—about the quality of teaching and learning and the consequent interest in creating learning environments that are more nurturing for undergraduates than that of the typical research-driven university; and the need to increase opportunity for individuals to pursue degrees in some newly emerging applied areas of study for which some colleges may possess the relevant expertise.

The foregoing points lead to the conclusion that it is time for Ontario to create a new category of university whose mission is the provision of high quality undergraduate education—a mission that is not seen as a temporary step on the way to becoming a research university. There is ample precedent for institutions of this type in other jurisdictions.

A THREE-YEAR UNDERGRADUATE DEGREE

The creation of a category of universities that offer only undergraduate programs might also provide an opportunity to explore an innovation that might justifiably cause many to recall the 1980s film "Back to the Future"—the three-year undergraduate degree. Keller (2008), a prominent American scholar of higher education, argued that a high quality, carefully designed and implemented three-year degree has a place among the range of programs offered by universities trying to respond to the varied needs and interests of students in a mass or universal post-secondary system. Although there is no doubt that the four-year degree program meets the requirements of many disciplines, it can also be argued that a carefully designed three-year program would serve students well as a pre-professional degree for those going on to professional study in disciplines such as law, education, journalism, business, social work, and media studies, and as a final degree for those who pursue on-the-job professional training in the financial, government, management, retail, public service, and other sectors. The three-year undergraduate degrees emerging in the European Union under the Bologna Accord further speak to the viability of such programs. Keller (2008) also pointed out that shortening the degree duration by a full year for a substantial number of students holds real financial efficiencies for both the public purse and the individual students and their families. Such considerations take on particular urgency in the financial situation facing Ontario as a result of the global economic recession.

Facing the fiscal and operational pressures discussed previously in this book, there has been less interest on the part of Ontario's research-intensive and aspiring research-intensive universities to sustain such high-quality, well-structured and supported three-year programs. The existing funding system provides clear incentives for universities to enrol students in four-year rather than three-year degree programs. As a result, the portion of students in three-year programs has declined dramatically across the province and, in fact, some major universities have simply stopped offering such degrees. The creation of a new category of undergraduate universities would provide a unique opportunity to reverse this trend through incentives that would encourage and reinforce the creation of three-year degree programs. Such programs should not be allowed to be developed into what was once referred to as "pass BAs" that involve little more than a credential earned after three years of unchallenging residency at the university. Rather, they would need to be designed as highly structured, demanding programs with high academic standards, perhaps initially aimed only at students with higher admission qualifications. If such programs could be developed and sustained, they would be of substantial benefit to both the province and its students and would serve as a clear signal of a turn toward educational innovation in Ontario.

A COMPREHENSIVE APPROACH TO FUNDING

At present the major funding decisions for universities are made piece by piece. The government determines the total operating grant for the university system (based on what the government thinks it can afford), and then determines the portion allocated to each institution (primarily by formula, with small amounts added to reflect diverse priorities that have arisen over the years). The government also sets tuition fees (based on what it thinks students can afford and voters will accept). Each university determines the level of spending necessary to educate students and to fulfill the other parts of its mission. The gap between revenues and expenses is addressed largely by increasing class sizes, hiring more temporary faculty to replace permanent faculty, or both.

If current arrangements continue, the outcome will almost certainly be that class sizes will continue to grow and a larger share of teaching will be done by temporary instructors. At the same time, faculty who are most actively involved in research and graduate studies will be spread more thinly across their teaching and research responsibilities. Although both the quality of undergraduate teaching and of scholarship and research are threatened, historic patterns suggest that, in the absence of systemic change, the former will suffer more.

Avoiding this outcome will require an open and explicit discussion between the institutions and the government about the rising costs of higher education. A starting point would be for the government and the institutions to agree each year how much money is needed simply to continue teaching and research operations at current levels. As we saw in Chapter 4, universities typically estimate their annual inflation rates to be 2-3 points higher than consumer price inflation. The government might choose to accept this higher rate of inflation as an unavoidable fact—just as Canadian governments implicitly accept that inflation in health care is unavoidably higher than in the economy as a whole—or, alternatively, the government might work with institutions to determine how the inflation rate can be lowered through efficiencies and productivity improvements.

Once the government and the institutions agreed on a "cost to continue," the annual funding process would then turn to a consideration of the additional funding required to increase enrolments, expand research and scholarship, or undertake other new priorities. Finally, there would be a need for the government to determine how the total costs will be paid—from higher government grants, higher tuition fees, or both.

The arithmetic of this approach is simple, but the change in the relationship between the government and the universities would be profound. Since the late 1960s, governments have determined the level of annual grants and have regulated tuition, which together comprise the lion's share of revenue; at the same time, the control of spending has been left to individual universities. Institutions can point to many cost-saving achievements during this period that have allowed funding to be re-directed for the purpose of increasing enrolment, meeting higher expectations for research, or other priorities. Yet the continued rise in class sizes and part-time instruction suggests that the current model of funding is reaching its limits. A larger role for government or a government advisory body would appear to be needed.

A similar approach might also be appropriate in the college sector, although there are important differences between the two sectors. As we saw in Chapter 4, colleges experienced an indisputable decline in per-student funding relative to consumer price inflation from the mid-1980s to the early 2000s, from which they are only now recovering. Colleges to date have a relatively modest role in research, and there is little to suggest that full-time college faculty have reduced their teaching responsibilities in order to pursue research expectations. Collective bargaining in the college sector is carried out province-wide, so the administrations of individual colleges have only partial ability to control their own costs. Despite these differences between the two sectors, colleges experience many pressures with respect to cost inflation, class sizes, and the use of temporary instructors that suggest a more explicit discussion of rising per-student costs would be worthwhile.

An example of a useful role for government in both the university and college sectors would be to reduce expenditures on zero-sum competitions among institutions. We noted in Chapter 4 a survey showing that more than half of students entering university from high school receive merit scholarships. Although nominally based on merit, the high percentage of students receiving the awards suggests that they are in effect a tuition subsidy to attract students with academic credentials that are average or higher—a far cry from the traditional intention that such awards recognize notable excellence. Any single institution that chose to withdraw from this competition would place itself at a disadvantage; most or all institutions, however, might agree that these funds would be better directed to needs-based financial aid or to improvements in the quality of students' education, while reserving a much smaller portion for scholarships for students who are truly outstanding. The government would perform a service by working with the institutions to articulate this agreement and enforce it.

A more controversial role for government would be to require detailed public reporting on compensation, teaching loads, class sizes, the use of temporary instructors, and other domains related to efficiency, effectiveness, and quality. For example, a full accounting of changes in compensation costs would incorporate standardized reporting of across-the-board salary increases, progress-through-the-ranks, performance-based increases, adjustments to reflect labour market demand, and employee benefits costs. An accounting of changes in teaching loads would need to reflect across-the-board changes plus individual reductions in teaching that allow faculty to pursue administrative or research duties. Such information would provide a factual basis for discussion on why inflation in higher education exceeds consumer price inflation, and it would allow governments to decide either to fund this level of inflation or to offer to work with institutions to develop specific ways of controlling it. The publication of such information might also have a salutary effect on those institutions that wished to motivate change internally, without government involvement.

While strong arguments can be made for increasing government funding and reducing the growth in per-student costs, these two steps will need to be supplemented by increasing contributions from students and their families. The Ontario government's 2009 budget pledged to eliminate the deficit by 2016 and said that, to do so, program expense growth will be held to an average annual growth rate of 2.3 percent (Ontario, Ministry of Finance, 2009, 89). Given the pressures from health care and other public services, the government over the next several years will at best be able to fund the cost of enrolment increases and a small portion of the cost of inflation in higher education. A substantial increase in tuition fees therefore seems unavoidable in order to fund rising per-student costs. We distinguish between across the board fee increases and fee deregulation; the latter, especially in a period when post-secondary spaces will be in short supply, might lead to very sharp fee increases that may have the perverse effect of diverting attention from the need to curb rising per-student costs. But, whether regulated or not, in the absence of a public appetite to pay higher taxes or to divert funds from other public programs, tuition increases appear to be inevitable.

A key weakness of the funding process within the post-secondary sector has been that it has served as an impediment to institutional diversity. The absence of planned and complementary diversity among the province's post-secondary institutions limits the system's effectiveness in both education and research. Examples of more diverse systems of higher education are available elsewhere in Canada and in other parts of the world. Although these systems have used different means to achieve diversity, they share two essential features: first, a clear policy framework, tenaciously applied; and, second, a funding system that recognizes, encourages, and reinforces diverse institutional missions and visions. We describe below a more differentiated system of funding that would allow for a balance between reasonable constraints in the public interest and the preservation of institutional autonomy.

Finally, maintaining and increasing participation rates in a higher-tuition environment will require continuing changes in federal and provincial student support programs. The two levels of government will need to adjust the programs for inflation every year so students have access to the up-front cash required to pay for the rising costs of tuition, books, and living expenses. The growing body of evidence about how accessibility is affected by upfront grants and flexible repayment programs will need to be analyzed and acted on to ensure that higher education becomes more accessible to low-income and middle-income families.

FOSTERING INCREASED EFFICIENCY AND EFFECTIVENESS IN THE UNIVERSITY SECTOR

A new teaching-focused university sector could serve as an escape valve to release pressures that have been building up within the existing university sector. Some might then see it as enabling the existing universities to continue on without having to make any significant changes. However, the assumption of "business as usual" in the existing sector would be unfortunate and, in fact, unsustainable—even with the creation of a new undergraduate-focused sector.

One factor that is likely to demand changes of the existing university sector is that financial viability has rested in considerable part in recent years on the use of contract, particularly part-time, faculty. With the increased militancy of the unions that represent contingent faculty, the wide gap between the compensation of contract and tenured faculty that makes the practice profitable is likely to diminish.

The diminished financial advantage of employing large numbers of contract faculty is but one factor that will make it imperative for the university sector to seek ways of increasing its efficiency. Ontario universities face continued enrolment pressure, and a significant increase in grant levels is unlikely in the foreseeable future. Substantial increases in tuition over the past decade have provided vital offsets to reductions in government support during the same period. Although we have noted that further tuition increases are inevitable, the government's and public's appetite for substantial increases, particularly in an economically challenging period, is likely to constrain this source of funds in the foreseeable future.

Improvements in efficiency and effectiveness may be sought both through modification of the division of roles and responsibilities among institutions and through internal changes within institutions. Regarding the former, assertions of the need for greater institutional differentiation in the university sector date back at least to 1980; many of the reasons why greater institutional differentiation in the university would be desirable have been discussed earlier in this book. We have also argued that the culture of the academy contributes to homogeneity, and that both the existing funding and quality assurance systems exert powerful influences toward convergence. There have been few initiatives to encourage universities to pursue differentiated missions not related to research.

If there is a genuine will to promote institutional differentiation, the place to start would undoubtedly be the funding system. The present "one-size fits all" approach to funding exerts an essentially irresistible force toward institutional homogeneity, reinforcing the tendency within academic culture for all institutions to aspire toward a uniform activity profile in which discovery research and graduate education hold clear pride of place. Although the government has experimented with differentiation grants in the past, such initiatives have not involved significant funding and have never become a systemic feature of the funding system. There is considerable potential for increasing institutional differentiation by using substantial portions of the total operating grant for distinct mission-related envelopes which would provide a real incentive for institutions to excel in both different areas and types of activity. For example, one envelope might support innovation and excellence in student learning and development particularly with respect to historically underserved populations; another might relate to resource-intensive research and aim to bring the corresponding resources for a subset of universities to the level enjoyed by their peers in other jurisdictions.

Integrating funding with the Multi-year Accountability Agreements that have been implemented in Ontario's university sector in recent years could provide a framework for relating an institution's funding more effectively to its mission and priorities. Even irrespective of funding, the Multi-year Accountability Agreements could contribute to institutional differentiation by giving formal recognition and an endorsement of institutional differences. Strategic application of differential tuition fees would serve as a further policy change promoting institutional differentiation. Although such a policy change may be a critical element of system differentiation, tuition policy, of course, must be managed carefully in order to ensure it does not impede access and so that other less obvious downsides are avoided. We recognize, also, that the current predominant conception of quality in higher education has an additional homogenizing influence. Thus, a later section of this chapter urges the creation of a dialogue about the meaning of educational quality in an effort to foster an appreciation of the legitimacy of different views, and to stimulate efforts to avoid the homogenizing influence of quality assurance processes.

Besides differentiation *among* universities, a form of greater differentiation *within* universities could be very helpful in enabling these institutions to cope with the diverse demands that they face. We are thinking here of the creation and widespread utilization of different appointment categories that promote role differentiation among members of faculty. In Chapter 4, we described the efforts that some universities have made to establish teaching-only positions, i.e., faculty positions in which the predominant role is teaching, engaged, in Boyer's (1990) terms, in "scholarship of teaching" without a substantial expectation of applied or discovery research within their discipline. A small portion of time could be provided for research in such positions, but it might be most appropriately focused on research that will improve teaching and learning. We noted that such positions do not exist at all universities; where they do, they are very limited in number except at a few institutions, and they make up a very small percentage of full-time faculty positions system-wide, generally not in the tenure stream.

A compelling case can be made, both in regard to efficiency and quality of teaching (and research) for expanding the number of such positions and making them part of the tenure stream. There are many Ph.D. holders who have an overriding love and commitment to undergraduate education, and who would gladly concentrate their academic effort on teaching if such stable, respected, full-time positions were available. Although these individuals would make excellent teachers of undergraduates, many of them are now working outside the university in places where they are not required to conduct research. Others who do work in universities currently devote time to research that could be spent more productively in teaching. One of the consequences of forced research is a torrent of pedestrian publishing that very few people read. If, instead, gifted teachers could spend more time teaching and gifted researchers could spend more time on research, the effectiveness of both teaching and research would be increased.

Lest these remarks be—accidentally or constructively—misinterpreted, we hasten to add that what is suggested is not the compartmentalization of the entire full-time professoriate into two separate camps. Rather, it is a move away from the uniform model of how faculty should allocate their time, and a move incrementally to foster more variation among faculty in this regard. Given current and anticipated levels of participation in undergraduate education, the proliferation and acceptance of such predominantly teaching full-time appointments would complement the typical teacher-researcher role to the benefit of members of faculty, students, the university, and the society at large. Creating appropriate numbers of such teaching positions in all universities would be part of this movement.

The presence of substantially more members of full-time faculty holding predominantly teaching appointments also would reduce the reliance of universities on part-time, contract instructors. Three related further points must be made. First, it would be both unrealistic and undesirable to imagine that part-time contract positions would be eliminated entirely. Such instructors often provide outstanding instruction in subject areas that are not represented by full-time faculty or where sufficient numbers of full-time faculty are unavailable. In addition, these same appointments provide welcome experience and funding for some senior graduate students. These situations are unlikely to disappear entirely under any foreseeable modifications to the university system. Second, it is important that universities more fully acknowledge and embrace the central role that part-time contract faculty play in the fulfillment of their teaching and, indirectly, their research mission. Such a change would involve an increased level of engagement of part-time instructors in the academic life of the institution, the provision of adequate resources to support their teaching, and the application of high standards for appointment and performance evaluation of their teaching.

Finally, although the model suggested here, involving more full-time predominantly teaching faculty and fewer part-time contract instructors, has many substantial advantages, it is undeniably likely to involve increased net costs relative to the current heavy reliance on course-by-course instructors. Our argument is that current circumstances are not sustainable and do not best serve the interests of undergraduate students nor, indeed, many of those filling these teaching positions. Moreover, it is unrealistic to continue to argue that the traditional teacher-researcher model is capable of meeting the needs of the increasingly large number of students quite rightly seeking access to undergraduate education. This model, in which those who also are devoting an equal amount of their time to discovery research do essentially all instruction, in fact, has not been a reality for some time. It is time to adopt an approach that is capable of delivering an undergraduate education of high quality within the reasonable limits of funding available from the individual student and the government faced with the challenges of supporting a post-secondary educational system that is quickly approaching universal participation.

Most of the effort that has gone into increasing efficiency in universities has been on the non-academic side of the enterprise. Many faculty members believe that in contrast to the settings in which most other professionals practice, the teaching-learning situation is not amenable to significant innovation. It has been said that if a 15th century physician were transplanted to a modern operating room, he might run away screaming in shock, while a university lecturer from the 15th century would feel right at home in the typical classroom of today. Critics of the way that teaching is conducted in the modern university maintain that it does not have to be this way, and that pedagogical research has identified a number of innovations that would make undergraduate teaching more effective and/or more efficient. In its Second Annual Review, the Higher

Education Quality Council of Ontario said that "[t]here is much to learn about effective teaching and learning but there is much we already know that is not widely put into practice" (HEQCO, 2009, 77).

While an analysis of the ways in which the efficiency of the core undergraduate teaching and learning enterprise in the university (and college) could be increased is beyond the scope of this book, we would like to reiterate the comment attributed earlier to William Massy, that it is essential for universities to "mount systematic and well-resourced programs for analyzing and continuously improving the processes of teaching and learning" (Massy, 2009, A26).

Although the focus of the suggestions for change in this, and the preceding, section of this chapter might reasonably be taken as focusing on baccalaureate education, our intention is that the introduction of an undergraduate university sector and of differentiation within and between existing universities would have broad beneficial impacts. In previous chapters, we outlined how pressures for increased enrolment and for far greater contributions to research aimed at supporting the province's and country's wealth and well-being under a one-size-fits-all funding, undifferentiated system are threatening all aspects of the universities' function, including their capacity to fulfill research expectations and to sustain high-quality graduate education. We suggest that an evolution towards substantial institutional differentiation, the employment of more predominantly teaching full-time faculty, and greater innovation in pedagogy will relieve pressures on these areas of functioning at the same time as they address issues of access and quality in baccalaureate education.

BALANCE AND DIFFERENTIATION IN THE COLLEGE SECTOR

Because we have placed priority on finding sustainable ways to offer baccalaureate education in Ontario, our discussion about the colleges has concentrated on their role in the provision of these programs and associated credit courses. However, it is important to appreciate that the colleges offer a highly diverse array of programs and courses, of which those pertaining to the baccalaureate are only a small portion, rather larger for some colleges and tiny to almost non-existent for others. Decisions about the role or involvement of colleges in baccalaureate activity must take into account how this might affect their other activities.

In fact, involvement in baccalaureate activity is one of the ways in which institutional differentiation among the colleges has been increasing. Since the colleges first began offering baccalaureate programs, some colleges that had obtained approval to offer the baccalaureate have decided not to do so while some have expanded their baccalaureate offerings considerably. With respect to provision of baccalaureate programs, colleges can now be divided into three groups: those that offer none; those that offer just one or two in areas of unique expertise, where in some cases they may have the only diploma program of its type in the province; and those that offer three or more, and seem intent on increasing their number of baccalaureate programs. Those in the second group might be termed "niche providers," and those in the third group, "general providers" of baccalaureate programs.

Relatively few colleges have the strength in liberal arts and the tradition of integration of liberal and applied studies to be regarded as credible providers of baccalaureate programs on a broad scale. More substantial involvement in baccalaureate programming would be a natural next step in the evolution of these colleges, and they could make a significant contribution to meeting the province's needs for more spaces. The baccalaureate programs of these institutions would be career-focused, and anchored in the expertise that has enabled them to run valuable, high demand diploma programs. These colleges would extend to the baccalaureate realm the learning-centered, nurturing environment that has characterized the Ontario colleges in their sub-baccalaureate programs, and thereby add this dimension to Ontario's opportunities for undergraduate study. Some of these colleges might become teaching-focused universities; some might be designated as polytechnic institutes; or they could be colleges whose mission is formally redefined to include substantial provision of baccalaureate programs. In the latter two cases, the institutions would continue to offer the other types of programs that they have been offering as part of their college mandate. Perhaps, even if one of these colleges becomes a teaching-focused university, it would be sensible for it to continue some of its sub-baccalaureate programming.

We hasten to emphasize that being substantial providers of baccalaureate programming, in any of the three situations indicated in the previous paragraph, is not a mission that we would envisage for more than a handful of colleges. A factor that would complicate the selection of colleges for these enhanced roles in provision of baccalaureate programs is geographical location. Four of the five ITALs are in the GTA, and were all of these institutions to shift a major proportion of their activity to baccalaureate provision, it could leave the GTA short of the other types of college programming that are so vital to meeting the needs of individual learners and so essential to the local and provincial economy. For example, alarm has been expressed about weaknesses in Ontario's apprenticeship system and the fact that Ontario ranks last in Canada in the proportion of the work force with apprenticeship or trades certificates or diplomas (HEQCO, 2009, 21). The Ontario government has recently announced steps to breathe new life into the apprenticeship system, and this may increase the demand for that sphere of college activity. Because much of the province's industry that would employ apprentices is located in the GTA, colleges in this region would have an important role in an expansion of apprenticeship training.

Whether apprenticeship training in the colleges would be more effective if it were concentrated in fewer colleges is a question of provincial organization of education and institutional specialization that warrants some consideration. Alberta concentrates apprenticeship training in one college in each of its two largest cities, and it has the most robust apprenticeship training system in Canada. As we have noted repeatedly in this book, questions about how to distribute different types of post-secondary and tertiary educational programming among institutions rarely get asked in Ontario, let alone become the subject of serious analysis.

While we envisage a greater role in providing baccalaureate programs for a small number of colleges, what we envisage for the college system as a whole is a reaffirmation of the importance to the province of their original mission of educating and training workers in a wide range of levels and fields for the provincial economy, and offering opportunities for career and personal development for individuals. Within that broad mission, there should be greater emphasis on ways in which this role might be enhanced and the whole system made more efficient through institutional differentiation and specialization. This differentiation could take a variety of forms including greater emphasis on trades training, more focus on serving underprepared learners, or greater involvement in the provision of career-focused baccalaureate programs that rest on a solid liberal arts foundation.

IMPROVING OPPORTUNITIES FOR COLLEGE TO UNIVERSITY TRANSFER

The issue of transfer from college to university has been the subject of considerable discussion since the Vision 2000 review of the colleges' mandate gave prominence to the issue nearly two decades ago. It was hoped that the College University Consortium Council (CUCC), which was created in 1996, would spearhead a movement for improving opportunities for transfer. In addition to stimulating some useful research on transfer, the CUCC's efforts related to transfer included two significant projects. One was making a substantial improvement in the Ontario College University Transfer Guide, an online resource that enables students to explore existing transfer arrangements.

The other project was the Port Hope Accord, an agreement between representatives of the college and university sectors that set out parameters, a timetable, and a process for improving transfer. However, there has been little follow-up on the process, and confusion about the parameters. Indicating amounts of transfer credit for students moving from, for instance, a two year program in a college to a four-year program in a university, the parameters were regarded by those who negotiated the agreement on behalf of the colleges as a starting point from which improvements would ensue. Instead, the universities have tended to re-gard the Port Hope parameters as fixed norms. As a consequence of the failure to implement the process outlined in the Accord and confusion over the parameters, little improvement in transfer opportunities has resulted from the Accord.

Most of the energy of the CUCC has gone into promoting collaborative programs between universities and colleges rather than into promoting improvements in transfer opportunities. As we noted earlier, these col-laborative programs are a useful addition to the post-secondary system, but they have two serious limitations. First, they tend to improve op-portunities for the university-bound student to benefit from the career education expertise of the colleges, but they do not enable the college-bound student to benefit from the resources of the university. Second, whatever their successes, the collaborative programs benefit only a tiny proportion of the number of students who would be affected by systemic improvements in transfer.

As we noted in Chapter 6, in discussing transfer it is important to dis-tinguish between programs in the arts and sciences and career programs. General Arts and Sciences programs constitute only a small fraction of college enrolment the vast bulk of which is in career programs. However, it has proven far more difficult to develop successful transfer arrangements for career programs than for arts and sciences programs. The experi-ence of other jurisdictions suggests that there are two principal ways of improving transfer opportunities for students in college career programs. One involves the establishment of provincial committees that consist of representatives of the colleges and universities and have a specific man-date to improve transfer opportunities; the other is the development in universities of specific programs aimed to facilitate transfer for students from college career programs.

Transfer arrangements for students in these programs are better in Alberta, British Columbia, and many American states than in Ontario, not just because of the explicit transfer mission of colleges in those juris-dictions, but also because of the existence of provincial or state mech-anisms to support that mission. Typically these mechanisms include jurisdiction-wide committees that develop policies for transfer, monitor transfer activity, and hold institutions accountable for making improve-ments. British Columbia and Alberta both have provincial councils on transfer. The mission of the Alberta Council is "to be a catalyst for neces-sary change and an advocate for learners in the areas of admission and transfer to educational programs" (Alberta Council on Admission and Transfer, 2009). The membership on the Alberta Council includes two students and two members of the general public. British Columbia has a similar type of council with several committees, including a broadly based provincial committee on transfer and articulation. It also has had commit-tees whose job it was to improve transfer arrangements for students in career programs such as business. Quebec also has a provincial committee to oversee mobility arrangements from its colleges to its universities. Stakeholders in these three provinces believe that these provincial bodies have made important contributions to improving transfer opportunities (Skolnik and Jones, 1993; Jones, Skolnik, and Soren, 1998).

In Chapter 6 we noted that one of the problems faced by students who wish to move from a career program in a college to a university is that the programs are so different between the two types of institutions. We also described three new types of programs that some universities in the United States have developed in order to deal with this problem. This is a development that would be well worth considering in Ontario, along with the establishment of better provincial funding mechanisms to serve as catalysts for transfer. Advances on both measures require stronger provincial leadership in post-secondary education policy than the province has exercised to date, a subject that is addressed in a later section of this chapter. To provide an incentive to universities to offer such programs, and recognizing that they would involve only third and fourth year students, the programs could be given a higher weight in the funding formula than the regular weight for undergraduate arts and science programs.

An Open University for Ontario

In Chapter 6 we noted the important contribution that an open university could make to Ontario's post-secondary education system. We observed that although today open universities deliver much, if not all, of their courses online or through other electronic media, it is not the technology through which courses are provided that defines an open university. Rather, it is an educational philosophy, a key element of which is open admissions, i.e., although students must meet traditional course requirements and standards once enrolled, admission to programs and courses is not based upon prior academic achievement, but on learners' needs and aspirations (Jones and Skolnik, 2009). Further, an open university provides the flexibility to enable learners to utilize its resources and infrastructure in whatever way will best meet the learner's needs.

Although all Ontario universities offer many of their courses online, none perform the function of an open university. In fact it would be impossible for them to do so, because the educational philosophy of an open university is so different from that of a conventional university. Hence, no Ontario university offers the open admissions or flexible credit recognition features of open education that are central to the idea of an open university. This can be provided only by an institution that is differentiated from the others in having the special mission of an open university.

An open university could play a particularly important role in facilitating degree completion for graduates of the colleges. As we noted earlier, a large number of Ontario residents are enrolled in Canada's leading English language open university, Athabasca University in Alberta. A significant portion of the demand for Athabasca's programs among Ontario's residents is from students and graduates of Ontario's colleges. A 2001 survey by the Ontario College University Consortium Council (CUCC, 2002) showed that 19 colleges in Ontario had degree completion agreements with Athabasca University. There were 190 agreements in total covering a wide variety of subjects. No other university in Ontario or elsewhere had degree completion agreements with as many Ontario colleges. It was estimated that program registrations of Ontario residents in Athabasca included about seven hundred from the CAATs who were utilizing the articulation agreements between Athabasca and their college (Jones and Skolnik, 2009). Besides providing a valuable degree completion option for graduates of the colleges, an open university could address the needs of learners in a variety of situations where individuals are unable to take advantage of the opportunities provided by the existing university sector.

RETHINKING THE IDEA OF QUALITY IN HIGHER EDUCATION

There are at least five agencies in Ontario that are concerned with quality in higher education, and there appear to be significant differences among them in the way that quality is conceptualized. The Ontario Council on Graduate Studies and the Undergraduate Program Review and Audit Committee seem to take the traditional view of quality—one that concentrates on inputs, selectivity, and educational processes. The Post-secondary Education Quality Assessment Board places its greatest emphasis on educational processes and policies. Both the PEQAB and the Ontario university agencies have accepted the same learning outcome standards as those adopted by the Council of Ministers of Education, Canada. However, it is difficult to obtain the data that would be required to determine whether these outcomes are actually achieved, and thus the program assessments of these agencies reveal little, if anything, about the actual learning outcomes achieved. The Ontario College Quality Assurance Service employs an audit process that evolved from an earlier approach to quality assessment that focused exclusively on learning outcomes. However, like the processes of the other agencies, the attention given to outcomes pertains primarily to intentions rather than results. In its *First Annual Review*, the Higher Education Quality Council of Ontario indicated that it had adopted the value added conception of quality, but in its *Second Annual Review* it gave considerable attention to the student experience and educational practices that are reflected in the NSSE survey. Of course, unlike the other agencies it does not conduct program assessments, so it would not have the same type of *direct* influence that the agencies that do program assessments have—though its stature and expertise may still enable it to have considerable influence.

Despite the nominal and various responsibilities assigned to these provincial institutions, it is arguable that the views about quality that matter most are those that are predominant within the university sector itself. That is, decisions made by these institutions on the basis of their ideas about quality have the greatest and most direct impact on students and faculty in the province. These institutions have the power to make decisions that determine whether students are able to pursue further study and control the opportunities of faculty for career advancement. The dominant views about quality within these institutions exert an influence on higher education in Ontario that extends beyond the walls of the institutions. For example, the idea that only faculty who have significant involvement in research can be high quality teachers of undergraduate students is a core tenet of universities in Ontario and has had ripple effects on the post-secondary system that have been discussed earlier in this book. The attention given to learning outcomes in recent years has not been matched by significant efforts to actually collect data on the achievement of those learning outcomes. Thus, while rhetorical references are made to learning outcomes conceptions of quality, the real judgments about quality continue to be made on the basis of data about inputs, selectivity, and conformity to traditional educational processes. As the director of an organization that advises states' post-secondary education spending priorities for the *U.S. Recovery and Reinvestment Act* of 2009 stated in an interview: "Universities aspire to prestige, and that is achieved by increasing selectivity, getting a research mission and having faculty do as little teaching as possible, not by teaching and learning, and taking students from Point A to Point B" (Lewin, 2009). Australia's Minister of Education hopes to attack this mindset through a new quality agency which would encourage academics "to value teaching as much as their passion for research" (Maslen, 2009).

The traditional conception of quality in higher education is not without some virtues; otherwise it would not have persisted as long as it has. However, in addition to whatever strengths this conception has, it also produces dysfunctional side effects that were described in Chapter 5. Because of these dysfunctional effects, and because of the increasingly apparent disparities in views about what constitutes quality in higher education, it would be valuable to have a structured dialogue among key stakeholders concerning the idea of quality and quality assurance practices in higher education that are appropriate for the 21st century. Ideally, this dialogue should go beyond restating the slogans and shibboleths found in most universities' statements about quality in higher education and begin to grapple with the differences among stakeholders in views about quality, and also consider the consequences of different conceptions of quality. Because it has the broadest purview on the subject of quality and has no attachment to an existing quality assurance process, the Higher Education Quality Council of Ontario would be the ideal agency to initiate such a dialogue. Catalyzing a dialogue on quality in higher education is well within the legislated mandate of HEQCO.

Research on various approaches to measuring quality, especially related to some of the newer conceptualizations, could do much to inform this dialogue. HEQCO's Second Annual Review describes several research projects related to academic quality that are under way and offers many valuable suggestions for mining existing data sources. Should the new type of teaching-focused, baccalaureate granting institution that we have described in this book be established, it would provide an ideal setting for testing various methods of measuring value added and examining their relationships with other types of quality measures such as input and NSSE measures.

RESPONSIBILITY FOR LEADERSHIP AND DIRECTION OF THE HIGHER EDUCATION SYSTEM

In 1965 when the Minister of Education, William Davis, introduced the legislation to establish a system of colleges, he stated that the Ministry would monitor the role of the colleges and their relationship with the universities and on this basis make changes in those aspects of the post-secondary system that were warranted. In fact, the monitoring that Mr. Davis referred to was short-lived and no significant changes have been made in the design of Ontario's post-secondary system since the establishment of the colleges over forty years ago. Although there have been occasional task forces and commissions that have examined particular issues in post-secondary education, usually related to, or stimulated by, funding issues, there has been a distinct absence of continuous oversight and systematic policy guidance of Ontario's post-secondary system over the more than four decades since Davis's 1965 commitment.

Post-secondary education is an enterprise that absorbs a great deal of public money, and is vitally important to the province's current and future well-being. Yet from the perspective of stewardship of this expensive and strategic public resource, for much of the time it has not been apparent that anyone has been minding the store. At other times there were some noteworthy initiatives, but they were not followed to completion. Frequently when serious, thoughtful ideas for reform have been put forward, the vociferous response of any group whose interest might be threatened by the proposed change has stifled debate. It is hard to imagine a thoroughgoing policy analysis in which ideas that are unpalatable to at least some stakeholders do not surface. However, that is no reason for not undertaking systematic policy analysis, especially within a realm of society that celebrates the free flow of ideas.

We do not wish to suggest that providing policy direction to a sector as large, complex, and often fractious as post-secondary education is an easy or straightforward undertaking. Probably no jurisdiction does a perfect job in this area, whatever that would mean, but many do a better job than Ontario. For example, looking at the history of post-secondary education in Alberta, some logic and order is evident in the way that the post-secondary system in that province has evolved. One can see both the antecedents of, and the public policy rationale for, the establishment of the Campus Alberta Quality Council and the policy on roles and mandates of the colleges that was announced in November 2007, described in Chapter 6. This is not to suggest that everything is rosy in Albertan post-secondary education, or that all decisions in that sphere have been based purely on rational considerations. Policy making is an inevitably messy business that often involves agonizing trade-offs between the principles that were outlined at the beginning of this chapter. But these difficulties and complicating factors make it even more necessary to have a systematic framework for policy oversight and direction, and someone with the designated responsibility for leadership in the policy process.

The global economic recession has made such policy leadership all the more urgent and may make an increased government role more acceptable to interested parties. It will be obvious to all serious observers that many aspects of the current system cannot be sustained in a period when both governments and institutions will have to rebuild their balance sheets. It should also be obvious that people employed in Ontario's post-secondary institutions cannot expect to continue with business as usual when so many of their fellow citizens—and some of their academic colleagues in other jurisdictions—are facing dramatic adjustments in their work and remuneration. Throughout the developed world, the financial turbulence and economic contraction has led governments to intervene in areas like banking and company restructuring that would have been inconceivable before the crisis. The current circumstances make it easier to imagine sustained government action, supported by enlightened institutional leadership, to facilitate the next phase of transformation in Ontario's post-secondary education system.

In general, there are two options for providing that policy leadership: the government itself or an arms-length agency of which there are many variants, the chief ones of which were discussed in Chapter 6. Since the consolidated governing board model in which all institutions in each sector or in total are under the jurisdiction of a single board is probably out of the question for Ontario, most of the important policy decisions will necessarily be made by government. That being the case, the choice is between relying solely on in-house staff and making use of an arms-length agency for policy advice. The latter offers more scope for transparency and diversity, but some such bodies have a tendency to offer advice that is more political than practical. Either approach can work well or poorly, depending upon commitment and competence. It all depends on the government developing a clear view of what it wants post-secondary education in Ontario to do and how it wants the system organized to do it. A special commission might be useful in developing a set of detailed recommendations and an implementation plan.[38] After that, it is important to recognize that providing systematic policy guidance for post-secondary education is a long term undertaking that requires development of appropriate capacity, structures, and processes.

This book argues that the present approach to the provision of baccalaureate education in Ontario is not sustainable and is in need of significant modification. The global recession, combined with the need to respond to dramatic increases in GTA-based enrolment demand, is bringing the underlying problems into stark relief. Although the Ontario government has, in recent decades, declined to engage in system design, we believe that the current circumstances make a stronger government role imperative. While the required changes will be difficult and controversial, it is easier to make system adjustments during a time of enrolment expansion. We think the time is right for sustained government action, supported by enlightened institutional leadership, to guide Ontario's post-secondary education system through its next transformation.

---

[38] Building on the lessons learned in the successful Rae Review (Clark and Trick, 2006), one model would be for the Premier to appoint a commission headed by a former premier or senior minister, advised by a former university president and a former college president, to consult on and develop within six months a detailed funding formula and specific legislative and regulatory amendments to drive the transformation.

GLOSSARY OF ACRONYMS AND TERMS

Aboriginal: Those people who belong to recognized indigenous groups in the Canadian Constitution Act, 1982, sections 25 and 35, respectively as First Nations, Métis, and Inuit.

ACAATO—Association of Colleges of Applied Arts and Technology: The former name of the advocacy organization for the province's 24 colleges of applied arts and technology which is now known as Colleges Ontario.

Accreditation: The recognition by an appropriate body that an institution or a program meets or exceeds certain standards. The principal type of accreditation in higher education in Canada is program accreditation, which exists mainly in regard to professional programs.

ATOP—Access to Opportunities Program: The three-year program announced by the Ontario Ministry of Education and Training in May 1998 to help universities and colleges dramatically increase the number of students enrolling in computer science and high-demand engineering programs. In the 1999 provincial budget, the initial $150 million in ATOP funding was expanded by $78 million.

AUCC—Association of Universities and Colleges of Canada: The Association that represents (in 2009) 94 Canadian public and private not-for-profit universities and university-degree level colleges. The AUCC's stated mandate is to facilitate the development of public policy on higher education and to encourage cooperation among universities and governments, industry, communities, and institutions in other countries.

Auditor General of Ontario: The Auditor General Act gives the Auditor the mandate to examine the government's financial accounts and trans-actions and to report his findings to the Legislature. Following the 2005 amendments to the Act, publicly financed colleges and universities in Ontario are included in the Auditor's remit.

Baccalaureate: Another name for most bachelor's degrees which are awarded by a university or a college upon completion of a program of undergraduate studies, normally of four or three years' duration. Al-though the expression "baccalaureate degree" is widely used, it is a literal redundancy, since the word baccalaureate by itself refers to a particular kind of degree. However, this redundancy has probably been legitimized by the extent of its use. Until the 1990s in Canada, baccalaureates were awarded only by universities and their affiliated colleges. However, community college type institutions in four provinces (Alberta, British Columbia, Manitoba, and Ontario) now also may award baccalaureates provided that they meet certain conditions established by their respective provinces.

BIU—Basic Income Unit: The funding weight per student used in cal-culating the university operating grant in Ontario. Values range from 1 for students in first year arts courses to 6 for students in PhD programs.

CAAT—College of Applied Arts and Technology: There are 24 colleges of applied arts and technology in Ontario. These colleges receive public funding from the Ontario government and many colleges have more than one campus location. These institutions offer the types of programs indicated in the definition of College (see College).

CAUT—Canadian Association of University Teachers: Founded in 1951, CAUT aims to be the national voice for academic staff representing (in 2009) 65,000 teachers, librarians, researchers, and other academic profes-sionals and general staff.

CCL—Canadian Council on Learning: An organization created by the federal government in 2004. CCL aims to provide Canadians with cur-rent information about effective approaches to learning for learners, educators, employers, and policy-makers. Its work focuses on three key areas: research and knowledge mobilization, monitoring and reporting on progress in learning and the exchange of knowledge about effective learning practices among learning stakeholders.

CFI—Canada Foundation for Innovation: An independent corporation created by the Government of Canada to fund research infrastructure.

CIHR—Canadian Institutes for Health Research: The Canadian Institutes for Health Research (CIHR) is the Government of Canada's agency responsible for funding health research in Canada. CIHR was created in 2000 under the authority of the CIHR Act and reports to Parliament through the Minister of Health.

College: A tertiary educational institution that offers programs of instruction from very short duration to three years in length for secondary school graduates and adults who are beyond the compulsory school leaving age. It offers programs of the following types: vocational and career education; adult upgrading and developmental education; general education and general interest courses; community education and related community services; and it may also offer programs for transfer to universities. In some jurisdictions, some colleges also offer bachelor's degree programs.

Colleges Ontario: The advocacy organization for the province's 24 colleges of applied arts and technology (see ACAATO). Besides advocacy, Colleges Ontario also provides services to its members including research, information, professional development, and central processing of applications.

Council of Ontario Universities (COU): The advocacy organization for the province's universities. Dating from 1962, COU represents the interests of Ontario's universities and provides services to its members and the community including research, communications, and the central processing of university applications.

CRC—Canada Research Chair: In 2000, the Government of Canada created a new permanent program to establish 2000 research professorships—Canada Research Chairs—in universities across the country by 2008. The Canada Research Chairs Program invests $300 million a year on chairs in natural sciences, engineering, health sciences, humanities, and social sciences.

CSAC—College Standards and Accreditation Council: CSAC was established in 1993 with a mandate to develop program standards and provide quality assurance for the college system. In August 1996, as part of a government restructuring of agencies, boards, and commissions, CSAC was closed down, and responsibility for the continuing development of program standards was transferred to the Ministry of Education and Training, now the Ministry of Training, Colleges and Universities.

CSSHE—Canadian Society for the Study of Higher Education: Founded in 1970, the CSSHE is a scholarly and professional organization whose aim is to advance knowledge of higher education in Canada. It publishes the *Canadian Journal of Higher Education.*

CSTA—Council of Science and Technology Advisors: A federally appointed group of advisors outside the government who provide expert science advice to the federal cabinet.

CUCC—College University Consortium Council: The body created in 1996 by the Ontario Minister of Education and Training to facilitate, promote, and coordinate joint education and training ventures by Ontario's colleges and universities. The Consortium Council is appointed jointly by its sponsors, the Council of Ontario Universities (COU), the Council of Presidents (Colleges Ontario), and the Ministry of Training, Colleges and Universities (MTCU) to act on behalf of Consortium members in the selection and management of Consortium projects.

Degree: An academic credential awarded by a post-secondary institution that has the legal authority to award degrees upon completion of a program of study that meets appropriate requirements. Academic degrees include Bachelor, Master, and Doctor. In Ontario, universities derive their authority to award degrees from their respective acts, and colleges obtain their authority, on a program by program basis, from ministerial consents under the *Post-secondary Education Choice and Excellence Act, 2000.*

Diploma: An academic credential awarded by a post-secondary institution upon completion of a program of study that meets appropriate requirements. Diplomas are normally of a duration between one and three years, and are offered mainly in technical and career focused fields. The awarding of diplomas is not regulated to the same extent as is the awarding of degrees. Thus, no specific legal authority is necessary for an institution to award diplomas, although diploma programs may be subject to various quality assurance procedures.

EPF—Established Programs Financing: The federal-provincial transfer scheme introduced by the federal government in 1977 that combined the federal transfers for post-secondary education, hospital insurance, and medical care into a single transfer payment, calculated based on population and economic growth rates.

FTE—Full-time Equivalent: A measure of student enrolment that is the equivalent of one student being enrolled full time for a normal (two term) post-secondary year of study.

Faculty Association: The association (which may or may not be a certified bargaining agent) that represents the interests of faculty members in each university and negotiates with the university administration on a range of matters relating to compensation and other employment matters.

G-13: A group of 13 research-intensive universities in Canada who meet regularly to share information and develop advocacy positions. The members are: University of Alberta, University of British Columbia, University of Calgary, Dalhousie University, Université Laval, McGill University, McMaster University, Université de Montréal, University of Ottawa, Queen's University, University of Toronto, University of Waterloo, and University of Western Ontario.

G.A.S.—General Arts and Science: College programs that are designed to introduce students to all vocational areas in a college (business, technology, applied arts, and health sciences) and to help students develop academic skills and knowledge they need to succeed in the career program of their choice, either at the college or university level. Some G.A.S. program provide first and second year university level arts and sciences courses for which universities award credit to transfer students.

GTA—Greater Toronto Area: The most populous metropolitan area in Canada. The GTA is a provincial planning area, and is the eighth largest metropolitan area in North America. In addition to the City of Toronto, it includes the Regional Municipalities of York, Halton, Peel, and Durham.

Higher Education: Often used interchangeably with "post-secondary" education (see "Post-secondary Education") to refer to education for which completion of secondary school is normally required or expected. However, some commentators use higher education to refer only to that portion of post-secondary education which involves earning credit towards the attainment of degree.

Indirect Costs of Research: The hidden, or indirect, costs of administering and managing research activities. Indirect costs include everything from upgrading library computer systems, and the construction, maintenance, and renovation of research space to helping universities promote their research programs to the public.

ITAL—Institute of Technology and Advanced Learning: The new designation created in 2003 by the Ontario government for selected colleges. Institutes of Technology and Advanced Learning may have up to 15 percent of programming in applied degrees.

Ministerial Consent: The regulatory approval, granted by the Minister of Training, Colleges and Universities, that is required by all public or private degree-granting organizations, either for profit or non-profit, based outside the province to offer all or part of a degree program in Ontario. Ministerial consent is also required by all private organizations in Ontario, either for profit or non-profit, and by all Ontario public organizations that are not empowered to grant degrees by Ontario statute to offer all or part of degree programs. Consent is also required to use the word "university" relating to an educational institution in Ontario.

MTCU—Ministry of Training, Colleges and Universities: The Ontario ministry responsible for higher education. The *Constitution Act* gives exclusive authority to each province in Canada to make laws in relation to education. In Ontario, the Minister of Education and the Minister of Training, Colleges and Universities are responsible for the administration of laws relating to education and skills training.

MYAA—Multi-Year Accountability Agreement: The Government of Ontario introduced MYAAs in stages in the mid 2000s. The Agreements, signed with each post-secondary education institution, articulate the government's goals for the system, and roles and responsibilities in meeting those goals. This agreement confirms the commitments expected from each institution and the sector-wide indicators that will be used to report on results achieved.

NSERC—Natural Sciences and Engineering Research Council of Canada: The federal agency that provides grants for research in the natural sciences and in engineering. The agency supports some 26,500 university students and postdoctoral fellows in their advanced studies.

NSSE—National Survey of Student Engagement: A survey instrument that is used to gauge the level of student involvement in activities that are thought to particularly enhance learning at universities in Canada and the United States. The comparable survey instrument in the college sector is the Community College Survey of Student Engagement, CCSSE.

OCAS—Ontario College Application Service: The college application service operated by Colleges Ontario. The Council of Ontario Universities operates a comparable service known as the Ontario Universities Application Centre, OUAC.

OCGS—Ontario Council on Graduate Studies: The arms-length affiliate of the Council of Ontario Universities that conducts quality reviews of proposed and existing graduate programs in Ontario universities according to the OCGS By-laws and Procedures Governing Appraisals.

OCUA—Ontario Council on University Affairs: The "buffer body" advisory council created by the government in 1974 following the recommendations of the 1972 Commission on Post-secondary Education. OCUA provided the government with reports and recommendations on an annual basis until it was wound up in 1996.

OSAP—Ontario Student Assistance Program: The student assistance program run by the Ontario Ministry of Training, Colleges and Universities, and funded by the provincial and federal governments. OSAP is a needs-based program, meaning that it provides loans, grants, scholarships, and bursaries based on a formula that compares a student's educational costs to expected contributions from his or her parents or spouse (if applicable) as well as his or her own income and assets.

PEQAB—Post-secondary Education Quality Assessment Board: The arms-length advisory agency that makes recommendations to the Minister of Training, Colleges and Universities of Ontario on applications for Ministerial Consent to offer degree programs under the terms of the *Post-secondary Education Choice and Excellence Act, 2000.*

Polytechnics Canada: An alliance of eight (in early 2009) Canadian post-secondary institutions whose aim is to advance the type of post-secondary education that combines practical learning with critical thinking and theoretical knowledge.

Post-secondary Education (also called "tertiary education" or "higher education"): Education that sequentially comes after secondary school and for which completion of secondary school or the equivalent is normally required or expected. Thus, post-secondary education includes programs offered by universities, colleges, and technical institutes. However, some of the programs and courses provided by these institutions do not require completion of secondary school and are not considered as post-secondary, for example, literacy and basic skills, short-term vocational training, and general interest courses.

PQAPA—Program Quality Assurance Process Audit: The self-regulatory mechanism for program quality assurance in Ontario's CAATs. PQAPA supports the responsibility of each college and its board to manage the quality of their programs.

Quality Assessment: A process in which a group of experts examines a college or university program, identifies its strengths and weaknesses, and determines whether the program is of an appropriate standard. The experts who conduct the examination normally are from outside the institution that offers the program, and their examination normally includes a visit to the institution.

Quality Assurance: A process through which the public can be assured that the programs of a post-secondary institution are of an appropriate standard. Quality assurance may involve quality assessment by an external agency, or it may concentrate on auditing the procedures employed by post-secondary institutions to ensure the quality of their programs.

Rae Review: The review of Ontario's post-secondary education system commissioned by the McGuinty Government in 2004, and led by former Ontario Premier Bob Rae. The "Rae Report" was released in 2005.

SSHRC—Social Sciences and Humanities Research Council of Canada: The federal agency that promotes and supports university-based research and training in the humanities and social sciences.

Teaching Load: The average number of teaching units (courses) that a faculty member is expected to assume during a year in addition to faculty- and department-related duties.

University College: A hybrid post-secondary institution which combines some of the functions of a college with some of the functions of a university. University colleges in Canada have been created by authorizing a college to take on some of the functions of a university, particularly substantial provision of baccalaureate programs in core university subjects, or less commonly through the merger of a college and a university. The largest number of university colleges in Canada, five, were created in British Columbia between the late 1980s and the mid 1990s, but these have all been converted into, or merged into, universities.

University: An institution of higher learning that has broad legal authority to award degrees at least at the level of the baccalaureate, and the vast majority of its programs of instruction are at the baccalaureate or higher degree levels. Besides having a faculty of arts and sciences, it may have professional schools and a school of graduate studies. In addition to offering degree programs, universities may be involved to varying extents in the conduct of research.

UPRAC—Undergraduate Program Review and Audit Committee: The body that oversees the system of regular audits of the Ontario universities' policies and procedures for the periodic quality reviews of undergraduate programs conducted by individual universities.

CHRONOLOGY OF KEY EVENTS IN ONTARIO HIGHER EDUCATION, 1950-2009

Date	Event	Main Result
1943-1985	Progressive Conservative governments of Premiers George Drew, Thomas Kennedy, Leslie Frost, John Robarts, William Davis and Frank Miller	
1951	Royal Commission on National Development in the Arts, Letters and Sciences (Vincent Massey, chair)	Recommendation for federal financing
1958	Committee on University Affairs created to advise the Premier on university budget proposals and related matters	Regular advice on governance and funding
1960	Federal Technical and Vocational Training Act, 1960	Provision of funding for training
1962	Founding of Council of Ontario Universities	New organization to support universities' collective autonomy

Date	Event	Main Result
1962	University presidents prepare *Post-secondary education in Ontario, 1962¬1970.* (John Deutsch report)	Plan for 1960s expansion of higher education
1963	Premier Robarts declares a moratorium on creating new universities	No further universities created until 1990s
1964	Department of University Affairs created	Permanent government organization to manage relationships with universities
1965	Legislation enacted to authorize the creation of the college system	A new set of institutions, parallel to the universities
1966	Creation of integrated Canada-Ontario student assistance program (OSAP)	Better accessibility for low-income students
1966	Commission to Study the Development of Graduate Programs in Ontario Universities (John Spinks, chair)	Identified lack of planning in Ontario post-secondary education
1967	Federal-Provincial Relations Act	Set terms for federal transfers on post-secondary education
1967	University operating grants formula introduced	Reduced government role in setting university budgets
1971	Creation of Ministry of Colleges and Universities	Brought both sectors within a single ministry
1972	Commission on Post-secondary Education in Ontario (Douglas Wright, chair)	Options for structure and funding
1974	Ontario Council on University Affairs created	Buffer body to advise on allocation of resources among institutions
1981	Committee on the Future Role of Universities in Ontario (Harry Fisher, chair)	Recommendations to rationalize number of universities to match resource availability

Date	Event	Main Result
1984	Commission on the Future Development of the Universities of Ontario (Edmund Bovey, chair)	Recommendations to rationalize roles of universities, including research intensity
1985-1990	Liberal governments of Premier David Peterson	
1990	Vision 2000: a review of the mandate of Ontario's colleges	Recommendations to revise role of colleges to support accessibility, program quality, and linkages to universities
1990-1995	NDP government of Premier Bob Rae	
1990	Report of the Provincial Auditor on accountability in universities	Declaration of lack of clarity in objectives and accountability to government
1993	Task Force on University Accountability (William Broadhurst, chair)	Recommendations to strengthen relationship between government objectives and university actions
1993	Task Force on Advanced Training (Walter Pitman, chair)	Recommendations for a formal mechanism for the recognition of credentials between colleges and universities
1993-1995	Ontario Council on University Affairs Resource Allocation Review (Joy Cohnstaedt, chair)	Recommendations to separate the funding for research and teaching
1995-2003	Progressive Conservative governments of Premiers Mike Harris and Ernie Eves	
1995	Operating grants cut by 15%, more tuition flexibility	Reduced government spending and increased student tuition
1996	Creation of College University Consortium Council	Consortium to promote college-university cooperation
1996	Ontario Council of University Affairs wound up	Elimination of the "buffer body"

Date	Event	Main Result
1996	Advisory Panel on Future Directions for Post-secondary Education (David Smith, chair)	Recommendations for reform organized around the themes of investment, quality, and accountability
1997-2003	Series of federal budgets that included substantial initiatives in support of research and student assistance	Creation of new agencies and increases in all research funding budgets
1997	Creation of Canada Foundation for Innovation and Ontario R&D Challenge Fund	Competitively allocated research funding
1998	Introduction of Key Performance Indicators (KPIs) for colleges and universities	New accountability mechanisms
1998-2003	Planning for "double cohort" and additional capital and operating funds	System expansion
2000	Post-secondary Education Choice and Excellence Act	Colleges and private institutions permitted to award degrees
2001	Investing in Students Task Force (Jalynn Bennett, chair)	Search for cost savings through administrative rationalization
2003-	Liberal governments of Premier Dalton McGuinty	
2005	Post-secondary Review (Bob Rae)	Recommendations for increased investment, quality measurement, and tuition flexibility
2005	Reaching Higher plan	Increased investment and quality measurement including expansion of graduate programs
2006	Higher Education Quality Council of Ontario created	New body to conduct research and provide evidence-based policy advice

UNIVERSITIES AND COLLEGES IN ONTARIO, 2009

University	Year Estab-lished[39]	Main Campus	FT Under-grad[40]	FT Grad	PT Under-grad	PT Grad	Prof. Schools[41]
Algoma University	2008	Sault Ste. Marie	1,080	0	260	0	
Brock University	1964	St. Catharines	12,800	750	2,700	590	
Carleton University	1952	Ottawa	16,600	2,700	4,100	780	E
University of Guelph	1964	Guelph	18,400	2,200	2,100	200	E
Lakehead University	1965	Thunder Bay	5,700	650	1,300	20	M,E
Laurentian University	1960	Sudbury	4,620	350	2,040	390	M,E

[39] For most universities, this is the year the Legislature authorized them to grant degrees and to be called a university. Many universities evolved from antecedent institutions.

[40] All enrolment numbers are Fall preliminary counts, as posted on the web site of the Association of Universities and Colleges of Canada on 23 July 2009. The Algoma numbers have been deducted from the Laurentian numbers.

[41] Universities with a medical school, law school, or engineering school are indicated with M, L, and E respectively.

University	Year Estab-lished	Main Campus	FT Under-grad	FT Grad	PT Under-grad	PT Grad	Prof. Schools
McMaster University	1887	Hamilton	20,500	2,800	2,900	540	M,E
Nipissing University	1992	North Bay	3,600	20	1,000	170	
University of Ontario Institute of Technology	2002	Oshawa	5,200	130	230	50	E
University of Ottawa	1848	Ottawa	25,900	3,900	5,800	1,400	M,E,L
Queen's University	1841	Kingston	14,300	3,700	3,200	310	M,E,L
Ryerson University	1993	Toronto	17,300	1,500	13,400	470	E
University of Toronto	1827	Toronto	53,800	12,400	7,000	1,900	M,E,L
Trent University	1963	Peter-borough	5,900	330	1,600	60	
University of Waterloo	1957	Waterloo	19,100	3,200	1,700	800	E
The University of Western Ontario	1878	London	25,900	4,300	3,600	560	M,E,L
Wilfrid Laurier University	1960	Waterloo	12,200	800	2,000	330	
University of Windsor	1963	Windsor	11,300	1,500	2,700	180	E,L
York University	1959	Toronto	39,500	3,900	6,800	2,100	E,L
Ontario College of Art and Design (related institution)	1912	Toronto	2,600	20	790	0	

College	Year Established	Main Campus	Enrolment[42]	ITAL[43]
Algonquin College	1966[44]	Ottawa	14,888	
Collège Boréal	1994	Sudbury	1,519	
Cambrian College	1966	Sudbury	3,894	
Canadore College	1973	North Bay	2,688	
Centennial College	1966	Toronto	9,410	
La Cité Collégiale	1989	Ottawa	3,461	
Conestoga College	1966	Kitchener	7,588	ITAL
Confederation College	1966	Thunder Bay	2,926	
Durham College	1966	Oshawa	7,313	
Fanshawe College	1966	London	12,650	
George Brown College	1966	Toronto	16,964	ITAL
Georgian College	1966	Barrie	7,549	
Humber College	1966	Toronto	16,671	ITAL
Lambton College	1966	Sarnia	2,329	
Loyalist College	1966	Belleville	3,307	
Mohawk College	1966	Hamilton	10,716	
Niagara College	1966	Welland	6,807	
Northern College	1966	Timmins	1,164	
St. Clair College	1966	Windsor	7,153	
St. Lawrence College	1966	Kingston	5,487	
Sault College	1973	Sault Ste. Marie	1,965	
Seneca College	1966	Toronto	19,139	ITAL
Sheridan College	1966	Oakville	14,409	ITAL
Sir Sandford Fleming College	1966	Peterborough	5,934	

[42] Full-time equivalents for 2007-08, excluding apprenticeship students.

[43] Colleges designated as an Institute of Technology of Advanced Learning are indicated by ITAL.

[44] The original college boards were created in 1966, although some colleges did not enrol their first students until 1967.

References

Abada, T., F. Hou, and B. Ram, eds. (2008). *Group Differences in Educational Attainment Among the Children of Immigrants*. Ottawa: Statistics Canada.

Alberta Advanced Education and Technology. (2007). *Roles and Mandates. Policy Framework for Alberta's Publicly Funded Advanced Education System*. Edmonton.

Alberta Council on Admission and Transfer. (2009). *About ACAT*. At http://www.acat.gov.ab.ca/acat_information/acat_information.htm (accessed 21 February 2009).

Alberta Department of Advanced Education and Manpower. (1975). *The Report of the Alberta Task Force on Nursing Education*. Edmonton.

Anderson, G. (2006). Assuring Quality/Resisting Quality Assurance: Academics' Responses to Quality in Some Australian Universities. *Quality in Higher Education* 12 (2):161-173.

Anderson, R.E. (1983). *Finance and Effectiveness: A Study of College Environments*. Princeton, NJ: Educational Testing Service.

Association of Colleges of Applied Arts and Technology of Ontario. (2004). *Applied Research and Innovation: Ontario's Colleges—An Underutilized Resource*, 2-3, Toronto.

Association of Colleges of Applied Arts and Technology of Ontario. (2005). *Student Mobility within Ontario's Post-secondary System*. Toronto.

Association of Universities and Colleges of Canada. (2005). *Momentum: The 2005 Report on University Research and Knowledge Mobilization*. Ottawa: AUCC.

Association of Universities and Colleges of Canada. (2007). *Trends in Higher Education, Volume 1: Enrolment*. Ottawa: AUCC.

Association of Universities and Colleges of Canada. (2008a). *Background Document. The Bologna Process: Implications for Canadian Universities*. Ottawa: AUCC.

Association of Universities and Colleges of Canada. (2008b). *Universities: Addressing Canada's Challenges*. Ottawa. At http://www.aucc.ca/_pdf/english/publications/univ_challenges_2008_e.pdf (accessed 27 September 2009)

Association of Universities and Colleges of Canada. (2008c). *Momentum: The 2008 Report on University Research and Knowledge Mobilization*. Ottawa: AUCC.

Astin, A.W. (1980). When Does a College Deserve to be Called "High Quality"? *Current Issues in Higher Education* 2(1):1-9.

Astin, A.W. (1985). *Achieving Educational Excellence*. San Francisco: Jossey-Bass Publishers.

Athabasca University. (2005). *Submission to the Rae Review*. Athabasca, AB: Athabasca University.

Bartram, P. (1980). The Ontario Colleges of Applied Arts and Technology—Review and Analysis of Selected Literature 1965-1976. Ed. D. Thesis. Toronto: University of Toronto.

Barzun, J. (1991). *Begin Here: The Forgotten Conditions of Teaching and Learning*. Chicago, IL: University of Chicago Press.

Baumol, W.J. (1996). Children of Performing Arts, the Economic Dilemma: The Climbing Costs of Health Care and Education. *Journal of Cultural Economics* 20:183-206.

Baumol, W.J. and W.G. Bowen. (1966). *Performing Arts: The Economic Dilemma*. New York: Twentieth Century Fund.

Berger, J., A. Motte, and A. Parkin, eds. (2007). *The Price of Knowledge: Access and Student Finance in Canada*, 3rd ed. Montreal: Canada Millennium Scholarship Foundation.

Birnbaum, R. (1983). *Maintaining Diversity in Higher Education*. San Francisco: Jossey-Bass Publishers.

Bok, D. (2003). *Universities in the Marketplace: The Commercialization of Higher Education*. Princeton, NJ: Princeton University Press.

Bowen, H.R. (1980). *The Costs of Higher Education*. San Francisco: Jossey-Bass.

Boyer, E.L. (1990). *Scholarship Re-Considered: Priorities of the Professoriate*. Princeton, NJ: Carnegie Foundation for the Advancement of Teaching.

Bragg, D.D., B.K. Townsend, and C.M. Rudd. (2008). *The Adult Learner and the Applied Baccalaureate: National and State-by-state Inventory*. Office of Community College Research and Leadership, University of Illinois at Urbana-Champaign. At http://occrl.ed.uiuc.edu/Projects/lumina/AppBaccInventory.pdf (accessed 24 February 2009).

Brint, S., J.A. Douglass, R. Flacks, G. Thomson, and S. Chatman. (2007). *A New Generation: Ethnicity, Socioeconomic Status, Immigration and the Undergraduate Experience at the University of California*. Berkeley: University of California Center for Studies in Higher Education.

British Columbia Ministry of Advanced Education. (2008). Legislation Paves the Way for New Universities in B.C. News Release. 19 April.

Brubacher, J.S. (1977). *On the Philosophy of Higher Education*. San Francisco, CA: Jossey-Bass Publishers.

Bruneau, W. and D.C. Savage. (2002). *Counting out the Scholars: The Case Against Performance Indicators in Higher Education*. Toronto: James Lorimer & Company.

CAAT Academic Negotiating Team. (2006). Memorandum to CAAT Academic Faculty Members. 28 June.

Cameron, D. (2002). The Challenge of Change: Canadian Universities in the 21st Century. *Canadian Public Administration* 45 (2):145-174.

Canadian Association of University Teachers. (1993). *Governance and Accountability. Report of the Independent Study Group on University Governance*. Ottawa.

Canadian Council on Learning. (2007). *Report on Learning in Canada, 2007. Post-secondary Education in Canada–Strategies for Success*. Ottawa.

Chapman, L. and D. Kirby. (2008). A Critical Analysis of the Benefits and Limitations of an Applied Degree in Undergraduate Nursing. *Nursing Leadership* 21 (4):73-84.

Church, E. (2007). "Will There Be Space for Your Child?" *Globe and Mail*, 30 July 2007.

Chung, L. (2006). Education and Earnings. *Perspectives on Labour and Income* 7:6 (Ottawa: Statistics Canada, catalogue 75-001-XIEIE, June 2006), Table 4.

Clark, I.D. (2002a). Advocacy, Self-Management, Advice to Government: The Evolution of the Council of Ontario Universities. In *The University: International Expectations*, eds. F.K. Alexander and K. Alexander, 32-50. Montreal: McGill-Queen's University Press.

Clark, I.D. (2002b). Comments on "The Challenge of Change: Canadian Universities in the Twenty-first Century" by David M. Cameron. *Canadian Public Administration* 45 (3):410-421.

Clark, I.D. and D. Trick. (2006). Advising for Impact: Lessons from the Rae Review on the Use of Special-purpose Advisory Commissions. *Canadian Public Administration* 49 (2):180-195.

Codling, A. and V.L. Meek. (2006). Twelve Propositions on Diversity in Higher Education. *Higher Education Management and Policy* 18 (3):1-24.

College Compensation and Appointments Council. (2008). *Full-time Academic Employees by Classification, February 6, 2008*. Toronto.

Colleges Ontario. (2005). *Environmental Scan 2005*. Toronto.

Colleges Ontario. (2007). *2007 Environmental Scan*. Toronto.

Colleges Ontario. (2008). *Environmental Scan 2008*. Toronto.

College-University Consortium Council. (2002). *Colleges of Applied Arts and Technology: Out-of-Province Degree Completion Arrangements*. Toronto.

Commission Appointed by Secretary of Education Margaret Spellings. (2006). *A Test of Leadership: Charting the Future of U.S. Higher Education*. Washington, DC: U.S. Department of Education.

Commission on Non-Traditional Study. (1973). *Diversity by Design*. San Francisco: Jossey-Bass Publishers.

Commission on Post-Secondary Education in Ontario. (1972). *The Learning Society*. Toronto: Ministry of Colleges and Universities. [Wright Commission report].

Commission on the Future Role of Universities in Ontario. (1984). *Ontario Universities: Options and Futures*. Toronto: Ministry of Colleges and Universities.

Commission to Study the Development of Graduate Programs in Ontario Universities. (1966). *Report*. Toronto: Department of University Affairs. [Spinks Commission report].

Committee on the Future Role of Universities in Ontario. (1981). *Report* Toronto: Ministry of Colleges and Universities.

Committee on the Healing Arts. (1970). Volume 2. Toronto: Queen's Printer.

Corry, J.A. (1981). *My Life and Work, a Happy Partnership*. Kingston: Queen's University.

Côté, J.E. and A. Allahar. (2007). *Ivory Tower Blues: A University System in Crisis.* Toronto: University of Toronto Press.

Council of the Federation. (2006). *Competing for Tomorrow. A Strategy for Post-secondary Education and Skills Training in Canada.* Ottawa.

Council of Ministers of Education, Canada. (2007). *Ministerial Statement on Quality Assurance of Degree Education in Canada.* At http://www.cmec.ca/Publications/Lists/Publications/Attachments/95/QA-Statement-2007.en.pdf (accessed 27 September 2009).

Council of Ontario Universities. (1982). *Squeezing the Triangle: Review of 1978-79 to 1981-82.* Toronto.

Council of Ontario Universities. (1984). *Brief to the Ontario Council on University Affairs on Operating Grant Requirements for 1985-86.* Toronto.

Council of Ontario Universities. (2003). *Advancing Ontario's Future through Advanced Degrees—Report of the COU Task Force on Future Requirements for Graduate Education in Ontario.* Toronto.

Council of Ontario Universities. (2004). *Enhancing Ontario's Competitiveness through Investment in Higher Education.* Toronto.

Council of Ontario Universities. (2004). *Proposed University Accountability Framework. Submitted by COU to the Post-secondary Review.* Toronto.

Council of Ontario Universities. (2006a). News release, 8 March 2006. Toronto.

Council of Ontario Universities. (2006b). Fact sheet, 23 March 2006. Toronto.

Council of Ontario Universities. (2006c). UPRAC Review and Audit Guidelines. At http://www.cou.on.ca/content/objects/UPRACGuidelineswithDegree-ExpectationsFinal.pdf (accessed 19 February 2009).

Council of Ontario Universities. (2007). *Resource Document 2007.* Toronto.

Council of Science and Technology Advisors. (1999). *Building Excellence in Science and Technology.* Ottawa: Government of Canada, Industry Canada.

Crimmel, H.H. (1984). The Myth of the Teacher-Scholar. *Liberal Education* 70 (3):183-198.

Davis, The Hon. W.G. (1966). Statement by the Minister in the Ontario Legislature, 21 May 1965. Reprinted in *Colleges of Applied Arts and Technology Basic Documents,* 5-16. Toronto: Ontario Department of Education.

Davis, W. (2008). National Strategy Vital for Advanced Education. *College Voice.* January. At http://www.co-media.org/documents/2008/College_Voice_January_2008.pdf (accessed 27 September 2009).

Dennison, J.D. (1995). Conclusion. In *Challenge and Opportunity: Canada's Community Colleges at the Crossroads,* ed. J.D. Dennison, 275-284. Vancouver: University of British Columbia Press.

Dennison, J.D. and P. Gallagher. (1986). *Canada's Community Colleges: A Critical Analysis.* Vancouver: University of British Columbia Press.

Deutsche Welle Online. (2006). Germany Chooses Munich, Karlsruhe as Elite Universities. 13 October. http://www.deutschewelle.de/dw/article/0,2144,2203600,00.html. (accessed 26 January 2009).

Doern, B. (2008). *"Polytechnics" in Higher Education Systems.* Toronto: Higher Education Quality Council of Ontario.

Dougherty, K.J. (1994). *The Contradictory College: The Conflicting Origins, Impacts, and Futures of the Community College*. Albany: State University of New York Press.

Drea, C. (2003). *Ontario Government Policy on Accessibility to the Colleges of Applied Arts and Technology: 1965-1995*. Ed.D. thesis, Ontario Institute for Studies in Education, University of Toronto.

Drolet, M. (2005). *Participation in Post-secondary Education in Canada: Has the Role of Parental Income and Education Changed over the 1990s?* Ottawa: Statistics Canada Catalogue No. 11F0019MIE No. 243.

Educational Policy Institute. (2008). *Institutional Student Financial Grants in Ontario*. Toronto: Higher Education Quality Council of Ontario.

Emberley, P.C. (1996). *Zero Tolerance: Hot Button Politics in Canada's Universities*. Toronto: Penguin.

Emery, H. (2004). Total and Private Returns to University Education in Canada: 1960 to 2000 and in Comparison to Other Postsecondary Training. In *Higher Education in Canada*, eds. C.M. Beach, R.W. Boadway, and R.M. McInnis, 77-111. Kingston and Montreal: McGill-Queen's University Press.

Engle, J. and C. O'Brien. (2008). *Demography Is Not Destiny: Increasing the Graduation Rates of Low-Income College Students at Large Public Universities*. Washington: Pell Institute for the Study of Opportunity in Higher Education.

Fallis, G. (2005). *Multiversities, Ideas and Democracy*. Toronto: University of Toronto Press.

Feam, H. (2008). Funding Focus on Research Elite Set to Split Sector. *Times Higher Education Supplement*. 27 November. At http://www.timeshighereducation.co.uk/story.asp?storycode=404503 (accessed 12 March 2009).

Finnie, R. and A. Usher. (2005). *Measuring the Quality of Post-secondary Education: Concepts, Current Practices and a Strategic Plan*. Ottawa: Canadian Policy Research Networks.

Fisher, D. and K. Rubenson. (1998). The Changing Political Economy: The Private and Public Lives of Canadian Universities. In *Universities and Globalization: Critical Perspectives*, eds. J. Currie and J. Newsom, 77-98. London: Sage Publications.

Fleming, W.G. (1971). *Ontario's Educative Society, Vol. IV, Post-secondary and Adult Education*. Toronto: University of Toronto Press.

Flexner, A. (1930). *Universities: American, English, German*. New York: Oxford University Press.

Florida Laws. (2008). *Chapter 2008-52*. At http://laws.flrules.org/files/Ch_2008-052.pdf (accessed 23 September 2008).

Floyd, D.L. and K.P. Walker. (2009). The Community College Baccalaureate: Putting the Pieces Together. *Community College Journal of Research and Practice* 33:90-124.

Floyd, D.L., A.M. Garcia-Falconetti, and M.R. Hrabak. (2009). Baccalaureate Community Colleges: The New Florida System. *Community College Journal of Research and Practice* 33:195-202.

Floyd, D.L., M.L. Skolnik, and K.P. Walker, eds. (2005). *The Community College Baccalaureate: Emerging Trends and Policy Issues*. Sterling, VA: Stylus Publishing, LLC.

Frenette, M. (2005). *The Impact of Tuition Fees on University Access: Evidence from a Large-scale Price Deregulation in Professional Programs*. Ottawa: Statistics Canada.

Frenette, M. (2007). *Why Are Youth from Lower-Income Families Less Likely to Attend University? Evidence from Academic Abilities, Parental Influences, and Financial Constraints.* Ottawa: Statistics Canada.

Geiger, R.L. (1986). *Private Sectors in Higher Education: Structure, Function, and Change in Eight Countries.* Ann Arbor: The University of Michigan Press.

Globe and Mail. (1955). 11 June, p. 1.

Goldin, C. and L.F. Katz. (2007). The Race Between Education and Technology: The Evolution of U.S. Educational Wage Differentials, 1890 to 2005. NBER Working Paper No. W12984. Cambridge, MA: National Bureau of Economic Research.

Government of Canada. (2001). *Achieving Excellence: Investing in People, Knowledge and Opportunity.* Canada's Innovation Strategy. Ottawa: Government of Canada.

Government of Canada. (2002*). Knowledge Matters: Skills sand Learning for Canadians.* Ottawa: Government of Canada.

Government of Canada. (2007). *Mobilizing Science and Technology to Canada's Advantage.* At http://www.ic.gc.ca/eic/site/ic1.nsf/vwapj/S&Tstrategy.pdf/$file/S&Tstrategy.pdf (accessed 27 September 2009).

Greenslade, M.V. (2003). *Faculty Practice as Scholarship in University Schools of Nursing.* Ph.D. Thesis, University of Toronto, Toronto.

Guba, E.G. and Y.S. Lincoln. (1989). *Fourth Generation Evaluation.* Newbury Park, CA: Sage Publications.

Hackl, F. (2008). The Role of the Non-University Sector in Austrian Higher Education. In *Non-University Higher Education in Europe,* eds. J.S. Taylor, J. Brites Ferreira, M. de Lourdes Machado, and R. Santiago, 15-41. Dordrecht: Springer.

Halliwell, J. (2008). *The Nexus of Teaching and Research: Evidence and Insights from the Literature.* Toronto: Higher Education Quality Council of Ontario.

Harley, S. (2002). The Impact of Research Selectivity on Academic Work and Identity in U.K. Universities. *Studies in Higher Education* 27 (2):187-205.

Harley, S. and F.S. Lee. (1997). Research Selectivity, Managerialism, and the Academic Labor Process: The Future of Non-mainstream Economics in U.K. Universities. *Human Relations* 50 (11):1427-60.

Harris, R.S. (1976). *A History of Higher Education in Canada, 1663-1960.* Toronto: University of Toronto Press.

Hattie, J. and H. Marsh. (1996). The Relationship Between Research and Teaching: A Meta-analysis. *Review of Educational Research* 66 (4):507-542.

Higher Education Quality Council of Ontario. (2007). *2007 Review and Research Plan.* Toronto. At http://www.heqco.ca/SiteCollectionDocuments/101_EN.pdf (accessed 27 September 2009).

Higher Education Quality Council of Ontario. (2009). *Second Annual Review and Research Plan.* Toronto. At http://www.heqco.ca/SiteCollectionDocuments/Second%20Annual%20Review%20and%20Research%20Plan.pdf (accessed 27 September 2009).

Hoffmann, F. and P. Oreopoulos. (2009). Professor Qualities and Student Achievement. *The Review of Economics and Statistics* 91 (1):83-92.

Homer-Dixon, T. (2001). *The Ingenuity Gap.* Toronto: Random House.

Huisman, J. (1998). Differentiation and Diversity in Higher Education Systems. In *Higher Education: Handbook of Theory and Research*, Vol. XIII., ed. C. Smart, 75-109. New York: Agathon Press.

Hurtubise, R. and D.C. Rowat. (1970). *The Report of the Commission on the Relations Between Universities and Governments*. Ottawa: University of Ottawa Press.

Inside Higher Education. (2008). *Whose Job Is It?* At http://insidehighered.com/news/2008/06/16/florida (accessed 12 March 2009).

Institute for Competitiveness and Prosperity. (2005). *Realizing Canada's Prosperity Potential*. Toronto.

Institute for Competitiveness and Prosperity. (2007a). *Agenda for Canada's Prosperity: Report on Canada 2007*. Toronto.

Institute for Competiveness and Prosperity. (2007b). Prosperity, Inequality and Poverty, Working Paper No. 10. Toronto.

Jackson, R.W.B. (1963). *The Problem of Numbers in University Enrolment*. Bulletin No. 18. Toronto: Department of Educational Research.

Johnson, D. (2008). How is Variation in Tuition Across Canadian Provinces Related to University Participation in the Youth-in-Transition Survey? Working Paper 2005-09 EC. Department of Economics, Wilfrid Laurier University, Waterloo, ON.

Johnson, D. and F. Rahman. (2005). The Role of Economic Factors, Including the Level of Tuition, in Individual University Participation Decisions in Canada. *Canadian Journal of Higher Education* 35 (3):101-127.

Jones, G.A. (1997). Preface. In *Higher Education in Canada: Different Systems, Different Perspectives*, ed. G.A. Jones, ix-xi. New York: Garland Publishing, Inc.

Jones, G.A. and M.L. Skolnik. (2009). *Degrees of Opportunity: Broadening Student Access by Increasing Institutional Differentiation in Ontario*. Toronto: Higher Education Quality Council of Ontario.

Jones, G.A., P.L. McCarney, and M.L. Skolnik. (2005). *Creating Knowledge, Strengthening Nations*. Toronto: University of Toronto Press.

Jones, G.A., M.L. Skolnik, and B. Soren. (1998). Arrangements for Coordination between University and College Sectors in Canadian Provinces: 1990-1996. *Higher Education Policy* 11 (1):15-27.

Keller, G. (2008). *Higher Education and the New Society*. Baltimore: Johns Hopkins University Press.

Kerr, C. (1978). Higher Education: Paradise Lost? *Higher Education* 7 (3): 261-278.

Kerr, J.C. (1982). The Shouting Starts. *The Canadian Nurse* 78 (2):42-43.

Kezar, A.J., T.C. Chambers, and J.C. Burkhardt, eds. (2005). *Higher Education for the Public Good*. San Francisco: Jossey-Bass Publishers.

Klumpp, M. and U. Teichler. (2008). German Fachhochschulen: Towards the End of a Success Story? In *Non-University Higher Education in Europe*, eds. J.S. Taylor, J. Brites Ferreira, M. de Lourdes Machado, and R. Santiago, 99-122. Dordrecht: Springer.

Kuh, G.D. (2003). The National Survey of Student Engagement: Conceptual Framework and Overview of Psychometric Properties. At http://nsse.iub.edu/pdf/conceptual_framework_2003.pdf (accessed 16 February 2009).

Kuh, G.D., J. Kinzie, J.A. Buckley, B.K. Bridges, and J.C. Hayek. (2006). *What Matters to Student Success: A Review of the Literature*. Washington, DC: National Post-secondary Education Cooperative.

Lang, D.W. (2005). The Political Economy of Performance Funding. In *Taking Public Universities Seriously*, eds. F. Iacobucci and C. Tuohy, 236-237. Toronto: University of Toronto Press.

Lazaridis, M. (2004). The Importance of Basic Research. Keynote Address at the Fourth Annual RE$EARCH MONEY Conference. 9 November 2004. At http://www.cou.on.ca/content/objects/Lazardis%20Speech%202004.pdf (accessed 27 September 2009).

Leslie, P. (1980). *Canadian Universities 1980 and Beyond: Enrolment, Structural Change, and Finance*. AUCC Policy Study No. 3. Ottawa: Association of Universities and Colleges of Canada.

Levin, J.S. (2001). *Globalizing the Community College: Strategies for Change in the 21st Century*. New York: Palgrave.

Levy, D.C. (1999). When Private Higher Education does not Bring Organizational Diversity. In *Private Prometheus: Private Higher Education and Development in the 21st Century*, ed. P.G. Altbach, 15-44. Santa Barbara, CA: Greenwood Press.

Lewin, T. (2009). State Colleges Also Face Cuts in Ambitions. New York Times Online. 17 March. At http://www.nytimes.com (accessed 22 March 2009).

Lewis, C. (2007). Post-secondary Accreditation Called Arbitrary. *The National Post*, A7. 6 November.

Lewis, D.R. and H. Dunbar. (1998). Costs and Productivity in Higher Education: Theory, Evidence and Policy Implications. In *Higher Education: Handbook of Theory and Research*, Vol. 14, ed. J.C. Smart, 39-102. New York: Agathon.

London, H.B. (1980). In Between: The Community College Teacher. *Annals of the American Academy of Political and Social Science* 48.

Lucas, C.J. (1996). *Crisis in the Academy: Rethinking Higher Education in America*. New York: St. Martin's Press.

Macdonald, J.B. (1962). *Higher Education in British Columbia and a Plan for the Future*. Vancouver: University of British Columbia Press.

Machado, M., J. Ferreira, R. Santiago, and J.S. Taylor. (2008). Reframing the Non-University Sector in Europe: Convergence of Diversity. In *Non-University Higher Education in Europe*, eds. M. Machado, J. Ferreira, R. Santiago, and J.S. Taylor, 245-260. Dordrecht: Springer.

Maclean's On Campus. (2009). University Students Grade their Schools. At http://oncampus.macleans.ca/education (accessed 16 February 2009).

Martin Prosperity Institute. (2009). *Ontario Competes: Performance Overview Using the 3Ts of Economic Development*. Toronto.

Maslen, G. (2009). Australia: Bold Plan to Reshape Higher Education. University World News Online. 8 March. At http://www.universityworldnews.com (accessed 22 March 2009).

Massy, W.F. (2009). It's Time to Improve Academic, Not Just Administrative, Productivity. *Chronicle of Higher Education* 55 (18):A26.

Matthews, D.D. (2006). "Can Immigration Compensate for Below-Replacement Fertility?: The Consequences of the Unbalanced Settlement of Immigrants in Canadian Cities, 2001-2051." Unpublished PhD thesis, Department of Sociology, University of Western Ontario, London, ON.

McCarney, P.L and M.L. Skolnik, eds. (2005). *Creating Knowledge, Strengthening Nations: The Changing Role of Higher Education*. Toronto: University of Toronto Press.

Meek, V.L., L. Goedegebuure, O. Kivinen, and R. Rinne, eds. (1996). *The Mockers and the Mocked: Comparative Perspectives on Differentiation, Convergence, and Diversity in Higher Education*. Oxford: Pergamon/IAU Press.

Mendelson, M. (2006). *Aboriginal Peoples and Post-secondary Education in Canada*. Ottawa: Caledon Institute.

Monahan, E.J. (2004). *Collective Autonomy: A History of the Council of Ontario Universities, 1962-2000*. Waterloo, ON: Wilfrid Laurier University Press.

Morley, L. (2003). *Quality and Power in Higher Education*. Buckingham, UK: Society for Research into Higher Education/Open University Press.

Munroe-Blum, H., with G. Davies and J. Duderstadt. (1999). *Growing Ontario's Innovation System: The Strategic Role of University Research*. Ontario Ministries of Colleges, Training and University, Energy Science and Technology and the Ontario Jobs and Investment Board. Toronto.

Mussallem, H.K. (1965). *Nursing Education in Canada*. Ottawa: Queen's Printer.

National Center for Public Policy and Higher Education. (2006). *Measuring Up 2006: The National Report Card on Higher Education*. San Jose, CA: National Center.

Neuman, S. (2005). Creating Knowledge, Strengthening Nations: The Role of Research and Education in the Humanities and Social Sciences in Government Agendas for Innovation. In *Creating Knowledge, Strengthening Nations*, eds. G.A. Jones, P.L. McCarney, and M.L. Skolnik, 227-245. Toronto: University of Toronto Press.

Newman, F., L. Couturier, and J. Scurry, eds. (2004). *The Future of Higher Education: Rhetoric, Reality, and the Risks of the Market*. San Francisco: Jossey-Bass Publishers.

Nossal, K.R. (2006). A Question of Balance: The Cult of Research Intensivity and the Professing of Political Science in Canada: Presidential Address to the Canadian Political Science Association, Toronto, Ontario, June 2, 2006. *Canadian Journal of Political Science* 39 (4):735-754.

Odum, E.P. (1992). Great Ideas in Ecology for the 1990s, *Bioscience* 42 (7):542-545.

OECD. (2006). *Education at a Glance 2006*. Paris.

OECD. (2007). *Education at a Glance 2007: Briefing Note for the United States* (18 September, 2). Paris.

OECD. (2008). *Education at a Glance 2008*. Paris.

Ontario College Quality Assurance Service. (2007). *Program Quality Assurance Process Audit Orientation Manual: Quality Assurance and Improvement in Ontario's Colleges*. Toronto.

Ontario Confederation of University Faculty Associations. (2008). *Career-Limiting Move? Teaching-Only Positions in Ontario Universities*. Toronto.

Ontario Council on University Affairs. (1981). *Seventh Annual Report*. Toronto.

Ontario Council on University Affairs. (1985). *Eleventh Annual Report*. Toronto.

Ontario Council on University Affairs. (1995). *21st Annual Report*. Toronto.

Ontario Council on University Affairs Task Force on Resource Allocation. (1994). *Sustaining Quality in Changing Times: A Discussion Paper*. Toronto.

Ontario Minister of University Affairs (1967). *Annual Report*. Toronto.

Ontario Ministry of Finance. (2005). *Ontario Budget 2005: Backgrounder: Reaching Higher: The Plan for Post-secondary Education.* Toronto.

Ontario Minister of Finance. (2009). *Ontario Budget 2009.* Toronto.

Organization of Part-time and Sessional Employees of the Colleges of Applied Arts and Technology. (2007). *Compromising Quality.* Toronto.

Paquet, G. (2006). *Savoirs, Savoir-faire, Savoir-être: In Praise of Professional Wroughting and Wrighting. A Think-Piece Prepared for Campus 2020—an Inquiry into the Future of British Columbia's Post-secondary Education System.* Victoria, BC: Ministry of Advanced Education and Manpower Development.

Parker, S. (2005). Australian Higher Education: Crossroads or Crisis? In *Taking Public Universities Seriously,* eds. F. Iacobucci and C. Tuohy, 26-37. Toronto: University of Toronto Press.

Patterson, G. (2000). Findings on Economies of Scale in Higher Education: Implications for Strategies of Merger and Alliance. *Tertiary Education and Management* 6:259-269.

Perkin, H. (1991). History of Universities. In *International Higher Education: An Encyclopedia.* Vol. 1., ed., P.G. Altbach, 169-204. New York: Garland Publishing, Inc.

Piper, M. (2002). Building a Civil Society: A New Role for the Human Sciences. Killam Annual Lecture, Halifax, NS: The Killam Trusts.

Piper, M. (6 October 2008). A Five-Step Program for Change. University Affairs. Ottawa, Ontario: Association of Universities and Colleges of Canada. At http://www.universityaffairs.ca/a-five-step-program-for-change.aspx (accessed 27 September 2009).

Pocklington, T. and A. Tupper. (2000*). No Place to Learn: Why Universities Aren't Working.* Vancouver: UBC Press.

Polytechnics Canada. (2009). About Polytechnics Canada. At http://www.polytechnicscanada.ca/about (accessed 25 February 2009).

Post-secondary Education Quality Assessment Board. (2009). *Completed Applications.* Toronto. At http://www.peqab.ca/completed.html (accessed 9 April, 2009).

Powell, B. (2007). Stakeholders' Perceptions of Their Influence and that of Others on Decision-making Processes in Ontario CAATs and Public Universities. Ph.D. Thesis, University of Toronto, Toronto.

Prichard, J.R.S. (2000). "Federal Support for Higher Education and Research in Canada: The New Paradigm." The 2000 Killam Annual Lecture. Halifax, NS: The Killam Trusts. At http://www.killamtrusts.ca/docs/Killam_Lec_00.pdf (accessed 27 September 2009).

Rae, The Honourable Bob (Adviser to the Premier and the Minister of Training, Colleges and Universities). (2005, February). *Ontario A Leader in Learning. Report and Recommendations.* Toronto: Ministry of Training, Colleges and Universities. At http://www.edu.gov.on.ca/eng/document/reports/postsec.pdf (accessed 27 September 2009).

Ratcliff, J.L. (2003). Dynamic and Communicative Aspects of Quality Assurance. *Quality in Higher Education* 9 (2):117-131.

Readings, B. (1996). *The University in Ruins.* Cambridge, MA: Harvard University Press.

Registered Nurses Association of Ontario. (1986). *Education for Excellence: Report and Background Papers Concerning the Entry to Practice Position.* Toronto: RNAO.

Rhoades, G. (1990). Political Competition and Differentiation in Higher Education. In *Differentiation Theory and* Social *Change: Comparative and Historical Perspectives,* eds. J.C. Alexander and P. Colony, 187-221. New York: Columbia University Press.

Romer, P. (2007). Economic Growth. In *The Concise Encyclopedia of Economics,* ed. D.R. Henderson. Indianapolis, IN: Liberty Fund.

Royal Commission of Inquiry on Education in the Province of Quebec. (1963). Quebec: Queen's Printer.

Royal Commission on Higher Education in New Brunswick. (1962). Fredericton, NB: Government of New Brunswick.

Royce, D. (1998). University System Coordination and Planning in Ontario, 1945-1996, Ed.D. Dissertation, University of Toronto, Toronto.

Ryerson University. (2008). *Consultation Paper: Leading toward Ryerson University's Academic Plan: 2008-2013.* Toronto.

Schachner, N. (1938). *The Mediaeval Universities.* London: Allen.

Schumacher, C. (1983). The Problem of Scale in Higher Education. In *Economies of Scale in Higher Education,* ed., S. Goodlad, 55-72. Guildford, Surry: Society for Research into Higher Education.

Shaienks, D., T. Gluszynski, and J. Bayard. (2008). *Post-secondary Education—Participation and Dropping Out: Differences Across University, College and Other Types of Post-secondary Institutions.* Ottawa: Statistics Canada.

Skolnik, M.L. (1986). If the Cut is So Deep, Where is the Blood? Problems in Research on the Impact of Financial Restraint. *The Review of Higher Education* 9 (4):435-455.

Skolnik, M.L. (1989). How Academic Program Review can Foster Conformity and Stifle Diversity of Thought and Method in the University. *The Journal of Higher Education* 60 (6):619-643.

Skolnik, M.L. (1994). University Accountability in Ontario in the Nineties: Is There a Role for a Provincial Agency? *Ontario Journal of Higher Education* 108-127.

Skolnik, M.L. (1995). Upsetting the Balance: The Debate on Proposals for Radically Altering the Relationship Between Universities and Government in Ontario. *Ontario Journal of Higher Education* 4-26.

Skolnik, M.L. (1996). Design, Deregulation, or Just Drifting: Ontario Universities Need Firmer Direction. *The University of Toronto Bulletin* (9 December):12.

Skolnik, M.L. (1997). Putting It All Together: Viewing Canadian Higher Education from a Collection of Jurisdiction Based Perspectives. In *Higher Education in Canada: Different Systems, Different Perspectives,* ed., G.A. Jones, 325-342. New York: Garland Publishing Company.

Skolnik, M.L. (2000). Does Counting Publications Provide any Useful Information about Academic Performance? *Teacher Education Quarterly* 27 (2):15-26.

Skolnik, M.L. (2004). The Relationship of the Community College to Other Providers of Post-secondary and Adult Education in Canada and Implications for Public Policy. *Higher Education Perspectives* 1 (1):36-58. At http://hep.oise.utoronto.ca/index.php/hep/article/viewFile/574/653 (accessed 27 September 2009).

Skolnik, M.L. (2005a). Reflections of the Difficulty of Balancing the University's Economic and Non-economic Objectives in Periods when its Economic Role is Highly Valued. In *Creating Knowledge, Strengthening Nations,* eds. G.A. Jones, P.L. McCarney, and M.L. Skolnik, 227-245. Toronto: University of Toronto Press.

Skolnik, M.L. (2005b). The Case for Giving Greater Attention to Structure in Higher Education Policy Making. In *Higher Education in Canada,* eds. C. Beach, R. Boadway, and M. McInnis, 53-75. Kingston, ON: John Deutsch Institute, Queen's University.

Skolnik, M.L. (2005c). The Community College Baccalaureate in Canada: Addressing Accessibility and Workforce Needs. In *The Community College Baccalaureate: Emerging Trends and Policy Issues,* eds. D.L. Floyd, M.L. Skolnik, and K.P. Walker, 49-72. Sterling, VA: Stylus Publishing Company.

Skolnik, M.L. (2008). Community Colleges and Further Education in Canada. In *Global Development of Community Colleges, Technical Colleges, and Further Education Programs,* eds. P.A. Elsner, G.R. Boggs, and J.T. Irwin, 41-50. Washington, DC: Community College Press.

Skolnik, M.L. and G.A. Jones. (1992). A Comparative Analysis of Arrangements for State Coordination of Higher Education in Canada and the United States. *The Journal of Higher Education* 63 (2):121-142.

Skolnik, M.L. and G.A. Jones. (1993). Arrangements for Coordination between University and College Sectors in Canadian Provinces. *Canadian Journal of Higher Education* 23 (1):56-73.

Smith, S. (1989). *Skilled and Educated: A Solution to Ontario's Urgent Need for More Polytechnic Education. Vision 2000 Background Paper.* Toronto: Ministry of Colleges and Universities.

Smith, S. (1991). *Commission of Inquiry on Canadian University Education.* Ottawa: Association of Universities and Colleges of Canada.

Snowdon, K. (2007). The Abolition of Age-based Mandatory Retirement in Academe: Revisiting the "Value" of Older Faculty. Harrowsmith, ON: Snowdon and Associates. At http://www.snowdonandassociates.ca/presentations.htm (accessed 29 September 2009).

Spinks, J.W.T. (1966). *Report to the Committee on University Affairs and the Committee of Presidents of Provincially-assisted Universities of the Commission to Study the Development of Graduate Programs in Ontario Universities.* Toronto: The Commission.

Statistics Canada. (2006a). 2006 Census Data Products. At www12.statcan.ca/english/census06/datatopics (accessed 12 March 2009).

Statistics Canada. (2006b). Educational Portrait of Canada, 2006 Census: Aboriginal population. At http://www12.statcan.ca/census-recensement/2006/as-sa/97-560/index-eng.cfm?CFID=3297203&CFTOKEN=88546588 (accessed 27 September 2009).

Stoll, P. (1993). *A Question of Transfer: An Historical Review of the Ontario Colleges' Mandate*. M.Ed. Thesis. Brock University, St. Catharines, ON.

Sweet, R., P. Anisef, and D. Walters. (2008). *Immigrant Parents' Investments in Their Children's Post-Secondary Education*. Montreal: Canada Millennium Scholarship Foundation.

Tam, P. (2007). Universities Told to Revamp Arts Degrees. *The Ottawa Citizen*, 6 December. At http://www.canada.com/ottawacitizen/news/story.html?id=b7f593a3-65b4-45de-87e2-4b835ca57926&p=1# (accessed 22 October 2009)

Task Force on Advanced Training. (1993). *No Dead-Ends*. Toronto: Ministry of Education and Training.

Task Force on University Accountability. (1993). *University Accountability: A Strengthened Framework*. Toronto.

Taylor, J.S., J. Brites Ferreira, M. de Lourdes Machado, and R. Santiago, eds. (2008). *Non-University Higher Education in Europe*. Dordrecht: Springer.

Teixeira, P., B. Jongbloed, D. Dill, and A. Amaraleds. (2004). *Markets in Higher Education: Rhetoric or Reality*. Dordecht: Kluwer.

Townsend, B.K. (2004). The Upside Down Degree. Presented in the symposium "Democratization or Destruction of the Baccalaureate? The Upside Down Degree and the Community College Baccalaureate," Annual Meeting of the Association for the Study of Higher Education, Kansas City, MO, 4-7 November.

Townsend, B.K. (2007). Interpreting the Influence of Community College Attendance upon Baccalaureate Attainment. *Community College Review* 35 (2):135-146.

Trick, D. (2005). *Continuity, Retrenchment and Renewal: The Politics of Government-University Relations in Ontario, 1985-2002*. Ph.D. thesis, Department of Political Science, University of Toronto, Toronto.

Trow, M. (1973). *Problems in the Transition from Elite to Mass Higher Education*. Berkeley, CA: Carnegie Commission on Higher Education Reprint.

UN-HABITAT. (2008). State of the World's Cities, 2008/09. New York: United Nations.

University of Toronto. (2008). *Towards 2030: A Third Century of Excellence at the University of Toronto: Synthesis Report*. Toronto.

University of Toronto Scarborough. (2009). Joint Program: Journalism. Toronto. At http://www.utsc.utoronto.ca/~jtprogs/Journalism/index.html (accessed 12 March 2009).

Usher, A. (2008). *The Party's Over—What Now?* Educational Policy Institute. At http://www.educationalpolicy.org/pub/commentary/081010.html (accessed 27 September 2009).

Usher, A. and R. Dunn. (2009). *On the Brink—How the Recession of 2009 will Affect Post-secondary Education*. Educational Policy Institute. At http://www.educationalpolicy.org/pub/pubpdf/0902_Recession.pdf (accessed 27 September 2009).

Valimaa, J. and M.L. Neuvonen-Rauhala. (2008). Polytechnics in Finnish Higher Education. In *Non-University Higher Education in Europe*, eds. J.S. Taylor, J. Brites Ferreira, M. de Lourdes Machado, and R. Santiago, 77-98. Dordrecht: Springer.

Vision 2000. (1990). *Quality and Opportunity. The Final Report of the Vision 2000 Task Force*. Toronto: Ministry of Colleges and Universities.

Volkwein, J.F. and D.A. Carbone. (1994). The Impact of Departmental Research and Teaching Climates on Undergraduate Growth and Satisfaction. *Journal of Higher Education* 65 (2):147-167.

Walker, K.P. (2005). History, Rationale, and Community College Baccalaureate Association. In *The Community College Baccalaureate: Emerging Trends and Policy Issues*, eds. D.L. Floyd, M.L. Skolnik, and K.P. Walker, 9-24. Sterling, VA: Stylus Publishing Company.

Wolf, A. (2002). *Does Education Matter: Myths about Education and Economic Growth*. London: Penguin Books.

Wolf, A. (2004). Education and Economic Performance: Simplistic Theories and their Policy Consequences, *Oxford Review of Economic Policy* 20 (2):319-320.

Wood, M.J. (2003). Entry to Practice: Striving for the Baccalaureate Standard. In *Canadian Nursing: Issues and Perspectives*, 4th ed., eds. J. Ross-Kerr and M.J. Wood, 369-382. Toronto: Mosby.

Zha, Q. (2009). The Global Campus. Blog. *Academic Matters*. At www.academicmatters.ca/online_community.blogs.gk (accessed 12 March 2009).

About the Authors

Ian D. Clark is a professor in the School of Public Policy and Governance, University of Toronto, a former federal deputy minister, and past-president of the Council of Ontario Universities.

Greg Moran is a professor and member of both the clinical and developmental groups within the Department of Psychology, University of Western Ontario, and a former Chair of Psychology, Dean of Graduate Studies, and Provost and Vice-President (Academic) at Western.

Michael L. Skolnik is professor emeritus in the Ontario Institute for Studies in Education of the University of Toronto and held the William G. Davis Chair in Community College Leadership in the University of Toronto from its establishment in 1999 until 2007.

David Trick is president of David Trick and Associates, consultants in higher education strategy and management, and is the former assistant deputy minister for post-secondary education in the Government of Ontario.

INDEX

Queen's Policy Studies
Recent Publications

The Queen's Policy Studies Series is dedicated to the exploration of major public policy issues that confront governments and society in Canada and other nations.

Our books are available from good bookstores everywhere, including the Queen's University bookstore (http://www.campusbookstore.com/). McGill-Queen's University Press is the exclusive world representative and distributor of books in the series. A full catalogue and ordering information may be found on their web site (http://mqup.mcgill.ca/).

School of Policy Studies

The New Federal Policy Agenda and the Voluntary Sector: On the Cutting Edge, Rachel Laforest (ed.), 2009. Paper 978-1-55339-132-6

The Afghanistan Challenge: Hard Realities and Strategic Choices, Hans-Georg Ehrhart and Charles Pentland (eds.), 2009. Paper 978-1-55339-241-5

Measuring What Matters in Peace Operations and Crisis Management, Sarah Jane Meharg, 2009. Paper 978-1-55339-228-6 Cloth ISBN 978-1-55339-229-3

International Migration and the Governance of Religious Diversity, Paul Bramadat and Matthias Koenig (eds.), 2009. Paper 978-1-55339-266-8 Cloth ISBN 978-1-55339-267-5

Who Goes? Who Stays? What Matters? Accessing and Persisting in Post-Secondary Education in Canada, Ross Finnie, Richard E. Mueller, Arthur Sweetman, and Alex Usher (eds.), 2008. Paper 978-1-55339-221-7 Cloth ISBN 978-1-55339-222-4

Economic Transitions with Chinese Characteristics: Thirty Years of Reform and Opening Up, Arthur Sweetman and Jun Zhang (eds.), 2009. Paper 978-1-55339-225-5 Cloth ISBN 978-1-55339-226-2

Economic Transitions with Chinese Characteristics: Social Change During Thirty Years of Reform, Arthur Sweetman and Jun Zhang (eds.), 2009. Paper 978-1-55339-234-7 Cloth ISBN 978-1-55339-235-4

Dear Gladys: Letters from Over There, Gladys Osmond (Gilbert Penney ed.), 2009. Paper ISBN 978-1-55339-223-1

Immigration and Integration in Canada in the Twenty-first Century, John Biles, Meyer Burstein, and James Frideres (eds.), 2008. Paper ISBN 978-1-55339-216-3 Cloth ISBN 978-1-55339-217-0

Robert Stanfield's Canada, Richard Clippingdale, 2008. ISBN 978-1-55339-218-7

Exploring Social Insurance: Can a Dose of Europe Cure Canadian Health Care Finance? Colleen Flood, Mark Stabile, and Carolyn Tuohy (eds.), 2008. Paper ISBN 978-1-55339-136-4 Cloth ISBN 978-1-55339-213-2

Canada in NORAD, 1957–2007: A History, Joseph T. Jockel, 2007. Paper ISBN 978-1-55339-134-0 Cloth ISBN 978-1-55339-135-7

Canadian Public-Sector Financial Management, Andrew Graham, 2007.
Paper ISBN 978-1-55339-120-3 Cloth ISBN 978-1-55339-121-0

Emerging Approaches to Chronic Disease Management in Primary Health Care,
John Dorland and Mary Ann McColl (eds.), 2007. Paper ISBN 978-1-55339-130-2
Cloth ISBN 978-1-55339-131-9

Fulfilling Potential, Creating Success: Perspectives on Human Capital Development,
Garnett Picot, Ron Saunders and Arthur Sweetman (eds.), 2007.
Paper ISBN 978-1-55339-127-2 Cloth ISBN 978-1-55339-128-9

Reinventing Canadian Defence Procurement: A View from the Inside, Alan S. Williams,
2006. Paper ISBN 0-9781693-0-1 (Published in association with Breakout Educational
Network)

SARS in Context: Memory, History, Policy, Jacalyn Duffin and Arthur Sweetman (eds.),
2006. Paper ISBN 978-0-7735-3194-9 Cloth ISBN 978-0-7735-3193-2
(Published in association with McGill-Queen's University Press)

Dreamland: How Canada's Pretend Foreign Policy has Undermined Sovereignty,
Roy Rempel, 2006. Paper ISBN 1-55339-118-7 Cloth ISBN 1-55339-119-5
(Published in association with Breakout Educational Network)

Canadian and Mexican Security in the New North America: Challenges and Prospects,
Jordi Díez (ed.), 2006. Paper ISBN 978-1-55339-123-4 Cloth ISBN 978-1-55339-122-7

*Global Networks and Local Linkages: The Paradox of Cluster Development in an Open
Economy*, David A. Wolfe and Matthew Lucas (eds.), 2005. Paper ISBN 1-55339-047-4
Cloth ISBN 1-55339-048-2

Choice of Force: Special Operations for Canada, David Last and Bernd Horn (eds.), 2005.
Paper ISBN 1-55339-044-X Cloth ISBN 1-55339-045-8

Force of Choice: Perspectives on Special Operations, Bernd Horn, J. Paul de B. Taillon, and
David Last (eds.), 2004. Paper ISBN 1-55339-042-3 Cloth 1-55339-043-1

New Missions, Old Problems, Douglas L. Bland, David Last, Franklin Pinch, and
Alan Okros (eds.), 2004. Paper ISBN 1-55339-034-2 Cloth 1-55339-035-0

*The North American Democratic Peace: Absence of War and Security Institution-Building in
Canada-US Relations*, 1867-1958, Stéphane Roussel, 2004.
Paper ISBN 0-88911-937-6 Cloth 0-88911-932-2

Implementing Primary Care Reform: Barriers and Facilitators, Ruth Wilson, S.E.D. Shortt,
and John Dorland (eds.), 2004. Paper ISBN 1-55339-040-7 Cloth 1-55339-041-5

Social and Cultural Change, David Last, Franklin Pinch, Douglas L. Bland, and
Alan Okros (eds.), 2004. Paper ISBN 1-55339-032-6 Cloth 1-55339-033-4

Clusters in a Cold Climate: Innovation Dynamics in a Diverse Economy, David A. Wolfe and
Matthew Lucas (eds.), 2004. Paper ISBN 1-55339-038-5 Cloth 1-55339-039-3

Canada Without Armed Forces? Douglas L. Bland (ed.), 2004.
Paper ISBN 1-55339-036-9 Cloth 1-55339-037-7

Campaigns for International Security: Canada's Defence Policy at the Turn of the Century,
Douglas L. Bland and Sean M. Maloney, 2004. Paper ISBN 0-88911-962-7
Cloth 0-88911-964-3

Understanding Innovation in Canadian Industry, Fred Gault (ed.), 2003.
Paper ISBN 1-55339-030-X Cloth 1-55339-031-8

Delicate Dances: Public Policy and the Nonprofit Sector, Kathy L. Brock (ed.), 2003.
Paper ISBN 0-88911-953-8 Cloth 0-88911-955-4

Beyond the National Divide: Regional Dimensions of Industrial Relations, Mark Thompson,
Joseph B. Rose, and Anthony E. Smith (eds.), 2003. Paper ISBN 0-88911-963-5
Cloth 0-88911-965-1

The Nonprofit Sector in Interesting Times: Case Studies in a Changing Sector, Kathy L. Brock
and Keith G. Banting (eds.), 2003. Paper ISBN 0-88911-941-4 Cloth 0-88911-943-0

Clusters Old and New: The Transition to a Knowledge Economy in Canada's Regions,
David A. Wolfe (ed.), 2003. Paper ISBN 0-88911-959-7 Cloth 0-88911-961-9

The e-Connected World: Risks and Opportunities, Stephen Coleman (ed.), 2003.
Paper ISBN 0-88911-945-7 Cloth 0-88911-947-3

Knowledge Clusters and Regional Innovation: Economic Development in Canada,
J. Adam Holbrook and David A. Wolfe (eds.), 2002. Paper ISBN 0-88911-919-8
Cloth 0-88911-917-1

Lessons of Everyday Law/Le droit du quotidien, Roderick Alexander Macdonald, 2002.
Paper ISBN 0-88911-915-5 Cloth 0-88911-913-9

*Improving Connections Between Governments and Nonprofit and Voluntary Organizations:
Public Policy and the Third Sector*, Kathy L. Brock (ed.), 2002.
Paper ISBN 0-88911-899-X Cloth 0-88911-907-4

Centre for the Study of Democracy

The Authentic Voice of Canada: R.B. Bennett's Speeches in the House of Lords, 1941-1947,
Christopher McCreery and Arthur Milnes (eds.), 2009. Paper 978-1-55339-275-0
Cloth ISBN 978-1-55339-276-7

*Age of the Offered Hand: The Cross-Border Partnership Between President George H.W. Bush
and Prime-Minister Brian Mulroney, A Documentary History*, James McGrath and
Arthur Milnes (eds.), 2009. Paper ISBN 978-1-55339-232-3
Cloth ISBN 978-1-55339-233-0

*In Roosevelt's Bright Shadow: Presidential Addresses About Canada from Taft to Obama in
Honour of FDR's 1938 Speech at Queen's University*, Christopher McCreery and
Arthur Milnes (eds.), 2009. Paper ISBN 978-1-55339-230-9
Cloth ISBN 978-1-55339-231-6

*Politics of Purpose, 40th Anniversary Edition, The Right Honourable John N. Turner 17th
Prime Minister of Canada*, Elizabeth McIninch and Arthur Milnes (eds.), 2009.
Paper ISBN 978-1-55339-227-9 Cloth ISBN 978-1-55339-224-8

*Bridging the Divide: Religious Dialogue and Universal Ethics, Papers for The InterAction
Council*, Thomas S. Axworthy (ed.), 2008. Paper ISBN 978-1-55339-219-4
Cloth ISBN 978-1-55339-220-0

Institute of Intergovernmental Relations

The Democratic Dilemma: Reforming the Canadian Senate, Jennifer Smith (ed.), 2009.
Paper 978-1-55339-190-6

Canada: The State of the Federation 2006/07, vol. 20, *Transitions – Fiscal and Political Federalism in an Era of Change*, John R. Allan, Thomas J. Courchene, and Christian Leuprecht (eds.), 2009. Paper ISBN 978-1-55339-189-0 Cloth ISBN 978-1-55339-191-3

Comparing Federal Systems, Third Edition, Ronald L. Watts, 2008.
Paper ISBN 978-1-55339-188-3

Canada: The State of the Federation 2005, vol. 19, *Quebec and Canada in the New Century – New Dynamics, New Opportunities*, Michael Murphy (ed.), 2007.
Paper ISBN 978-1-55339-018-3 Cloth ISBN 978-1-55339-017-6

Spheres of Governance: Comparative Studies of Cities in Multilevel Governance Systems, Harvey Lazar and Christian Leuprecht (eds.), 2007. Paper ISBN 978-1-55339-019-0
Cloth ISBN 978-1-55339-129-6

Canada: The State of the Federation 2004, vol. 18, *Municipal-Federal-Provincial Relations in Canada*, Robert Young and Christian Leuprecht (eds.), 2006.
Paper ISBN 1-55339-015-6 Cloth ISBN 1-55339-016-4

Canadian Fiscal Arrangements: What Works, What Might Work Better, Harvey Lazar (ed.), 2005. Paper ISBN 1-55339-012-1 Cloth ISBN 1-55339-013-X

Canada: The State of the Federation 2003, vol. 17, *Reconfiguring Aboriginal-State Relations*, Michael Murphy (ed.), 2005. Paper ISBN 1-55339-010-5 Cloth ISBN 1-55339-011-3

Canada: The State of the Federation 2002, vol. 16, *Reconsidering the Institutions of Canadian Federalism*, J. Peter Meekison, Hamish Telford, and Harvey Lazar (eds.), 2004.
Paper ISBN 1-55339-009-1 Cloth ISBN 1-55339-008-3

Federalism and Labour Market Policy: Comparing Different Governance and Employment Strategies, Alain Noël (ed.), 2004. Paper ISBN 1-55339-006-7 Cloth ISBN 1-55339-007-5

The Impact of Global and Regional Integration on Federal Systems: A Comparative Analysis, Harvey Lazar, Hamish Telford, and Ronald L. Watts (eds.), 2003.
Paper ISBN 1-55339-002-4 Cloth ISBN 1-55339-003-2

Canada: The State of the Federation 2001, vol. 15, *Canadian Political Culture(s) in Transition*, Hamish Telford and Harvey Lazar (eds.), 2002. Paper ISBN 0-88911-863-9
Cloth ISBN 0-88911-851-5

Federalism, Democracy and Disability Policy in Canada, Alan Puttee (ed.), 2002.
Paper ISBN 0-88911-855-8 Cloth ISBN 1-55339-001-6, ISBN 0-88911-845-0 (set)

Comparaison des régimes fédéraux, 2ᵉ éd., Ronald L. Watts, 2002.
Paper ISBN 1-55339-005-9

John Deutsch Institute for the Study of Economic Policy

The 2006 Federal Budget: Rethinking Fiscal Priorities, Charles M. Beach, Michael Smart, and Thomas A. Wilson (eds.), 2007. Paper ISBN 978-1-55339-125-8
Cloth ISBN 978-1-55339-126-6

Health Services Restructuring in Canada: New Evidence and New Directions, Charles M. Beach, Richard P. Chaykowksi, Sam Shortt, France St-Hilaire, and Arthur Sweetman (eds.), 2006. Paper ISBN 978-1-55339-076-3 Cloth ISBN 978-1-55339-075-6

A Challenge for Higher Education in Ontario, Charles M. Beach (ed.), 2005.
Paper ISBN 1-55339-074-1 Cloth ISBN 1-55339-073-3

Current Directions in Financial Regulation, Frank Milne and Edwin H. Neave (eds.), Policy Forum Series no. 40, 2005. Paper ISBN 1-55339-072-5 Cloth ISBN 1-55339-071-7

Higher Education in Canada, Charles M. Beach, Robin W. Boadway, and R. Marvin McInnis (eds.), 2005. Paper ISBN 1-55339-070-9 Cloth ISBN 1-55339-069-5

Financial Services and Public Policy, Christopher Waddell (ed.), 2004.
Paper ISBN 1-55339-068-7 Cloth ISBN 1-55339-067-9

The 2003 Federal Budget: Conflicting Tensions, Charles M. Beach and Thomas A. Wilson (eds.), Policy Forum Series no. 39, 2004. Paper ISBN 0-88911-958-9
Cloth ISBN 0-88911-956-2

Canadian Immigration Policy for the 21st Century, Charles M. Beach, Alan G. Green, and Jeffrey G. Reitz (eds.), 2003. Paper ISBN 0-88911-954-6 Cloth ISBN 0-88911-952-X

Framing Financial Structure in an Information Environment, Thomas J. Courchene and Edwin H. Neave (eds.), Policy Forum Series no. 38, 2003. Paper ISBN 0-88911-950-3
Cloth ISBN 0-88911-948-1

Towards Evidence-Based Policy for Canadian Education/Vers des politiques canadiennes d'éducation fondées sur la recherche, Patrice de Broucker and/et Arthur Sweetman (eds./ dirs.), 2002. Paper ISBN 0-88911-946-5 Cloth ISBN 0-88911-944-9

Money, Markets and Mobility: Celebrating the Ideas of Robert A. Mundell, Nobel Laureate in Economic Sciences, Thomas J. Courchene (ed.), 2002. Paper ISBN 0-88911-820-5
Cloth ISBN 0-88911-818-3

Our publications may be purchased at leading bookstores, including the Queen's University Bookstore (http://www.campusbookstore.com/) or can be ordered online from: McGill-Queen's University Press, at
http://mqup.mcgill.ca/ordering.php

For more information about new and backlist titles from Queen's Policy Studies, visit http://www.queensu.ca/sps/books or visit the McGill-Queen's University Press web site at: **http://mqup.mcgill.ca/**